Beyon

Beyond Adaptation

*Essays on Radical Transformations
of Original Works*

Edited by PHYLLIS FRUS *and*
CHRISTY WILLIAMS

McFarland & Company, Inc., Publishers
Jefferson, North Carolina, and London

LIBRARY OF CONGRESS CATALOGUING-IN-PUBLICATION DATA

Beyond adaptation : essays on radical transformations of
original works / edited by Phyllis Frus and Christy
Williams.
   p.   cm.
Includes bibliographical references and index.

ISBN: 978-0-7864-4223-2
softcover : 50# alkaline paper ∞

   1. Literature—Adaptations—History and criticism.
2. Intertextuality. 3. Parodies—History and criticism.
I. Frus, Phyllis. II. Williams, Christy, 1978–
PN171.A33B49   2010
809—dc22   2010004367

British Library cataloguing data are available

On the cover: Julia Roberts and John Malkovitch in *Mary Reilly*
(1996, TriStar Pictures/Photofest)

Manufactured in the United States of America

McFarland & Company, Inc., Publishers
  Box 611, Jefferson, North Carolina 28640
  www.mcfarlandpub.com

For our families

Acknowledgments

This project began formally with a letter to McFarland, calling their attention to the appearance of a new area of study and the need for a book that laid out its parameters and showed the quality of work being done in it. Our colleague Laurie Leach first broached the idea when she suggested collecting essays about novel and film revisions that go so far beyond adaptation that they ought to be called something else. This sparked our realization that disciplines in the humanities are moving away from traditional adaptation studies and toward the recognition that transformative works inhabit a unique place. We owe Laurie a huge debt for beginning the discussion of transformation and initiating the project. She was the first editor and wrote the first call for papers, and her essay for the collection was the first to arrive. She had to bow out as editor as her administrative duties at Hawai'i Pacific University increased, but she has remained an enthusiastic and helpful consultant on the book.

We are grateful to the contributors not just for their thoughtful and thought-provoking essays but for their willingness to engage in the back-and-forth necessitated by our process of pulling together a collection centered on a field that was still nebulous; we discovered its richness as the essays came in. Of the contributors, we single out for special appreciation Laurie Leach, who improved the introduction by reading a draft, and Alissa Burger for participating in our panel at the 2007 Hawai'i International Conference on the Arts and Humanities, the first public presentation of the project. We also appreciate our HPU colleague, Deborah Ross, who agreed to write an essay specifically for the collection. Other HPU friends and colleagues we would like to acknowledge are Bill Potter, Mark Tjarks, and Angela Gili, who asked helpful questions when we presented an overview of the book at HPU's Faculty Scholarship Day in 2009, and Houston Wood, for his enthusiastic encouragement. In addition, we thank Marilyn Schweitzer for her excellent editing and indexing skills.

We gratefully acknowledge the Hawai'i Pacific University Trustees' Scholarly Endeavor Program, which awarded the editors each a course reduction during sequential terms so that they could devote time to the collection, and the Faculty Development and Scholarship Activities Committee of the HPU Faculty Assembly for supporting the participation of the editors and Laurie Leach in the 2007 Hawai'i International Conference on the Humanities.

Phyllis was a fellow at a 2007 National Endowment for the Humanities Summer Seminar for College Teachers on Adaptation and Revision held at the University of California at Santa Cruz. The seminar, led by Professors Hilary Schor and Paul Saint-Amour, provoked her thinking about transformations of texts and resulted in two seminar members contributing essays, Antje Anderson and Marc DiPaolo. She thanks the NEH for the fortuitous coming together of all the seminar colleagues.

Finally, hats off to our families for their support, especially to William Williams III for his much appreciated generosity.

Table of Contents

Introduction: Making the Case for Transformation

The 2007 action film *Transformers* earned over $70 million in the United States its opening weekend and is currently among the top 25 box office hits of all time domestically. The 2009 sequel, *Transformers: Revenge of the Fallen*, did even better, despite poor reviews; it was tenth on the list at the beginning of 2010. The 2007 film was nominated for 43 awards in 2008 (three of them Oscars) and won ten. What makes the films so popular? Both feature robot-aliens and big action scenes, but many movies have had these. We hazard a guess: *Transformers* films are popular because of their depiction of metamorphosis. The appealing element of Transformers is not that they are cars or that they are robots, but that they are both and can change status depending on what is needed.

The feature film derives from both *Transformers* the Saturday-morning TV show that began in 1984 and the toy line introduced the same year (both had Japanese counterparts). The TV show was for all practical purposes a 30-minute cartoon advertisement for the toys, which are vehicles that turn into robots. It was one of many children's shows of the time with the marketing premise of cartoon and toy launched together. Surely the reason that Transformers have remained popular, with new toy releases every year, is the potential inherent in their dual status. Similarly, the film succeeds to the extent that it makes a virtue out of the way the larger-than-life characters can hide in the shape of vehicles—mundane cars or trucks—and then shift gears to become robots capable of wielding weapons. In both, the focus is on the action of transforming, not the end product. Perhaps Transformers appeal to kids because they tap into the great shape-shifters of myth, such as Zeus, who turned himself at various times into a lightning bolt, a bull,

1

and a swan. Other transformers are the trickster figures of Native American storytelling, such as Old Coyote and his descendant, Wile E. Coyote.

Like our robot-alien heroes (and villains) textual transformations contain within them other texts, and it is the combining of the texts into a new work, and the act of shape-shifting itself, that makes the new texts so appealing. This may also explain the charm of fairy tales, for they not only display many mechanisms of transformation, such as allusion, parody, and irony, but characters undergo physical, social, and emotional transformation as well. Besides, magic—often involving shape-shifting—is commonplace. As Marina Warner says, even more than the presence of fairies, a moral message, or the happy ending, "metamorphosis defines the fairy tale" (xx).[1] Because there are so many fairy tales and they are constantly being retold, they manage to exhibit most of the ways texts can be transformed: borrowing, mocking, challenging or correcting the ideology of their predecessor, glossing or explaining. In contemporary fairy tales, many authors and filmmakers challenge outdated attitudes (as in feminist fairy tales) or transpose their work into different genres (with horror and fantasy as the most common). Almost all create a new context. The film *Freeway* (1996) is just one fairy-tale transformation that does all three—challenges the victimization of Little Red Riding Hood, shifts genres to a suspense thriller, and makes Red a hitchhiker who is picked up by a child psychologist and serial killer named Dr. Wolverton while on her way to her grandmother's house.

Writers, filmmakers, and creators of video games alter texts and create new contexts in many different ways. They make something new out of previous material; they quote, echo, make fun of, bring out an overlooked layer, challenge the ideology of or simply comment on earlier texts. Parody—which involves many of these operations on a source text, particularly mocking and inversion—is a common type of transformation and can appear across modes and genres. Another kind of transformation that involves the reader in the process of creating the new text is intertextuality. It is particularly useful for unintentional transformations—those that audiences co-create simply by bringing their experiences of other texts to the new one—and in analyzing transformations of real-world stories, such as history films and historical novels.

Often, as in the case of *Transformers*, the stories move from one medium or mode to another—toy to animated figures, TV show to feature animated film, novel to Broadway musical, fairy tale to video game. Also, texts of every kind are transformed: popular as well as canonical, best-sellers like *Gone with the Wind* as well as Shakespeare, Brontë, and Dickens. Historical figures and stories are also often transformed, as when the story of Pocahontas is turned into a fairy tale when given the Disney treatment, or accounts of the

adaptation : > emphasis
> ages

attack on Pearl Harbor are filmed as epics when the more appropriate genre would be disaster movie.

she does not mention
> confinement to
> aging

What Is a Transformation?

It makes sense to use the term transformation to describe all these per-mutations, but we should define what we mean by it, for despite what we may seem to be saying, not every text is a transformation. At its most basic level, a transformation is a text that reworks an older story or stories, making a transformation very much like an adaptation. In fact, many of the works that are discussed in this collection have been called adaptations by other scholars. But in the vast range of texts that can be called adaptations, there are some that move beyond mere adaptation and transform the source text into something new that works independently of its source.

It may help to think of an analogy. In the 1830s, Charles Darwin observed a variety of species of finches when visiting the Galapagos Islands. One of the differences from species to species of finch was the beak sizes and shapes (some were good for cracking hard shells, others better at probing flowers, etc.), and eventually Darwin hypothesized that over time, all of the different species of finch had common ancestors, and that the differences in the finches' beaks were due to the way in which each species had adapted to the available food sources on its individual island. While this is a very simplified way of looking at adaptation in animals, it is similar to adaptation in literature. An adaptation is a text that has been changed to suit a new purpose or environment (like a classic novel updated to a twenty-first-century setting). But, like the finches, the new text is recognizable as a relation of the earlier text.

A transformation, however, is generally drastically different from its source text, so it may not be recognizable as a cousin. To keep with the highly reductive science analogies, think about metamorphosis. When a caterpillar has reached maturity, it transforms into a butterfly—an entirely new form that is based on the earlier form. In literary transformations, the new text may be based on an older one, but the reader or viewer may not recognize the connection. The 1995 film *Clueless*, for example, is a transformation of Jane Austen's 1816 novel *Emma*. It is possible to watch the movie and not recognize *Emma* at all, even if you have read it. The setting, characters, and plot are so different that the movie stands on its own. An adaptation of *Emma*, however, such as the 1996 film starring Gwyneth Paltrow in the title role, announces itself as an adaptation of Jane Austen's novel. It tells Austen's story, uses her characters, and even keeps the title, though like all film adaptations it selects and compresses the action and adds other ele-

here

popular ments to meet the needs of today's audiences. The creators of the film *Emma* want the audience to know about Jane Austen's novel and to see the two works as related because of the cultural cachet that attaches to any adaptation of a work of high culture.

Transformations may hide the fact that they are based on or related to earlier stories. They usually do not share their title with the earlier text, although they may play on the predecessor's title, as the novel *Wicked* and the Broadway musical *The Wiz* both allude to characters in *The Wizard of Oz*. The plot may be similar, but because its context may be completely different, the similarities may go unnoticed; for example, the plot of the 2008 film *Aquamarine* is very similar to that of the fairy tale "The Little Mermaid," but the modernization of the story hides those similarities. One common way to transform texts is to rework material in a significant way, such as by telling a story from a different perspective as a way to engage themes and issues left out of the previous version (as *Wicked* retells *The Wizard of Oz* or *Mary Reilly* retells *The Strange Case of Dr. Jekyll and Mr. Hyde*). These kinds of novels are sometimes called "parallel" novels, because they treat the same events from a different character's point of view. The appeal of a parallel transformation may be similar to that of a sequel: audiences want to know what happened to the characters later on—or earlier, in the case of a prequel.

Another way to transform a text is to use a familiar plot but vary the setting, situation, and/or characters (the 2001 film *O* uses the plot of *Othello* and *Clueless* uses the plot of *Emma*, but both make their sources relevant to contemporary American teenage audiences, not least because each source's language is translated into American slang of one kind or another). A writer or filmmaker may update the earlier text to reflect a new social, political, or cultural context (for example, Michael Almereyda's 2000 film version of *Hamlet*, which keeps Shakespeare's language and the characters' names but makes Denmark a corporation, not a kingdom). Yet another method of transformation is for an author or filmmaker to radically transform a source by using parallel plot events and similar characters without being constrained by the earlier plot (the Coen Brothers' *O Brother, Where Art Thou?* is loosely based on *The Odyssey*, and *A Thousand Acres* has many allusions to the plot and characters of *King Lear*). In a transformation the predecessor text is not regarded as the original that the transformation ought to remain true to. Critics of adaptation often spend time determining how faithful the adaptation is to the "original," sometimes with a comparison of which is "better" (a contest the new text rarely wins).[2] We usually refer to an earlier text as *a source,* or precursor text, parts of which the new text makes into something new. While knowing about the older text enriches our reading of a transformation, our interpretation does not depend on it.

here

Whereas adaptations are frequently "based on" another text, transformations are often "inspired by" another text. Because they are not limited
to representing a source text, they can re-imagine all sorts of new possibilities for the characters, settings, or plots that audiences have made popular.
Many transformations work from multiple texts, not just a single one. The
1998 film *Shakespeare in Love,* for example, uses many texts by and about
Shakespeare to create an imagined version of Shakespeare's life at a time in
his life when he was young and inexperienced and struggling with writer's
block. A variety of texts provide elements of the movie's plot, lines of dialogue, and information that seems biographical but probably is not. Precursor texts include *Romeo and Juliet, Twelfth Night,* his sonnets, and historical
narratives about Queen Elizabeth, other contemporaries, and Elizabethan
theater. The 2007 film *Becoming Jane* does the same kind of biographical
construction for Jane Austen, drawing on her novels and the few letters of
hers that survive. Biopics like *Ray* (2004) and *Walk the Line* (2005) are
inevitably transformations of multiple documentary and journalistic texts,
even when they credit a particular biography as a source.

This distinction between texts that adapt and texts that go beyond adaptation is not new, but few critics use the term *transformation*. Instead, they
stick with the tried-and-true *adaptation*, despite the many problems with the
term they invariably note (it does not cover unintended transformations and
is hamstrung by the comparison to the original that invariably ensues—the
so-called fidelity model). Or they use a variety of fancy terms—"intertextual dialogism" (Mask), "a mosaic of quotations" (Kristeva 37), even "non-
synchronous historicity" (Lim 164). While it is useful to have a variety of
terms to talk about the way texts are altered—revision, transmutation, recycling—it would help to have an umbrella word that points to texts that go
beyond adaptation. Instead, a handful of terms are used inconsistently by a
variety of critics and theorists across fields.[3]

We are not the first to claim use of the term *transformation*, or to point
out how many retellings go beyond adaptation into the realm of critical revision, appropriation, recycling, or transmutation—that is, transformation.
Jack Zipes suggests a pair of terms to classify texts that retell classical fairy
tales: *duplication*, which reproduces and reinforces the ideology, patterns,
and images of the classical tale, creating a "look-alike"; and *revision,* which
transforms the classical tale and "alters" its traditional values, patterns, and
images (*Fairy Tale as Myth* 9). While his distinction is quite useful, it too
could perpetuate the fidelity model because of its emphasis on the source
text. It might seem that we are also suggesting only two types of retellings—
adaptation and transformation—but we do not want to perpetuate the binary
categories implied by the use of the two terms. Instead of opposition, we

conceive of a range of transformations across a continuum and point out that many texts do both. After all, as Cristina Bacchilega argues, fairy-tale retellings can "reproduce" *and* "transform" the stories that they tell (10). For example, the recent film versions of Charles Dickens's *Great Expectations* and of Athol Fugard's novel *Tsotsi* both rely heavily on their source texts while critically commenting on them; they fall somewhere in the middle of the continuum, rather than fitting firmly in either category.

Fairy Tales and Transformation

Several essays in this collection analyze fairy tales that have been transformed or make use of fairy-tale allusions in the texts analyzed. Because fairy tales are frequently about metamorphosis and are often easily recognizable, they are popular sources for contemporary transformations. For fairy-tale retellings, there is rarely one "original" story, but rather a host of stories that inform the writing. There are earliest recorded stories, such as "Yeh-hsien," a version of "Cinderella" written down between A.D. 850 and 860, but no single ur-text that is the progenitor of Cinderella stories or any group of tales. This multiplicity of tales without a traceable "original" helps to explain why transformation is such a big part of the genre.

When we think of fairy tales as a genre, we tend think of their timeless quality, a model popularized by the Brothers Grimm (Wilhelm and Jacob) and Charles Perrault. Any fairy tale could happen at any time in any place to anyone. The tales take place in a dark wood or a kingdom far away ruled by unnamed kings and queens, not in Germany or France. Characters usually don't have names, but when they do, they are often descriptors like Sleeping Beauty (she's pretty and sleeps) or Cinderella (she's a girl covered in soot). But the identity of the characters is rather vague and left up to the audience's imagination. The lack of detail invites postmodern transformers to insert the context that is missing from the "universal" tales. This has meant a whole industry of what are sometimes called revisionist fairytales. Examples abound in postmodern literature by authors such as Angela Carter, Robert Coover, and Salman Rushdie; in fantasy and young adult literature by authors such as Jane Yolen, Kelly Link, and Robin McKinley; and in fantasy and horror for adults such as the fairy-tale retellings series edited by Terri Windling and Ellen Datlow.

Because we rarely have one original tale, rather a host of stories with similar plots or details, there is no one story to be faithful to, and the issue of fidelity is avoided completely. Nevertheless, it can be difficult to remember the wide range of stories from different cultures and historical periods when certain Western tales—those of Perrault, Grimm, and Hans Christian Andersen—are so canonized and reproduced so frequently that they carry the weight of an "original." For Americans, Walt Disney versions of classic fairy tales (*Sleeping Beauty, The Little Mermaid,* and *Beauty and the Beast*) often seem like the "originals" because they are the first, and sometimes the only, versions many American children know. Turning well-known stories— many of which are fairy tales—into animated Disney blockbusters is its own type of transformation—Disneyfication. The introduction of talking animal sidekicks and musical numbers, among other changes, helps to make legends (*Mulan*), myths (*Hercules*), history (*Pocahontas*), classic novels (*The Hunchback of Notre Dame*), and many other types of stories into formulaic films based on Disney's successful transformation of fairy tales like *Snow White and the Seven Dwarfs.*

The literary fairy tale has a long history of transformation. Not only that, but the early writers of fairy tales collaborated in an environment similar to the one in which authors of postmodern and speculative fiction write today[4]—borrowing from established tales, writing against another writer, trying to write a bigger and better fairy tale than has appeared before. Just as we can see elements of Bram Stoker's *Dracula* in vampire stories written today, the writers of the literary fairy tale build on what already works, adding their own distinctive touch to create new tales. Similarly, we have new vampire worlds like Anne Rice's *Interview with a Vampire* series and Joss Whedon's *Buffy the Vampire Slayer* television series that use much of what Stoker invented as vampire lore, though Stoker too relied on existing folklore and literature to create his vampire.

Many of these new fairy-tale texts transform the material by questioning or subverting the themes of the source stories, critiquing or updating, or even parodying them. They do not simply retell the story, but change the story in fundamental ways so that the types, motifs, and tropes of the source stories are used for a new purpose. In *Fairy Tales and the Art of Subversion,* Zipes explains that the ideologies of the classic literary tales stem from oral folktales "of late feudal and early capitalist societies," arguing that "the oral folktales were those symbolic acts in which [the folk] enunciated their aspirations and projected the magic possibility in an assortment of imaginative ways so that anyone could become a knight in shining armor or a lovely princess" (6, 7). Thus the enchantment of these tales is their promise of transformation and a better life. But fairy tales also carry ideology, socializing children and adults into the dominant ideologies of the day. The tales promise the possibility of class transformation, while at the same time socializing audiences into proper classed behaviors. Zipes explains that when institutionalized as literary tales, these same stories continued their ideological function, but also became a means of subverting dominant ideology. Fairy-tale transformations are a way for writers to "intervene in the civilizing process," such as by questioning patriarchal authority or the valuing of heterosexual marriage (Zipes 20).

Presumably tales that were popular were also particularly effective at socializing their audiences. Stephen Benson has pointed out that for the postmodern writer "committed to the overturning of conventions of inequality and restriction," fairy tales are an ideal canvas on which to work (12–13). Many feminist fairy-tale subversions, for example, attack the passive-princess tales by rewriting stories so that women save men or save themselves. One of the feminist interventions into fairy tales during the 1970s is this kind of role reversal designed to replace the sleeping beauties with active heroines. Along these lines, marriage is also removed as the happy ending in some retellings, so that heroines get to live independent lives. More recently, authors like Emma Donoghue question the heterosexist assumptions of fairy tales by challenging the conventional romantic relationships and presenting lesbian alternatives instead.

Parody and Transformation

Many fairy-tale retellings could be called parodies; examples are the *Shrek* series of films that rely on the audience's knowledge of fairy-tale conventions, particularly those of Disney. Through humor, the films offer a scathing critique of the Disney empire and its use of fairy tales.[5] Parody is a fruitful site at which to explore transformation because it is generally excluded from the category of adaptation, although it clearly has a transformative relationship to one or more source texts (Musser 234). Charles Musser explains that by making fun of a prior text a parody deflates or even destroys it, which means the new text cannot be an adaptation. In our framework, however, parody easily fits. Here Linda Hutcheon's theory comes in handy. She defines parody not as mocking a text, but imitating a text with ironic interventions. Thus parody becomes "repetition with critical distance, which marks difference rather than similarity"—a key difference between transformation and adaptation (6). Many postmodern retellings of fairy tales, such as those of Angela Carter in *The Bloody Chamber*, imitate the conventions of the fairy-tale genre to comment on modern ideological and social issues rather than to mock the fairy tale itself. For example, Carter's "Snow Child" does not make fun of the tale "Snow White," but uses the "Snow White" story to emphasize the sexual violence implied in many fairy tales that previous retellings have neglected to explore.[6] Parody thus may be the best example of why we need the term *transformation*: in parody, there is obviously a relationship between the texts, but it goes beyond adaptation.

Hutcheon gives the mock epic as an example of parody that uses a narrative form to comment on modern sensibilities, rather than critique the form (5). An example of mock epic that invokes its source rather than making fun of it is *O Brother, Where Art Thou?* (2000). The filmmakers Joel and Ethan Coen insert characters from Homer's *Odyssey* into the film, set in the Depression-era South. One of the villains, played by John Goodman, has an eye patch, like the Cyclops, and he acts monstrously; women doing laundry at the river who seduce the three fugitives from a chain gang are the Sirens; and there are other allusions to the *Odyssey*. But the epic tale serves little other purpose than to make viewers feel good about recognizing the characters' Homeric equivalents and perhaps to justify the film's episodic plot. Thinking of the *Odyssey* while watching *O Brother* might also inflate the men's search for safety and freedom to the level of quest. But as three critics writing in *Film Quarterly* demonstrate, it is more productive to view the film as an allegory of the Great Depression, the period in which it is set. This reading emphasizes the tension that the failure of the banks and then the entire economy brought about between "the government and its citizens, between the haves and the have-nots" (Content, Kreider, and White 42). To interpret the movie as bearing an allegorical relationship to events and processes of the 1930s in the southern United States is to add a layer of complexity by substituting a different set of texts for the merely surface analogies of characters from the *Odyssey*. This doesn't mean that the parody isn't also quite funny as the film goes about its critical engagement with both genre and history.

In fact, many parodies are humorous and critical; they are funny even if you don't know the specific sources. All it takes is for the source material to have filtered down into popular culture so that motifs, characters, and dialects or accents are familiar, even though far removed from the precursor text(s) where they originated. Mel Brooks' 1974 film *Young Frankenstein* (written by Brooks and Gene Wilder) is a good example of a parody that many people find hilarious even if they are unfamiliar with the sources—the series of *Frankenstein* movies made in the 1930s and Mary Shelley's gothic novel of 1818. Although viewers innocent of knowledge of the earlier films obviously enjoy it, they are not viewing it as much of a transformation. When exposed to the earlier movies, first-time viewers must be very surprised at the seriousness of these films about a man who assumes God's powers to make life—and some probably first learn that Frankenstein is the name of the creator, not his creation. *Young Frankenstein* makes fun of the old horror films such as *Frankenstein* and *Bride of Frankenstein* by imitating some of their features, but in an ironic way. The result is a film that comments critically on the horror genre and on its popularity by changing its genre to comedic satire. It inverts relationships; exaggerates the monomania of Dr. Frankenstein, thereby deflating him; and invokes many other conventions of Frankenstein movies only to upend them.

However, for many parodies, an intimate knowledge of the model is required to enjoy the new work. For example, take Margaret Atwood's short story "Gertrude Talks Back" in which Atwood gives Hamlet's mother a monologue that becomes an opportunity to explain to her son why she prefers Claudius, her second husband, to Hamlet's father and to reply to his charges that her remarrying was untimely. Unless Atwood's readers have studied the play or seen a stage or film version of *Hamlet*, they will not see the wit in Gertrude's spirited self-defense, as she quotes lines that her son has hurled at his mother about her "polluted sheets." The setting for the imaginary monologue, as those familiar with *Hamlet* will recognize, is Act IV Scene iv of *Hamlet*. The story does not work for the reader unable to recognize the allusions to Gertrude's behavior in over-hastily marrying her brother-in-law.

Transformation is the only term that applies here, for no scholar of adaptations would call this two-page story an adaptation of Shakespeare's most famous tragedy. Yet it clearly depends on *Hamlet*, and the term we choose to describe the relationship is part of our interpretation of Atwood's story. We might say that "Gertrude Talks Back" is parasitic on the host text, or a satirical comment on Gertrude's mostly passive role in the unfolding tragedy. In the latter case, we realize that the story enables Gertrude to talk back not just to Hamlet, who is pleading with her to refuse to share Claudius's bed, but to all the directors and critics who have interpreted the relationship between Hamlet and his mother as Oedipal. The story then is not just a transformation of a scene and themes from *Hamlet*, but a critical commentary on *Hamlet*'s interpreters—critics and adapters—who vie to establish the dominant meaning of Shakespeare's great play.

Intertextuality and Transformation

So far we have been describing deliberate transformations. What about unintentional ones? For cases when the filmmaker or writer seems not to have deliberately reworked or commented on an earlier work we can use the concept of intertextuality. In general, intertextuality is the study of how texts are related irrespective of chronology. One way to describe the relationship is to say that texts converse with one another. They have a dialogue with prior texts, consciously or unconsciously. Mikhail Bakhtin's term for such plural texts is "dialogic." It takes a reader or spectator to bring this dimension out in the open, for texts become dialogic when they are read or viewed, as the reader of a print text or viewer of a film shapes its meanings through noticing connections with other texts. The author may have intended for us to see the relationship, but we can also see resemblances of one text to another without prompting from the author. For example, one critic watching *The Stepford Wives*, a 1975 film about housewives in a suburban town who were being killed one by one and turned into domestic robots, was reminded of Bluebeard, the fairy-tale villain who serially murdered his wives, and she interpreted it as an intertextual transformation of the tale—although neither the novel it is based on nor the film refers to Bluebeard specifically (Lim 165). Anyone who has been shown the parallels is likely to view the film through the prism of the fairy tale, thus co-constructing it as a transformation whether the filmmakers had Bluebeard in mind or not.

Calling a story in any medium a transformation draws our attention to the new text rather the one that has been modified or represented. Intertextuality carries this concept further; the emphasis is not on either text, the new one or its predecessor(s), but on the relations between them, the act of transformation itself. Film theorist Deborah Cartmell describes the difference as going from addressing the question of how faithful to the original a text is to figuring out how many meanings are generated in the new text (qtd. in Leitch 167). The opportunity to find a plurality of meanings makes transformations much richer and more complex by suggesting multiple interpretations, depending on which other text the viewer emphasizes or notices in the first place. But it makes a difference which intertext a reader knows. Nabokov's *Lolita* is a prime example of how interpretation is radically different depending on the intertexts the reader brings to her reading. Emily Collins explains that readers of *Lolita* familiar with Disney's film and not Andersen's "The Little Mermaid" will read the allusions to the story in that novel quite differently, possibly resulting in a wholly different interpretation of the novel, one in which the teenaged Lolita is responsible for her own exploitation at the hands of the much older Humbert Humbert (98).

Here is where we can turn to adaptation studies, for Robert Stam and his colleagues have been reading films, novels, plays, documentary films, and even genres through the prism of intertextuality.[7] This inevitably results in generating many antecedents in the process of comparing differences, additions, and innovations of the new text. This is particularly useful in the case of texts with historical referents. For example, once we realize that Conrad's novel *Heart of Darkness* was merely a point of departure for Francis Ford Coppola in the epic film *Apocalypse Now*, we see that he was interested in the historical parallels between Belgium as colonial power in the Congo in the novel and French and U.S. colonial actions in Vietnam—that is, in the historical intertexts—rather than in updating the plot and characters with a new setting. The war in Vietnam that began as an attempt to shore up a colonial power dominates the film. There is no analogue for it in *Heart of Darkness*, which depicts brute force resulting in total suppression of an "other." Both novel and film are similar, however, in laying bare the racist actions of both powers. Recognizing the relationship between film and novel, even if the only parallels are colonialism and a journey up a river to stop a rogue officer, brings the historical intertexts behind Conrad's text to light.

A benefit of reading films with nonfictional antecedents as intertextual transformations, especially history films like *Apocalypse Now*, is that we can begin to change our habitual way of treating history as a text that has been adapted, always imperfectly.[8] Instead we should acknowledge that our only access to the past is through narrative accounts. Dudley Andrew's claim that every representational film is in some sense an adaptation is useful here, although we would substitute the term "transformation" for "adaptation." Andrew writes, "Every representational film adapts a prior conception" (29), that is, renders in a different way some previous "whole, some concept of person, place, event, or situation" (28). Although in this often-cited essay Andrew focuses on what most critics and viewers have in mind when they use the term adaptations—those related loosely or closely to a "well-constructed original text" (29)—it applies most clearly to history and reality-based films. He implies that no filmic representation is ever truly original, but always interprets some preexisting formation or understanding—in other words, some textualization. This means that all films that tell true stories are transformations, even those with an original screenplay. The script refers to some interpretation of what happened, from someone's point of view— that is, to previous texts either close to the events referred to or at some remove of distance or time.[9]

It may seem from these examples that we are valuing transformations over mere adaptations, suggesting that a text that cites a plethora of other texts is better than one that does not. The presence of intertextual features does not make a text good (nor does their absence make it a failure), but at least it moves the criteria of evaluation off the poles of fidelity—the text is faithful to its source or departs too far from it. Transformation is not about making a comparative value judgment: which is better? It is about understanding relationships and their effects—how they work together and why they differ when they do. The particular sources or citations that the viewer or reader chooses to focus on can support a richer, more complex reading, and in turn provide pleasure to the audience.

Although there is no simple equation between kind or degree of transformation and the "greatness" of a text, highlighting the process of transformations in so many texts in popular culture does explain the fascination of literary and media studies with popular cultural texts. So many twenty-first-century texts borrow freely—citing, sampling, quoting, parodying, even exploiting—that lack of originality is no longer considered a weakness. Hip-hop is only the most obvious case where sampling is commonplace. Quotation and imitation are admired tactics, and critics have fun showing readers and viewers how to find echoes and citations of other texts. Many of us have experienced pleasure in detecting a plurality of voices. We believe that the more echoes we can hear, the richer the text, and in the ways literary criticism has been practiced for nearly a century, since modernism, richness is a sign of value.

The Essays

The essays in this collection approach transformed texts in a variety of ways, as the texts studied variously update, subvert, recover, challenge, and remake the conventions of a prior text or the texts themselves. The approaches the contributors take and the texts they treat are so diverse that we decided not to group the essays in any of the usual ways, such as by kind of transformation studied. There are many collections that do that already, particularly by focusing on the move from book to film. Our collection displays an amazing variety of modes and media analyzed by the contributors; they include video games, comic books, plays, novels, films, short stories, poetry, television miniseries, musicals, and animated films. We begin with essays that discuss the texts least likely to be called transformations—one that has been rewarded for originality, two that appear to be cinematic adaptations of novels, a transformation actually titled "Adaptation," and two novels that transform nonfictional sources.

Phyllis Frus, in interpreting Jane Campion's film *The Piano* as a retelling of other stories, has set herself a challenge, for Campion's script won an Academy Award for best original screenplay. In order to account for the dozens of contradictory interpretations of this much-lauded film, she treats it as an intertextual transformation. Frus chooses two apparently dissonant readings resulting from very different intertexts—historical narratives and fairy tales—and mediates between the two. She concludes that the historical referents are subsumed by the fairy-tale and gothic elements, making it more satisfactory to interpret the film as a historical romance than as a history film.

Devin Harner too has taken on a challenging task—treating a film that names itself as *Adaptation*. Clearly the film does far more than adapt Susan Orlean's journalistic account in *The Orchid Thief*, making the title of the film a misnomer. Harner looks at the way Charlie Kaufman and Spike Jonze subvert Hollywood conventions by drawing attention to the spectatorial pleasure inherent in conventional films. He also explores the film's metafictional commentary on the process of adapting a book to film, especially difficult when the main characters—the subjects of the transformation—are around to protest their treatment.

Marni Gauthier takes up two novels—*Free Enterprise* and *I, Tituba, Black Witch of Salem*—that not only offer new depictions of women marginalized by history due to their race and gender, but transform the genre of the historical novel as well. Both novels do double duty in reclaiming historical figures that have been blanketed in shadow, making them central to the historical accounts retold while at the same time calling attention to the process of creating history. Gauthier also argues that these novels are part of a transnational shift in academia from American Studies to Americas Studies.

Anne M. Reef chose to write about what most critics would call a straightforward adaptation: the 2000 film *Tsotsi*, directed by Gavin Hood, which is based on the only novel by famed South African playwright Athol Fugard. Reef argues that the film is both a linguistic transformation, in that the English language of Fugard's book that makes it accessible world-wide becomes Tsotsitaal, a street language specific to townships like Soweto, and a post-colonial gesture that critiques the neocolonialism that persists in post-apartheid South Africa. Applying the post-colonial theory of Bill Ashcroft, Reef analyzes what she calls the film's representation of a "class-stratified, crime-ridden, and HIV/AIDS-plagued, but still creatively competent post-apartheid South African society."

Antje S. Anderson takes as her topic Charles Dickens' *Great Expectations*, a classic novel that has been adapted many times, arguing that Alexander Cuarón's 1999 film is a transformation rather than simply an updating. Besides moving the setting from 1820s and 1830s England to Florida and New York City in the 1980s and 1990s, Cuarón focuses on the love affair between the main character, Finn (Pip in the novel), and the woman he has loved since childhood, Estella. Anderson argues that the film also alters the genre into which Dickens' novel is inevitably placed, the *Bildungsroman*, or novel of education and growth, by making the film into an anti–*Bildungsroman*, a narrative of circularity and stasis.

Laurie F. Leach, like Gauthier, is concerned with the effect of making a minor figure in one text the protagonist of another. She takes as her case study Valerie Martin's novel *Mary Reilly*, which retells Stevenson's *The Strange Case of Dr. Jekyll and Mr. Hyde* from the viewpoint of a housemaid who rates only two lines in the source text. This is a transformation in three ways: the background becomes the foreground, the class station of the characters is inverted, and the events narrated parallel the account given by Stevenson's narrators. Using the work of Gerard Genette, Leach argues that these make *Mary Reilly* an intertextual transformation.

Julia Round's essay considers a translation across the widest possible range of classic to popular text, that is, from Shakespeare to comics. She analyzes the incorporation of two plays by William Shakespeare, *A Midsummer Night's Dream* and *The Tempest*, into Neil Gaiman's award-winning fantasy series *The Sandman*, noting the blending of fact and fiction, the allusion to performance legacy and interpretation, and the use of metafiction. She makes the astute observation that Gaiman's transformation returns Shakespeare's plays to the popular realm where he started, as the playwright, one of the most canonical writers of all time, is transformed by one of the most celebrated fantasy writers of today.

Deborah L. Ross's essay on gender impersonation, Orientalism, and metamorphosis takes as its starting point David Henry Hwang's play *M. Butterfly*. Hwang began the play in 1986 after hearing about a French diplomat on trial for espionage who claimed he had lived in intimacy for twenty years with a Chinese spy without knowing he was a man. Hwang, seeing the similarity to *Madama Butterfly*, took this occasion to expose Western attitudes towards Asians by making a "deconstructivist" transformation of Puccini's opera. Ross traces the path of the butterfly back to versions of the story that predate the opera, returning to Hwang's play to find it not so much influenced by the "true" story as by contemporary theories of gender and sexuality.

Alissa Burger takes a look at a marginalized character who is made to shine in reinventions of *The Wizard of Oz*. Her analysis of *Wicked*, both novel and musical, examines how gender and narrative are negotiated by the shift in focus when the witch, not the naïve girl from Kansas, becomes the heroine. Burger argues that through an intertextual critique of previous incarnations of Dorothy and the Wicked Witch of the West, *Wicked* reimagines the possibilities for female gender roles and female friendship and breaks the binaries set forth by the earlier incarnations of Oz.

Cathlena Martin examines the translation of classic children's novels, Lewis Carroll's *Alice's Adventures in Wonderland* and *Through the Looking Glass*, into an interactive video game for adults, *American McGee's Alice*. Her essay explores how audience, medium, and tone are transformed when making the jump from traditional to new media. She argues that *Alice* is a logical text to turn into a video game, as both novels employ a game structure and *Alice* is already part of an established tradition of transformation. The move to video game, she argues, provides a unique opportunity to revisit classic children's texts and perhaps create a deeper meaning by looking through an intertextual lens.

Jennifer Orme tackles a recent incarnation of one of the most transformed texts of all times, the *Arabian Nights*. Orme explains that the 2000 television miniseries of the same title does something that previous onscreen versions of the *Arabian Nights* have not—it reproduces the frame story of Scheherezade and focuses on the power of storytelling. But to make the story of Scheherezade as exciting to an American audience as the popular stories she tells, the makers of the miniseries transform the story of a clever woman who saves her people into a traditional love story. While Scheherezade's stories ultimately save the day, Orme argues that the framing of her stories undercuts their power, diminishing the apparent message of the series.

Lan Dong examines the Disneyfication of a Chinese legend in her analysis of *Mulan*. She joins the debates on this film that criticize it for its cultural appropriation and applaud it for its strong female heroine. Dong argues that the film is a transnational hybrid, featuring a heroine who appeals to American audiences while still retaining some of its Chinese roots. Part of the Americanization of the character is to play up her tomboyism and emphasize the cross-dressing and performance of gender. She argues that Disney makes an important deviation from other transformations of the Mulan legend by having the heroine achieve her success as a woman in woman's clothes rather than disguised as a man.

Marc DiPaolo approaches Disneyfication from another angle, examining how the marketing monster of the corporation undoes the feminist threads in Disney's *Beauty and the Beast*. DiPaolo compares the heroine Belle to her product counterpart, arguing that amidst a feminist backlash, the Disney team stripped its most feminist character of her depth, intelligence, and independence. He situates his reading of the character in feminist criticism of the film, which does not necessarily share his appreciation of Disney's attempt at a strong, independent heroine. Finally, DiPaolo takes up *Shrek* as an alternative to the Disneyfied fairy tale, but one that, for all its girl-power posturing, cannot match the feminism offered by the Disney screenplay written by Linda Woolverton.

Stella Bolaki also takes a feminist approach in reading four retellings of the "Snow White" fairy tale: Anne Sexton's "Snow White," Olga Broumas's "Snow White," Angela Carter's "The Snow Child," and Emma Donoghue's "The Tale of the Apple." She approaches the four texts as feminist transformations that challenge the patriarchal gender paradigms often supported by more traditional fairy tales, examining both the ideological and narrative revisions of each. For her, then, transformation is a critical move that reveals how politics can be an important part of stories, even those read for their entertainment value.

Just as the first essay illustrates the variety of ways texts can be transformed through the concept of intertextuality, the culminating essay illustrates the value of an intertextual approach while analyzing fairy-tale films that take as their subject the process of transformation. Christy Williams reads three mermaid films (*Splash*, Disney's *The Little Mermaid*, and *Aquamarine*) against the backdrop of Hans Christian Andersen's fairy tale "The Little Mermaid," suggesting that when read together, the four texts highlight important ideological shifts that might not be clearly visible when reading each film individually in relation to Andersen's tale. She tracks the films' engagement with representations of love and sacrifice as tied to gender and analyzes how the films present the acquisition and performance of gender. Ultimately, her argument is more about the value of reading the films together than presenting any single interpretation of the mermaid tales.

Finally, this collection is a beginning—an argument that it is time to change our language and our focus and start calling the innovative work being done on intertextual and critical adaptations what it is, a study of transformation.

Notes

1. Jack Zipes writes that the best way to account for the fairy tale's "major appeal" is its "celebration of miraculous or fabulous transformation in the name of hope" ("Cross-Cultural Connections" 849).

2. The critical literature on adaptation is filled with expressions of impatience over the persistence of the source-adaptation model. See Thomas Leitch for an overview of the problem (161–62).

3. To be fair, scholars of film adaptation like Dudley Andrew, Robert Stam, and Leitch have expanded adaptation studies to make it central to cinema studies and, Leitch argues, to textual studies itself (167).

4. Speculative fiction includes such genres as fantasy, horror, sci-fi, utopian, apocalyptic, and fairy-tale fiction.

5. See Marc DiPaolo's essay in this collection for more analysis.

6. This is further explored in Stella Bolaki's essay in this collection.

7. Mia Mask elaborates an astounding number of intertexts swirling around Toni Morrison's novel *Beloved* and the film adaptation produced by Oprah Winfrey; Robert Stam sketches out similar influences on Stephen Spielberg's film version of Alice Walker's *The Color Purple*; and Barton Palmer demonstrates an intertextual reading of the genre of *film noir*.

8. The novel *The Wind Done Gone*, by Alice Randall, an "unauthorized parody" of Margaret Mitchell's *Gone with the Wind*, illustrates an important function of transformations: to fill in the history that has been replaced by myth in a popular novel and has taken on the status of truth. Randall's novel tells a parallel story from the viewpoint of a black woman— the half-sister of Scarlett O'Hara and a slave—a "shadow" text written to fill in historical details that were completely left out of both novel and film. See Rimmer for Randall's summary of what was left out, and an overview of the lawsuit brought against publication.

9. The concept of the narrativization of history is by now well accepted. See Hayden White for a thorough explanation.

Works Cited

Andrew, Dudley. "Adaptation." *Film Adaptation*. Ed. James Naremore. New Brunswick: Rutgers University Press, 2000. 28–37.

Bacchilega, Cristina. *Postmodern Fairy Tales: Gender and Narrative Strategies*. Philadelphia: University of Pennsylvania Press, 1997.

Bakhtin, M. M. "Discourse in the Novel." Trans. Caryl Emerson and Michael Holquist. *The Dialogic Imagination: Four Essays by M. M. Bakhtin*. Austin: University of Texas Press, 1981. 259–422.

Benson, Stephen. "Introduction: Fiction and the Contemporaneity of the Fairy Tale." *Contemporary Fiction and the Fairy Tale*. Ed. Benson. Detroit: Wayne State University Press, 2008. 1–19.

Collins, Emily. "Nabokov's *Lolita* and Andersen's *The Little Mermaid*." *Nabokov Studies* 9 (2005): 77–100.

Content, Rob, Tim Kreider, and Boyd White. Rev. of *O Brother, Where Art Thou?* Dir. Joel Coen. *Film Quarterly* 55.1 (2001): 41–48.

Hutcheon, Linda. *A Theory of Parody: The Teachings of Twentieth-Century Art Forms*. New York: Methuen, 1985.

Kristeva, Julia. "Word, Dialogue and Novel." Trans. Alice Jardine, Thomas Gora, and Léon S. Roudiez. *The Kristeva Reader*. Ed. Toril Moi. New York: Columbia University Press, 1986. 34–61.

Leitch, Thomas. "Twelve Fallacies in Contemporary Adaptation Theory." *Criticism* 45.2 (2003): 149–71.

Lim, Bliss Cua. "Serial Time: Bluebeard in Stepford." *Literature and Film: A Guide to the Theory and Practice of Film Adaptation*. Ed. Robert Stam and Alessandra Regno. London: Blackwell, 2005. 163–90.

Mask, Mia. "*Beloved:* The Adaptation of an American Slave Narrative." *Literature and Film: A Guide to the Theory and Practice of Film Adaptation*. Ed. Robert Stam and Alessandra Regno. London: Blackwell, 2005. 272–94.

Musser, Charles. "Horace McCoy's Appropriation and Refiguration of Two Hollywood Musicals." *A Companion to Literature and Film*. Ed. Robert Stam and Alessandra Regno. London: Blackwell, 2004. 229–57.

Palmer, R. Barton. "The Sociological Turn of Adaptation Studies: The Example of *Film Noir*." *A Companion to Literature and Film*. Ed. Robert Stam and Alessandra Regno. London: Blackwell, 2004. 258–77.

Randall, Alice. *The Wind Done Gone*. New York: Houghton Mifflin, 2001.

Rimmer, Matthew. "Gone with the Wind: Copyright Law and Fair Use." *Australian Library and Information Association*. April 2003. 15 June 2009. <http://www.alia.org.au/publishing/incite/2003/04/wind.gone.html>.

Stam, Robert. "Beyond Fidelity: The Dialogics of Adaptation." *Film Adaptation*. Ed. James Naremore. New Brunswick: Rutgers University Press, 2000. 54–76.

Warner, Marina. *From the Beast to the Blonde: On Fairy Tales and Their Tellers*. New York: Farrar, Straus and Giroux, 1994.

White, Hayden. *The Content of the Form: Narrative Discourse and Historical Representation*. Baltimore: Johns Hopkins University Press, 1987.

Zipes, Jack. "Cross-Cultural Connections and the Contamination of the Classical Fairy Tale." *The Great Fairy Tale Tradition: From Straparola and Basile to the Brothers Grimm*. Ed. and Trans. Jack Zipes. New York: Norton, 2001. 845–69.

_____. *Fairy Tale as Myth/ Myth as Fairy Tale*. The Thomas D. Clark Lectures, 1993. Lexington: University Press of Kentucky, 1994.

_____. *Fairy Tales and the Art of Subversion: The Classical Genre for Children and the Process of Civilization*. 2nd ed. New York: Routledge, 2006.

1

Borrowing a Melody: Jane Campion's *The Piano* and Intertextuality

PHYLLIS FRUS

Jane Campion's 1993 film *The Piano* is one of the most widely reviewed and praised films of the 1990s. Nominated for nine Academy Awards and winner of the Palme d'Or, the top prize at Cannes, *The Piano* tells the story of Ada, a woman with a young daughter, who is sent by her father to marry a settler in the British colony of New Zealand. Given the film's period setting and its subjects—colonialism, the exchange of land and women, establishment of settler identity, sexual discovery and adultery—it is not surprising that it has been treated from various feminist, psychoanalytical, mythic, and historicist perspectives. In addition, fairy-tale scholars Maria Tatar and Cristina Bacchilega have read *The Piano* alongside retellings of the Bluebeard tale by Angela Carter and Margaret Atwood.[1] While many of these interpretations are admiring, the film has many detractors as well, and it has sparked a slew of questions and controversy (Johnson 145–52). Is *The Piano* misogynist or feminist? Does Ada resist being passed like property from father to husband, or does she accept being sent halfway across the world to marry a stranger as the best a woman who has had a child out of wedlock can do? Does her story represent sexual victimization or sexual awakening?[2]

The number of competing interpretations can be illustrated by noting various answers to the question, What is the significance of Ada's muteness? Barbara Johnson connects Ada to the silent woman of the English literary tradition, noting that muteness can be a form of resistance and subjecthood, as well as of oppression (141–43). Diane Hoeveler attributes Ada's silence to hysteria, a displaced response to the stereotype of women as "endless chatterer" (110). To Marina Warner, Ada's use of the piano as her voice signifies both "repression and rebellion: Ada resists and overcomes her constricted fate by her refusal to acquiesce, symbolized by her muteness" (405). Warner also connects the silence of the heroine to mermaid legends that link voice to identity and silence to submission (406).

Although intriguing, the plot of *The Piano* does not explain the many and varied interpretations. Ada McGrath, a mail-order bride, travels from Scotland in the mid–nineteenth century with her nine-year-old daughter, Flora, to marry a countryman who is busily acquiring land in the bush of New Zealand from its Maori owners. Ada does not speak; she communicates in writing, by making hand signals to Flora, who translates and speaks for her, and through the passionate music she plays on her piano. In the opening scenes this instrument is left on the beach rather than being carried to Stewart's hut with her trunks and boxes. Separating her from her piano as though it were just another possession proves to be Stewart's undoing. Feeling betrayed, Ada sleeps with her daughter rather than her husband and turns to Baines, a neighbor sympathetic to the Maori, for help in getting access to her piano.

Awakened to Ada's passionate nature by watching her happiness at playing her beloved instrument, Baines offers Stewart prime land in return for possession of the piano and lessons from Ada. Baines offers to trade the piano back to Ada, its rightful owner, a few keys at a time, in return for favors of a prurient sort. Although Ada is in effect simply being exchanged once again between men, she becomes aroused by being so passionately desired and begins an affair with Baines. Angry at being shut out by Ada and Baines during the music lessons, Flora betrays her mother to Stewart. After spying on the lovers, but keeping his voyeurism to himself, Stewart first tries to rape Ada and then shuts her and Flora up in his house. When Ada sends a note to her lover on a piano key she has ripped from the instrument, Flora betrays her again, taking the message to her stepfather, who attacks Ada's piano and then her hand with an axe, chopping off her index finger.

Simply by staring at her husband Ada stops him from raping her while she lies delirious with fever from her injury—and Stewart grants her unspoken wish to let her leave the settlement with Baines (he believes her mind has told him to let her go). When Ada impulsively orders the piano thrown overboard from the Maori canoe carrying them away, she places her foot in the coil of tethering rope and goes into the deep with it, until she frees herself and floats up to be rescued. The primary ending shows Ada living in

Nelson among other Pakehas with an apparently untroubled Flora, practicing speaking aloud, and playing her new piano with the prosthesis her new husband has fashioned for her.[3] The old piano lies buried at the bottom of the deep like the coffin one of the Maori sailors compared it to. In an epilogue Ada says that she dreams she lies there with the piano, imagining her death had her will not chosen life; the final shot is of Ada tethered to the instrument.

We can account for the contrasting and conflicting readings of the film by using the concept of intertextuality. The film refers to a variety of literary, historical, and folk texts; these create a complex web of allusions, making the film highly suitable to treat as a retelling of other stories. Locating *The Piano*'s sources helps us choose the most satisfactory way to interpret the film. It also helps to evaluate it, for if we do not recognize the film's many borrowings—of plot devices from genres such as gothic, motifs from fairy tales, characters' motivations and actions from psychoanalytic theory, and figures from New Zealand's colonial history—we are likely to see its combination of realist and romantic elements as flaws or simply confusing. Two particular readings seem most promising: Is it a history film—one that takes its subject seriously, representing some feature of social, political, or economic life in cinematic terms that bear scrutiny—or does it simply use its period setting as backdrop for a love story?

Critics have complained about the jarring contrast between the period look and the postmodern sensibility of the characters in *The Piano*. Diane Hoeveler sums up our experience of viewing the film as one of "historical dissonance, a sense that we are watching a contemporary drama played out in anachronistic costumes and setting" (116). Hoeveler has a very particular explanation for what she calls the "staged 'Victorian' quality" of the film that contrasts with its forward-driving plot; she believes the discordant notes struck by *The Piano* are the result of Campion's attempt to disguise the fact that her screenplay is an adaptation of a novel that she did not have the rights to—Jane Mander's *Story of a New Zealand River*, first published in 1920, which is a leisurely narrative of more than twenty years of a mismatched couple's marriage (116).[4] Hoeveler is so eager to prove that *The Piano* is derivative that she does not simply charge that Campion's film revises the novel without crediting it; she finds many other "blatant" debts: to sources as diverse as Browning's *The Ring and the Book* (for the removal of the heroine's finger and threat to dismember her if more suitors appear), feminist literary fairy tales by Atwood and Carter (for the "cunning, scheming feminist heroine" they share with Ada), and the tradition of women using silence as a form of protest against the patriarchy (112–13; 110).[5]

Although her intention in analyzing Campion's screenplay side by side with Mander's novel is to reveal *The Piano* to be unoriginal and therefore not deserving of its international accolades, we can interpret Hoeveler's comparison much differently—as evidence of the film's polyvocalism. The echoes she finds do not make *The Piano* an unacknowledged adaptation; they make it intertextual, and laying bare the many allusions, borrowings, and similarities to other texts does not make it derivative; it makes it a richer, more complex film, one that varies according to the antecedent texts the audience brings to it.

Mander's novel and the few other predecessors and influences Hoeveler mentions are just the tip of the iceberg so far as intertexts are concerned. From the earliest reviews of *The Piano*, critics have cited literary influences such as Poe, Hawthorne, and nineteenth-century Gothic (Hendershot 105n1). Campion herself identified Romantic novels by the Brontë sisters as influential, particularly *Wuthering Heights* (135).[6] Other likely precursors are film genres (mail-order bride films like *Picture Bride* and *Heartland* or a gothic romance like *Rebecca*) and the heroic or spiritual journey of mythology (Bussi). Like many other films made by auteurs, writer-directors who have control of all aspects of a film's production, *The Piano* also prompts readings based on certain patterns of interpretation developed by psychoanalysis, feminism, and post-colonial theory, for critics can find ample evidence of parallels in the case histories of Freud, feminist interpretations of films, and stories told by post-colonial subjects, such as a growing number of Maori films (for examples, see Modleski; Johnson; DuPuis). Acknowledging that all these are antecedent texts, and yet that none is the source of Campion's film, makes sense in an intertextual framework.

If we emphasize the period details and the historical referents, we expect a history film that comments in some way on the mid-nineteenth-century process of colonizing an island nation with an indigenous population that was resisting. *The Piano* is set sometime in the middle of the nineteenth century, while colonization of what was then Aoteoroa was underway by men and women from the British Isles. We can assume this time period from the clothes the characters wear and from Campion's expressed wishes to give her characters a Victorian sensibility, particularly the repressed sexuality we associate with Victoria's subjects. Campion told an interviewer she wanted to show a woman experiencing a powerful sexual awakening after she had been uprooted from familiar surroundings and sent to the farthest reaches of the empire (Ostria and Jousse 124–25). That may be why the film attempts to yoke the Maori, who are subjected to the might of a brutal colonizing power, with women, who are subject to men's power and control. As women are to men, Maori are to Pakeha.[7] Calling attention to parallels between women as Other and colonized subjects is a fairly good reason to treat *The*

Piano as a historical film. But at most it is what I call quasi-historical because of the indefinite time period, the few signs of Maori resistance to colonization, and the anachronistic music that Ada plays.

The quasi-historical film, as its name implies, barely belongs in the category of history film. While the setting and cultural processes are historical—that is, we recognize social movements and political institutions such as British colonialism and mail-order brides—the main plot incidents and all the figures are fictitious. In some quasi-historical films the period details are elaborate, and we can date the events approximately, but no major events or figures appear in the background. When we look for intertexts to support a historical reading, we do not find nonfictional sources from the period. Most of this film's antecedent texts and genre conventions come from fiction and romance, not from history.

Apparently the motives for making a period film or costume drama—getting just the right look with authentic costumes and setting details—differ from those driving the makers of a history film—getting the history right so that audiences will believe in the truth of the story. Campion's primary purpose seems to be exploration of an erotic triangle comprising an émigré couple and a man who has begun to "go bush," and then setting their relationship against a wild landscape that works more symbolically than historically. The location in the bush, Stewart's exploitative land trades with the local Maori, and the Maori themselves are merely background for those whom the filmmaker regards as the really interesting characters: white settlers coming to terms with their sexual identities and their role in the colony as owners of land and therefore holders of power.[8]

In these ways, an intertextual reading of *The Piano* with emphasis on its historical antecedents may explain why the film, despite its depiction of Maori characters speaking their own language and Campion's use of a Maori consultant, disappointed historians and others looking for a serious film on a period of colonization, the effects of which—Maori land claims and demands for autonomous status—were being hotly debated at the time the film was made (DuPuis 59). As Margaret Jolly points out, the effect of the cinematic and plot elements is to naturalize the settling of New Zealand rather than to historicize it; the film converts conquest of a people into romantic spectacle. All told the film presents a fantasy of successful colonization, rather than an interpretation of historical events.

A reading that focuses on fairy tales may be more satisfactory, particularly because these predecessor texts are compatible with gothic or historical romance.[9] The fairy-tale antecedents that color *The Piano* are the genre in general and the Bluebeard tale in particular, with background texture provided by closely related tales and mermaid legends. By emphasizing the motifs, echoes, and allusions from these stories with their qualities of magic or fantasy, it is easy to regard the film as a transformation of a fairy tale, with Stewart as Ada's axe-wielding "Bluebeard," but not as a deliberate retelling of the medieval tale first set down by Charles Perrault in 1697. Fairy-tale qualities pervade the plot, including elements of magic and a clear demarcation between good and evil. Closely related to this, characters represent types, as they do in romance as well as fairy tales. These characteristics are reinforced by the cinematic strategies employed, particularly the antirealism of the shooting style, the music track, and the setting in the woods.

In basic outline, "Bluebeard" is a simple tale. An unattractive rich man with a distinctive-colored beard that sets him off as "other" has taken a number of wives, all of whom have disappeared mysteriously. Bluebeard marries another and soon afterward leaves on a journey. Before leaving, he gives his bride a key to a chamber that she is expressly forbidden to enter. When out of curiosity she uses the key to open the door to the secret room, she sees the bloody heads of several previous wives. She drops the key, which is permanently stained with blood, thereby announcing her guilt. Bluebeard returns ahead of schedule to claim her as his next victim. She is rescued by, variously, her brothers, mother, or a sister. In closely related tales, such as "The Robber Bridegroom" and "Mr. Fox," the maiden promised in marriage pays a visit to her intended's house in the forest before the wedding, where she encounters him or his gang killing a woman while she is in hiding. The severed finger of one of her predecessors flies into her lap, but she is not discovered. She reveals the truth about the bridegroom the next day at a celebratory meal by narrating the story of the atrocities as though she had dreamed them, producing the severed digit as proof of her betrothed's true nature. He is then captured by friends and brothers or the other guests.[10]

Though the allusions to Bluebeard are clear—marriage to a stranger, forest setting, amputation of a finger—Campion's film is complicated by the presence of a child from the bride's former life and by various other omissions and substitutions. For example, the key is a piano key rather than a key to a chamber, and it is a metonym for Ada, whereas in most versions of the tale Bluebeard's key is a phallic substitute for his power of enforcement. Also, different characters act as voyeurs. Both Flora and Stewart peer into Baines' hut, where the piano lessons have turned into exploratory sessions between Ada and George. In closely related tales such as "The Robber Bridegroom" and "Fitcher's Bird," the wife or betrothed hides herself to keep from suffering the fate of the bridegroom's other victims and spies to learn how to save herself, whereas first Flora and then Stewart suffer the fate of those excluded from the primal scene: extreme jealousy and anger, leading to a desire for revenge. When we make the fairy-tale elements prominent we notice that Campion's screenplay has reversed the usual villain-victim pair; in this version Bluebeard becomes the weak figure; his is the "fatal curiosity" as he peeps through a crack in Baines' hut to watch a love scene between his wife and another man (Campion 83). This (in)version provides a substitute husband (Baines) who is not cruel but relinquishes his power over the wife, which he has gained by possessing the piano, so that she can come to him as an equal (Hendershot 100).

Because the film does not employ the basic kernel of "Bluebeard" in its classic tellings, it serves as a model of intertextuality quite different from that of Atwood's or Carter's literary fairy tales. Campion's film has direct allusions to motifs such as an axe and a husband who becomes a monster. It includes a rehearsal and a staging of the tale as a shadow-play. But the motifs are distributed among various characters so that the tale does not form the skeleton on which Campion's plot is hung. The fairy tale elements support the genre of gothic romance, whereas it is missing two of the major elements of the Bluebeard tale, perhaps even the defining ones. As Bliss Cua Lim has pointed out, Bluebeard is literature's first serial killer, but in *The Piano* neither husband nor lover—the two possible monsters here—have a prior record of violence. Neither does the female protagonist resemble the heroine of the Bluebeard tale, for in most variants of Bluebeard, the wife (or betrothed) enacts the role of "last girl" of horror films, in that she confronts the bloody bodies of his previous victim-wives and thus anticipates her own fate (Lim 170). The Bluebeard tale may better be viewed as a palimpsest, one of the layers revealed when the viewer reads the film critically, with attention to the way the various intertexts add dimensions and echoes.

To decide on a particular intertextual interpretation, we must do more than cite resemblances of plot and theme between the transformation and anterior texts. We should also compare narrative structures, analyze genre conventions, and pay attention to cinematic style. A film transformation like *The Piano* has even more layers of intertextuality than print texts, because movies are made up of what Robert Stam calls "tracks" or layers of communication: visual, verbal, and auditory (56). In the auditory track, the music that Holly Hunter as Ada plays to express her emotions and desires signifies different things to particular listeners. To some it brings to mind New Age, modal music, whereas others emphasize its impressionistic, atmospheric qualities.[11] A cinematographer's shooting style may refer to other texts, even those in other media, such as painting or photography (Hayward 201). Stuart Dryburgh, director of photography on Campion's film, says that the cinematography was inspired by autochrome, a nineteenth-century color stills process that results in strong colors—the dark blue-greens of the bush and the amber-browns of the mud and the interior of Baines' hut (qtd. in Bilborough 141). The effect gained may contribute to the historical look of the film, as Campion apparently intended, or it may add to the symbolic resonance of the settings—depending on the way one is interpreting the film.

The fairy-tale atmosphere is reinforced by cinematic details: the light and color are characterized by extremes of black and white, not subtle shades. Even the point of view of the camera, which goes up on the ceiling to look down at Stewart's teacup and inside the piano's packing case with Ada's hand to play a tune, reinforces the artificiality provided by the elements of fairy tale and magical realism. To take another example, the production designer of *The Piano*, Andrew McAlpine, points to the "dank darkness" of the clearing that Stewart has laboriously cleared for his hut by felling trees and burning stumps, laying creeping vines over all, which contrasts dramatically to the "green cathedral" of Baines's cabin, "a very gothic landscape, surrounded by this cool green light." According to McAlpine, these distinctive moods were deliberately created by altering the natural landscape (qtd. in Bilborough 140). But does the cinematic style support a fairy-tale or a historical reading? Apparently Campion wanted to have it both ways, to suggest both history and romance.

Campion says she instructed the crew to "improve" the wild setting of New Zealand in order to relate the bush to imagery of the unconscious. She used it, that is, for "its dark, inner world" (Bilborough 139). Also, she refers to the "epic style of the film and landscape" as suggesting "the romantic genre"; yet she also wanted it to be real, and authenticity was an important goal. (Campion instructed Holly Hunter not to shampoo her hair regularly, so that the heroine's greasy hair would counter the romanticism of the classic film beauty.) As Campion said, she wanted the audience never quite let off the hook "by any sense that the action is taking place in a fairy tale or romantic world" (qtd. in Bilborough 139). At the same time the lack of psychological depth and attention to surfaces and textures rather than the inner lives of the characters, common characteristics of fairy tales, suggest romance. In my view, these cinematic means tip the balance toward fairy tale and romance, away from historical realism.

Clearly, reading *The Piano* as an intertextual transformation of "Bluebeard" adds complexity. To give just four examples, looking at the film through the prism of the tale draws our attention to the husband as villain, as in some way monstrous, whereas most critics, particularly feminist readers, have focused on the movie as the heroine's story. Noting the Bluebeard parallels makes Ada's daughter Flora important, as she betrays her mother to her stepfather, causing the axe to come down on Ada in a symbolic decapitation. In a way, calling attention to the Bluebeard analogues paradoxically makes the characters' motives more complex: because Stewart is clearly not as monstrous as Bluebeard, the viewer may find it easier to blame Ada, as he does: "You broke my trust, you pushed me hard, too hard.... I only clipped your wing, that is all." (Campion 111–12).

The fairy tale of Bluebeard that is performed at the church, and which shadows the plot, helps to paint the husband as authoritarian and controlling if not evil, making the heroine's successful escape from him even more satisfactory, in the tradition of patriarchal husbands in nineteenth-century novels, such as Rochester in *Jane Eyre*.

Even if we concede that the fairy-tale reading is stronger than the interpretation of *The Piano* as a history film, we can still take cultural and historical lessons from it. This is because although the fairy-tale dimension complements a reading of the film as a historical romance, there is a historical dimension to fairy tales. Although the story of Bluebeard and his wives now appears in collections of children's fairy tales, it has its roots in adult entertainment. Campion may have deliberately sought to return the tale to its source as a moral cautionary tale of a woman punished for her failings: curiosity and disobedience (Tatar 124). Its performance as a shadow play put on in the church on Christmas Eve would have been not only historically appropriate, as shadow plays were common well into the twentieth century, but thematically apt as well, for stagings of Bluebeard, according to Tatar, functioned to reassert patriarchal power (123). Although the wife is rescued or saves herself in many versions, sometimes help comes too late. The variant performed as a shadow play may be one of these, for the rehearsals that Stewart witnesses show the axe falling on the bride's neck. We do not get to see the play's conclusion in performance, for a few Maori men in the audience come to the heroine's rescue before the axe can descend. This version may so fascinate Stewart because his masculinity needs shoring up. We also see him watching a rehearsal and the performance carefully; apparently it gives him a model for how to treat a recalcitrant bride, and may reinforce his sense of entitlement, his right to her body. We can still regard the movie, like many fairy tales, as a story of patriarchal power, which suits the historical theme of colonization. It is 1850s New Zealand, in the bush, and a husband is having problems domesticating his mute mail-order bride and persuading her to consummate their marriage. All told, the tale reminds audiences at the church as well as at the movie that men rule—their advantages are reinforced by narratives. In this view, we do not regard the Maoris who interrupt the play at the climax as naïve, but see their point in objecting to it as a lesson.

This is yet another reason *The Piano* is barely historical; it invokes a great many conventions of the romance genre. A rule of thumb might be: the more genre conventions a film displays, the less it is reality-based. Despite its director's feminist intentions, its international cast, its financing from a French corporation, and Campion's reputation as auteur, this "art film" has many romance conventions: a love triangle, a seduction, fetishization of a woman's (and yes, a man's) body through close-ups of various body parts (which, despite the fragmentation, contributes to the romance by promoting the myth of viewers' intimacy with the characters), and satisfying closure: a happy ending in marriage. These conventions are also the source of much of the pleasure of viewing *The Piano*. Viewers probably enjoy watching a woman try to maneuver gracefully through the bush to reach her lover in a hoop skirt big enough to use as a tent for two, and to watch mother and daughter looking similar in their shovel-head bonnets, which is echoed in scenes of the daughter's speaking for her mute mother, adopting her mannerisms, and playing at being a wife and mother.

Reading *The Piano* as a transformation of fairy tales in general, Bluebeard in particular, places imitation, allusion, and borrowing in a positive light. It can even explain the many contradictory interpretations, including accounting for the negative ones. For example, a fairy-tale framework would support a critical view that the film is all exterior, with little in the way of in-depth character realization. A fairy-tale reading is also compatible with postmodernist readings, those that find no definite or determinable meaning in *The Piano*. Sarah Kerr says that this glancing portrayal of characters who lack plausible motivation is the primary weakness of the film. In her view, it is all surfaces and sensations (30). The camera viewpoints and other aesthetic choices support that—or they may simply be Campion being reflexive, leaving her mark (Dryburgh qtd. in Bilborough 141). Once noted, the fairy-tale elements do not go away from the spectator's consciousness, no matter what conclusion one draws about their effects. A historical reading proves to be unsatisfying because of the film's reliance on fairy-tale and romance texts and its neglect of colonial issues. The interpretation that subsumes and complements others is the one that traces not only the many references to Bluebeard but the influence of fairy tales on the film's narrative structures, the genre conventions it displays, and its cinematic style.

Notes

1. Two books of essays on the film have been compiled (Coombs and Gemmell; Margolis). Also contributing to the phenomenon was the publication in 1993 of both the screenplay and a novelization of the film (the latter co-written by Campion and Kate Pullinger).
2. Johnson writes, "The genius of the movie lies in the fact that it can provoke such diametrically opposed readings" (147).
3. *Pakeha* is the Maori term for white colonizers and their descendants.
4. In Mander's novel, at the end of the nineteenth century, a woman with a young daughter and a piano meets a lumber entrepreneur in Auckland. She marries him and moves with him to the edge of the New Zealand bush near the mouth of a river, where the husband builds the first tram to get logs down to the harbor. The wife is attracted to her husband's

foreman, who is a surgeon on the side and highly educated (he falls in love with the wife while delivering her many babies), but the affair is platonic while the husband is alive. The husband is depicted as a womanizer, while his second-in-command refrains from any sex for the most part, in a kind of chivalric devotion to his boss's wife.

5. To be fair, Hoeveler stops short of charging Campion with plagiarizing Mander's novel; others in New Zealand did suggest that her borrowing met a legal definition of plagiarism and that Campion should at least return her Oscar for original screenplay (see Fox; Frey).

6. Hillary Frey says that Campion acknowledged *The African Queen* as well as *Wuthering Heights* as inspiring the film, and she reports that "Campion readily concedes a long-time familiarity with [Mander's] novel." All told, Campion says, about twenty novels influenced the film (Frey).

7. The parallels are not as obvious as they might be because certain scenes in the screenplay were left out of the film. These include passages in which the Maori display resentment and discuss plans to fight back with the guns they can secure only by trading their land. Ada rebels against her husband, but we don't see how profoundly and actively the Maori resisted; we don't know when the film is set—"before or after the 1840 signing of the Treaty of Waitangi in 1840, or before, during, or after the Anglo-Maori land wars of the 1860s" (DuPuis 55–56).

8. While Campion has been praised for using a Maori consultant and having the indigenous people speak their own language (only some of it is translated in subtitles), she has also been blamed for failing to depict the Maori resistance (DuPuis; Pihama). Whatever the director's intentions may have been, the result is that the Maori serve primarily as background color and as a means of differentiating the two British settlers: Stewart the utilitarian exploiter of natives and their land, and George Baines, a liminal figure halfway between colonizer and native (DuPuis 65). DuPuis calls the film a "colonialist fantasy" (63).

9. The richest readings of the film incorporate discussion of fairy-tale elements in support of a reading of the film as romance, gothic, or coming-of-age case study. For examples, see Quart; Hendershot; Modleski.

10. Tatar reprints various versions of the Bluebeard tale. An annotation of Perrault's "Bluebeard" and links to many variants can be found at surlalunefairytales.com/bluebeard.

11. A determining factor in its style is Hunter's ability as a talented amateur pianist who played the diegetic music for the film. Composer Michael Nyman sent her drafts of the music to learn what she could do well; he then wrote for her strengths as well as her tastes, which included arpeggi (chords with the notes played in sequence rather than all at once), repetition of motifs, and atmospheric sounds rather than "precise, rhythmic" patterns. See Gorbman (46–48).

Works Cited

Atwood, Margaret. "Bluebeard's Egg." *The Classic Fairy Tales*. Ed. Maria Tatar. New York: Norton, 1999. 156–78.

Bacchilega, Cristina. *Postmodern Fairy Tales: Gender and Narrative Strategies*. Philadelphia: University of Pennsylvania Press, 1997.

Bilborough, Miro. "The Making of *The Piano*." *The Piano*. New York: Hyperion, 1993. 135–53.

Bussi, Elisa. "Voyages and Border Crossings: Jane Campion's *The Piano* (1993)." *The Seeing Century: Film, Vision, and Identity*. Ed. Wendy Everett. 161–73.

Campion, Jane. *The Piano*. New York: Hyperion, 1993.

_____, and Kate Pullinger. *The Piano: A Novel*. New York: Hyperion, 1994.

Carter, Angela. "The Bloody Chamber." *The Bloody Chamber and Other Stories*. London: Penguin, 1979. 7–41.

Coombs, Felicity, and Suzanne Gemmell, eds. *Piano Lessons: Approaches to* The Piano. London: John Libbey, 1999.

DuPuis, Reshela. "Romanticizing Colonialism: Power and Pleasure in Jane Campion's *The Piano*." *Contemporary Pacific* 8.1 (1996): 51–79.

Fox, Alistair. "Puritanism and the Erotics of Transgression: The New Zealand Influence on Jane Campion's Thematic Imaginary." *Jane Campion: Cinema, Nation, Identity*. 23 August 2007. <http://www.otago.ac.nz/communicationstudies/campion/participants/fox.html>

Frey, Hillary. "The Purloined Piano?" *Lingua Franca* 10.6 (2000). 15 June 2009. <http://linguafranca.mirror.theinfo.org/print/0009/field-piano.html>.

Gorbman, Claudia. "Music in *The Piano*." *Jane Campion's* The Piano. Ed. Harriet Margolis. Cambridge Film Handbooks. Cambridge: Cambridge University Press, 2000. 42–58.

Hayward, Susan. *Cinema Studies: The Key Concepts*. 2nd ed. London: Routledge, 2000.

Hendershot, Cindy. "(Re)visioning the Gothic: Jane Campion's *The Piano*. *Literature/Film Quarterly* 26.2 (1998): 97–108.

Hoeveler, Diane Long. "Silence, Sex, and Feminism: An Examination of *The Piano*'s Unacknowledged Sources." *Literature/Film Quarterly* 26.2 (1998): 109–17.

Johnson, Barbara. "Muteness Envy." *The Feminist Difference: Literature, Psychoanalysis, Race, and Gender*. Cambridge: Harvard University Press, 1998. 129–53.

Jolly, Margaret. "Looking Back? Gender, Race, and Sexuality in Campion's *The Piano*." Lecture, University of Hawaii-Manoa, 16 Feb. 2006.

Kerr, Sarah. "Shoot the Piano Player." Rev. of *The* Piano, dir. Jane Campion. *New York Review of Books* 41.3 (3 Feb. 1994): 29–30.

Lim, Bliss Cua. "Serial Time: Bluebeard in Stepford." *Literature and Film: A Guide to the Theory and Practice of Film Adaptation*. Ed. Robert Stam and Alessandra Regno. London: Blackwell, 2005. 163–90.

Mander, Jane. *The Story of a New Zealand River*. 1920. Rpt. Christchurch, NZ: Whitcombe and Tombs, 1973.

Margolis, Harriet, ed. *Jane Campion's* The Piano. Cambridge Film Handbooks. Cambridge: Cambridge University Press, 2000.

Modleski, Tania. "Axe the Piano Player." *Old Wives' Tales and Other Women's Stories*. New York: New York University Press, 1998. 31–46.

Ostria, Vincent, and Thierry Jousse. *The Piano:* Interview with Jane Campion. Trans. Michael Curley. *Cahiers du Cinema May 1993*. Rpt. *Jane Campion Interviews*. Ed. Virginia Wright Wexman. Jackson: University Press of Mississippi, 1999. 124–32.

The Piano, Dir. Jane Campion. Perf. Holly Hunter, Sam Neill, Harvey Keitel, and Anna Paquin. Miramax, 1993.

Pihama, Leonie. "Ebony and Ivory: Constructions of Maori in *The Piano*." *Jane Campion's* The Piano. Ed. Harriet Margolis. Cambridge Film Handbooks. Cambridge: Cambridge University Press, 2000. 114–34.

Quart, Barbara. Rev. of *The Piano*. Dir. Jane Campion. *Cineaste* 20.3 (April 1994). 3pp. *Academic Search Premier*. EBSCO. 4 June 2009.

Stam, Robert. "Beyond Fidelity: The Dialogics of Adaptation." *Film Adaptation*. Ed. James Naremore. New Brunswick: Rutgers University Press, 2000. 54–76.

Tatar, Maria. *Secrets beyond the Door: The Story of Bluebeard and His Wives*. Princeton: Princeton University Press, 2004.

Warner, Marina. *From the Beast to the Blonde: On Fairy Tales and Their Tellers*. New York: Farrar, Straus and Giroux, 1994.

2

Adaptation, The Orchid Thief, *and the Subversion of Hollywood Conventions*

DEVIN HARNER

I tell my students that beginning an academic paper with a definition from Merriam-Webster is perhaps the worst opening move that they can make for a variety of reasons. However, in deference to the euphoric coloring outside of the lines of *Adaptation's* director, Spike Jonze, and writer, Charlie Kaufman, I'm inclined to begin this essay thus:

According to Merriam-Webster, or, more specifically, to www.merriamwebster.com, *Adaptation* is:

1. the act or process of adapting: the state of being adapted
2. adjustment to environmental conditions...
3. something that is adapted; specifically: a composition rewritten into a new form.

To this list, I'll add one of my own:

4. a feature film, released in 2002 and starring Nicholas Cage, that treats themes involving all the aforementioned definitions, and that self-consciously chronicles screenwriter Charlie Kaufman's attempts to turn *New Yorker* staff writer Susan Orlean's nonfiction book *The Orchid Thief* into a viable film script.

This definition only works for the first part of the film, however. Although according to its title and to its initial premise Kaufman is "adapting" Orlean's book, instead he transforms the source text in several ways:

31

adding a meta-level about the impossibility of adapting such a plotless tale, necessitating wholesale transformation; highlighting the intertextual relationship between book and film; trying out conventions borrowed from various popular film genres and subverting them; and interrogating spectatorial pleasure in traditional romantic comedies and buddy movies. As the film's plot diverges from the source text, it critiques the repressive, patriarchal generic conventions of mainstream Hollywood cinema. In light of the way in which Kaufman's screenplay departs so dramatically from the unglamorous meanderings of the book's narrative, perhaps a more accurate title for the film would be "Transformation."

As one of film's most intellectually engaging and elusive artists, Charlie Kaufman achieved critical acclaim and a bit of fame, at least on college campuses, with 1999's *Being John Malkovich*, his first collaboration with Spike Jonze. A former skateboarder, Jonze was known for directing high-concept videos for the likes of Bjork, the Beastie Boys, and Weezer that blur the line between irony, nostalgic reverence, and allusive hyper-referential representation. Jonze was also a producer of the MTV *Jackass* series before making his feature film debut with *Being John Malkovich*. The legend surrounding the origins of *Adaptation*, which Kaufman validates in an interview with *The Guardian's* Danny Leigh, is that it was a deliberate attempt by Kaufman to distance himself from the wildly successful postmodern strangeness of *Being John Malkovich*. Kaufman wanted to retreat into the relative comfort of adapting a book essentially about orchids, with little in the way of a love story, plot-level action, or the traditional, necessary entanglements of Hollywood features.

However, Kaufman ends up hampered by the book's rambling, orchid-centric structure in which not much happens, at least by mainstream Hollywood standards. Orlean herself notes that her book profiling John Laroche, a Florida nursery owner who was caught poaching orchids with a group of Seminoles, was "such a non-linear, eccentric story that I never imagined someone would picture it as a movie" (Foreword viii). The result is that *Adaptation* is a strange amalgam of fiction and fact that documents Kaufman's grappling with *The Orchid Thief's* shortcomings until he is forced to invent against his will. (His inventions include not only writing himself into the script as would-be adapter, but creating a twin brother, Donald, who tags along throughout the film, and who is himself writing a more conventional movie script, and having more success with women than Kaufman.)

As we witness onscreen, Kaufman's initial forays into turning the book into a film script prove to be horrible failures, and cause him to descend into a pit of self-loathing, insecurity, and compulsive masturbation—all of which center on his own lack of success with women and on his parallel creative impotence. These themes collide when Kaufman develops a crush on Orlean that is as much intellectual as sexual. The nature of their relationship evokes Orlean's relationship to John Laroche, the book's real-life subject. As the *New York Times*' Ted Conover puts it in a review of *The Orchid Thief*, there is not enough of Laroche to make a book; as a consequence, Orlean retreats into herself and into Victorian-era orchid history, and this affects both the book and the would-be film's style and plot. In the film, Kaufman's obsession with Orlean as subject upstages the orchids for the sake of the film's plot, and mirrors the writer-centered narration in the book that objectifies Laroche. By engaging with off-screen reality, fictionalizing the lives of its real-world characters, and imposing much more plot on Orlean's text, *Adaptation* responds directly to Orlean's subjective, and self-interested, first-person female narrator in *The Orchid Thief* and highlights the original text's seeming deficiencies of plot and character when held up against a Hollywood rubric. It is ironic that Kaufman's onscreen attempts to remain true to Orlean's original plotlessness ultimately fail and that his efforts to add plot to the script, and to objectify subjects—be they characters, orchids, or other texts—for the sake of a romantic subplot, provide the film with conventional plot-level conflict and resolution.

In its self-awareness, and its focus on the creative process as a secondary plotline that parallels, intersects, and ultimately upstages the source text's narrative, *Adaptation* creates multiple opportunities for dialogue between the two texts. The amazing thing about transformations like this—like cover versions of popular songs where the new version of the song adds something imperceptible, or takes something away, or shifts the tone, or the key, or the pacing—is that the two texts are dependent on each other, not to make meaning, but to make *further* meaning. Although each can stand alone, the later text comments somehow on the earlier one. These complementary trajectories project a "story" which shares neither a beginning nor an end with the earlier text. For the reader familiar with both, there is a haunted quality to the film through which *Adaptation* deliberately calls attention to *The Orchid Thief* by allowing its plot to turn on the dialogue between the two texts. In their foregrounding of the intertextual relationship that is at the heart of all re-envisioned or adapted texts, Kaufman and Jonze go beyond adaptation and into transformation mode.

Despite the onscreen Kaufman's best efforts, the film ultimately descends into sex, drugs, and car chases—all of which are lacking in Orlean's text. However, in its use of voice-over culled verbatim from *The Orchid Thief* and its documenting of onscreen Kaufman's frustration as he tries to remain faithful to Orlean's book, the film pays lip service to the goal of accurate representation. For example, the film evokes Orlean's representation of

Laroche in the book—aside from the way in which he meets his demise, and the fact that he is depicted as having a torrid affair with Orlean. One bit of support for this otherwise farfetched plot addition is that Donald (also played by Cage) finds what he suspects are hints in *The Orchid Thief* that Orlean is attracted to Laroche. Any romantic interest in her subject would compromise Orlean's reputed journalistic objectivity, and Donald's discovery serves conveniently as an explanation for the fictitious affair with Laroche in the movie. At the same time, as *The Orchid Thief* is transformed and enters the realm of fiction Orlean's onscreen desire to protect her professional reputation, and said journalistic objectivity, is the catalyst for the film's descent into familiar buddy movie tropes, and into the requisite plot-level climax and resolution.

Although the difficulty of the project is hinted at in the onscreen Kaufman's voice-over narration as the film opens, it is brought to the forefront in two parallel scenes that both establish the film's subversive aesthetic and provide the onscreen rationale for Kaufman to move out of adaptation and into transformation. In the first scene, Kaufman discusses his vision for the film with producer Valerie Thomas, and in the later he is suffering from writer's block and meets with his agent, Marty, in an attempt to get out of the contract. In the earlier scene at a posh Hollywood restaurant, Thomas is professional, complimentary, and enthusiastic. In contrast, Kaufman is nervous and worried that the producer will notice his sweating or his baldness. Throughout their conversation, Kaufman pauses, gestures, stumbles, and wipes his brow. He is pinned in the frame by the camera, and, as a consequence, we are uncomfortable for him. Despite Kaufman's fame, and the fact that Thomas gushes over his talent as a screenwriter, his insecurity is appropriated by Jonze aesthetically, and he is further objectified in the scene.

When prompted by Thomas to share his thoughts on Orlean's text, Kaufman says, "It's great, sprawling *New Yorker* stuff, and I'd want to remain true to that. You know? I'd want to let the movie exist, rather than be artificially plot driven" (Kaufman 5). But when he meets his agent in the later scene, Kaufman reads the sentence from Conover's *New York Times* review about Laroche being an inadequate subject for a book-length project. This time, though, he is in apparent agreement that the book lacks narrative drive, as he comments, "It's that sprawling *New Yorker* shit" (50). In echoing his earlier praise of Orlean's text, and in conceding a bit of his desire for fidelity to *The Orchid Thief*, Kaufman reverses himself ironically and humorously. In doing so, he allows the film to change direction and to take on a plot, as the off-screen Kaufman gives himself license to invent, finally.

By this point in the film not much has happened aside from Kaufman skulking around uncomfortably, having a near miss with his sort-of love interest Amelia, masturbating, and berating Donald for his own attempt to write a screenplay and for recommending the seminar he is taking from famed screenwriting teacher Robert McKee. The fictional Kaufman's onscreen wants aside, the real Kaufman and his counterpart, Jonze, must make a movie that is watchable and that adheres, at least nominally, to the same Hollywood conventions that both the onscreen and the real Kaufman had hoped to avoid. Jonze and Kaufman reach something of a compromise, and they ultimately temper their regression to plot-level conventionality with a subversive aesthetic that critiques mainstream cinema's mode of spectatorial pleasure. In the early scene with Thomas and in later scenes with Amelia, Kaufman's agent, and a waitress, Jonze objectifies Cage's Kaufman in the frame, inverting the conventional Hollywood male gaze in a manner that makes viewers question our own pleasure in watching.

What makes a book, or a film, pleasurable aside from plot? Most of us know: movie stars are attractive, jokes are witty, sets are bright and larger than life, and the soundtrack feels like a mixtape constructed by the love of our lives playing on that perfect rainy November day. Films are enjoyable because they take us out of our own reality and into a fictional reality that feels "more real than real" until the lights come back on. Daniel Dayan suggests that the familiar conventions of genre allow us to be "sutured" into the film, that is, to suspend our disbelief, and to live in the world of the film, rather than the "real" world, for its duration (118). Laura Mulvey asserts that the manner by which we are sutured into the film is not value neutral, and that mainstream Hollywood cinema implicitly maintains the phallocentric power structures of patriarchal society that subjugate women. In her essay "Visual Pleasure and Narrative Cinema" Mulvey suggests that the "male gaze" of the spectator, reinforced in the onscreen gaze of the protagonist, is the problem. The actor's look at the actress, which anticipates and answers the viewer's desires, is a gaze of control and of subjugation. For Mulvey, the paramount pleasure of cinema is the aesthetic pleasure of looking at a female subject who is powerless to move away from the controlling gaze, and who lacks agency. Her theory does not refer just to pornography; it addresses all cinematic scenes in which the woman is centered in the frame as subject.

Despite its being hailed as innovative, critics like Gaylyn Studlar argued that Mulvey's theory of spectatorship was bound by the conventions of the patriarchy that it sought to dismantle, in that it failed to account for female spectatorial pleasure. Simply put, Mulvey's ideal theorized spectator was a heterosexual male who gazed at an onscreen woman. Her model for spectatorial pleasure provided no provision for the female, or for the gay male moviegoer. In her essay "Masochism and the Perverse Pleasures of the Cinema," Studlar responded to Mulvey, suggesting that a mode of pre-phallic cinematic pleasure is possible that is masochistic, and that does not depend on the gender of the spectator. Mulvey suggests that it is possible to shoot a movie that does not resort to the objectifying male gaze, and she posits that independent cinema might fix the problem formally (844). This is what Jonze has done in the following scenes, which frame Cage-as-Kaufman subversively and which, even in their outright invention, paradoxically allow the transformed film to approximate the book's narrative perspective.

As Kaufman sits alone with Amelia at a party it feels like a scene from a typical romantic comedy. The camera cuts back and forth between them, and they do not share the frame at first. Kaufman is initially comfortable and smiling, but then the camera fixes on him with a close-up of his head from a bizarre angle. He is in the background and Amelia is in the foreground, and it looks like they are going to kiss, despite the fact that the camera seems to mimic their awkwardness. Abruptly, Kaufman says, "Thanks for coming out with me tonight, Amelia" (14). There is a close-up of him; her back is to the camera, and he is the one who is caught in the frame and objectified.

In a later scene in which the expected kiss is also subverted, Amelia is visibly disappointed, almost in tears, and her head is in the foreground so that we are looking at Kaufman through *her* gaze. This is the point in a romantic comedy where he should kiss her, and he is as aware of this as the viewer. Instead, he starts talking again, making excuses, and worrying about the script. Once he has blown it, he invites her to an orchid show over the weekend. We are uncomfortable for him, as the camera lingers on him, waiting for her rejection—which the viewer has already anticipated. "Good night, then," he mumbles, talking to the slamming car door, and to the empty space that she has left in the frame. The viewer's aesthetic pleasure has been subverted by framing Cage as Kaufman in the "female gaze" from Amelia's point of view. For the viewer, there is little conscious pleasure in watching Kaufman nervous, sweaty, and frustrated by his own inability to kiss Amelia.

The scenes with Amelia parallel the ones involving an anonymous waitress at a diner. In the first, the shot centers on Kaufman as he awkwardly attempts to order pie and coffee. The waitress is held at arm's length by the camera and is dressed modestly. Kaufman is reading *The Orchid Thief,* and he is initially more interested in the book than in her, evident in that the camera focuses on the book. She says, "I love orchids," which triggers a fantasy of them together at an orchid show. The fantasy scene adheres to Hollywood conventions: her shirt is much tighter, and the camera stays on her as she takes it off suggestively. This scene is mainstream cinema exaggerated, and it is made all the more unsettling because it is followed immediately by a scene where Kaufman is masturbating. The explicit link between the viewer's voyeuristic tendencies and the spectatorial experience as exploitive and essentially masturbatory has been made literal in a manner that makes the book's plotlessness feel like an improvement—in that its gaze is focused on orchids and on a fully-clothed Laroche. If Cage's onscreen Kaufman is objectifying Orlean via the book, then we are doing the same to Kaufman, and in turn to the waitress because the camera reflects the spectator's gaze. Or we are trying to, except that Jonze subverts this pleasure by making it ridiculous and by holding Kaufman in the frame for too long.

In a later scene at the diner, the viewer is initially more uncomfortable than the waitress, because we have had to witness him masturbating and because we know the nature of Kaufman's looking at her before she does. This feeling is heightened as the camera lingers a bit too long on the waitress. As Kaufman asks her to go to the orchid show with him, the camera pins him there in the diner's booth and we have to watch him squirm uncomfortably as he apologizes before he has even been rejected. The discomfort is furthered as she reports to the other waitresses about his creepiness. We do not hear what she says to another waitress, but the camera follows the other woman's gaze and it frames Kaufman uncomfortably. The fact that we do not hear what they are saying is significant because, like Kaufman, we have lost agency. This scene that deprives the viewer of agency figuratively inverts the exploitive male gaze of the earlier fantasy scene, and allows the waitress-as-subject to regain power, as Jonze further interrogates mainstream cinematic conventions.

In addition to its allusion to Laroche-as-subject in the original text, the scene also serves to distance *Adaptation* from romantic comedy conventions, and it points out that our pleasure in watching them is anything but benign. If this were a romantic comedy proper, then perhaps Kaufman would have had more luck, but it is not, and more problematic is the fact that the waitress is not even the love interest set up by the film's initial adherence to romantic comedy tropes. Rather, she is just a fetish object, a metaphorical orchid that parallels Orlean's relationship to Laroche, and Laroche's to orchids in the original text. And, as in the source text, the relationship is sexualized, but purely symbolic. If there were more plot in the book, the romantic subplot would not be as important to the film. However, at this point in *Adaptation* there is little chance for resolution because, given the restrictions that Jonze puts on the gaze for the sake of subversion, the onscreen Kaufman's lack of self-confidence is reinforced to the point of impossibility. Onscreen Kaufman makes both the women that he shares the scene with and the viewer uncomfortable because he is uncomfortable, but there is more to it. He is a victim of Jonze's aesthetic which conspires against him. On a plot level, both the onscreen Kaufman and the viewer need a way out.

Kaufman meets with his agent, Marty, to complain about the difficulties that he is having, and to see if he can get out of the deal. But Kaufman wanting out, like Kaufman not getting anywhere with his love interest, is not enough conflict-wise to keep the viewer engaged, and both of these points have nothing to do with the adaptation of *The Orchid Thief*—the movie's reason for being. As a consequence, as the film moves forward, it must remain faithful to the plot-trajectory that Kaufman has set out, however tedious this is for him onscreen or for the viewer. In an effort to salvage the movie that we are watching, as well as the movie that Kaufman is writing, the offscreen Kaufman is forced to engage in dialogue with the book's shortcomings as well as with Hollywood conventions. Kaufman writing himself into the script, and his making it self-consciously referential, is enough to keep the film from sputtering to a halt, but not enough to provide the conflict and resolution that viewers demand.

As he is talking to Marty, the gaze comes back into play, as Marty continually makes lewd references to women who pass by. Like the earlier scene where we were uncomfortable for Kaufman because of the way in which he was pinned in the frame and subjugated by the producer, in this scene we see Kaufman occupy the metaphorical position of the woman who is not in the frame, and who, while a victim of the agent's misogyny, does not hear the comments directly, as Kaufman and the viewer do. Because the agent is so crude, the viewer's discomfort is compounded, and, given Kaufman's position in the frame, the exploitative nature of mainstream cinema is further highlighted. At the same time, though, the meeting with the agent gives Kaufman license to invent, finally, and the plot moves forward. But from the perspective of the dominant male gaze, the spectatorial pleasure party is over.

Adaptation suggests a mode of spectatorial pleasure that is subversive to normative modes and that exemplifies Studlar's masochistic spectatorial experience, even as it deliberately calls attention to the "male gaze" by inverting it, and subjugating Cage as Kaufman and Cooper as Laroche. As the conversation at a New York dinner party turns to Laroche's missing front teeth, one of Orlean's yuppie friends says, "It seems almost sociopathic to make everybody look at that" (Kaufman 24). Yet this is exactly what Orlean does for most of the book and what the viewer of the film, in turn, must do. In showing Laroche this way, as *literal* subject of Orlean's book, with a gaping hole where his teeth should be, Jonze feminizes Laroche symbolically, putting him in the place of the woman-as-monster in a manner in keeping with Linda Williams' theories expressed in "When the Woman Looks." Our desire to look is driven, in part, by Laroche assuming the place of the woman—figuratively bound by a gaze that echoes Orlean's position as narrator in the original text.

The spectatorial pleasure built around Orlean and Laroche is foregrounded when the film's parallel plots finally collide, and the film regresses to generic norms. For all its originality and unpredictability, *Adaptation* ultimately trades heavily in the specific generic conventions that we already know, and it is dependent on its oscillation between closeness to and distance from the familiar as it makes meaning. *Adaptation* adheres nominally to the conventions of the romantic comedy and the buddy movie, although it is far more intellectually engaging and not as over-the-top funny. In fact, a good portion of its power depends on the degree to which it approaches these conventions of genre, but like a limit in calculus which gets ever closer to a point on a plane without crossing it, leaves our expectations unfulfilled. Simultaneously, the film calls our attention to the fact that our expectations of genre are often rooted in the somewhat unsavory and exploitive patriarchal conventions of the Hollywood studio system.

As the film becomes a buddy movie, it is transformed so much through plot-based invention that aside from the familiar characters, it is no longer recognizable as *The Orchid Thief,* and becomes, instead, a transformation built from the book's pieces. In a scene where Kaufman and Donald trail Orlean and Laroche to Laroche's house in Florida, and Kaufman is caught peeping through the window (as are we), Orlean is fully clothed, snorting lines of "orchid dust," and seemingly engaged in sex with a naked Laroche. Laroche occupies the frame as a woman would conventionally, but he is totally un-self-aware and confident. This paradox is important, particularly in light of Orlean's original narrative position and of the fact that in the film Laroche is "hunted" by Orlean as much as Orlean is by Kaufman. Their own hazy, green-lit sex scene mocks romantic comedy conventions and is as uncomfortable as Kaufman's waitress fantasy. The film subverts expectations of genre and problematizes the male gaze because Laroche is feminized, yet confident, and he even asks Kaufman, "Who's gonna play me?" in reference to the film (Kaufman 88). Our expectations are further troubled because the clothed Orlean is the one who is modest and offended as the film resorts to normal conventions with a vengeance.

In the film's final minutes, Laroche and Orlean march Kaufman and Donald into the Everglades where they intend to kill them for witnessing their drug-fueled tryst (which, to Orlean's thinking, will destroy her position as an objective journalist if it makes it into the film). They escape when Laroche is eaten by an alligator, but as they are driving away they are hit by a speeding park ranger and Donald is thrown from the car and killed.

Donald's death gives Kaufman a chance to engage in the clichéd "dying buddy" moment often seen in war movies ("So Happy Together" plays in the background as Kaufman pleads with his brother to live). It also gives him another chance with Amelia, in that it provides them an excuse to get together for lunch. Despite the fact that Amelia talks about her new boyfriend, Kaufman is uncharacteristically confident and relaxed. In a sense, they have picked up where they left off, and he kisses her, finally, as if out of nowhere. "Charlie, I'm with someone, why are you doing this now?" she replies. He mutters, "I love you." She departs, heading for the escalator, before exclaiming, "I love you, too, y'know," and descending (Kaufman 99). We have now switched back to romantic comedy-land—except that the romantic leads part ways. As Kaufman is driving away, he realizes, finally, that he knows how to finish the script. He exclaims, "It's done ... and that's something," and speaks into the cassette recorder, "Kaufman drives off from the encounter with Amelia, filled for the first time with hope." And then, "I like this. This is good," as surreal stop-motion shots of daisies and taillights fill the screen and "So Happy Together" plays once more (Kaufman 100).

In its buddy-movie ending, followed by its romantic-comedy ending, and in its transformed distance from Orlean's text, *Adaptation* seems to be doing a bit more ideologically than just giving the viewers what we want (or what we think we want) plot-wise. The voice-over and the deliberately referential song take us out of the narrative's action and another step away from the book in that we are left, finally, with a soundtrack, characters, and plot-level resolution, which are not present in *The Orchid Thief*. In this divergence, Jonze further highlights the film's constructedness and its allusive and intertextual relationship to Orlean's book and to offscreen reality. In Jonze and Kaufman's attention to plotlessness as plot, they highlight the difficulties of adapting texts, critique audience expectations for mainstream romantic comedies and buddy movies, and call attention to the often repressive subject-object relationships of conventional cinema. Specifically, through having Nicholas Cage star in a buddy movie with himself and inserting a romantic subplot involving Orlean and her book's subject, John Laroche, into the film, they interrogate dominant cinema's restrictive notion of male spectatorial pleasure and veer closer to *The Orchid Thief's* narrative perspective, even as they diverge plot-wise.

The filmmakers are clearly after referentiality with payoff, rather than parody or pastiche. Although critics were quick to note how easily Kaufman, Jones, and Cage poked fun at Hollywood conventions, Jonze cautioned in an interview with Sean O'Hagan, "I don't mind what people think as long as they don't just think we're being ironic." Irony may well be the default mode of discourse in twenty-first-century pop culture; after all, during the last election cycle pundits noted that most American college students got their news from satirist Jon Stewart. But Jonze and Kaufman suggest that we can have it both ways, that our contemporary tendency toward referentiality is not necessarily ironic and without meaning. Considering their body of work, individually as well as together on *Being John Malkovich*, Jonze and Kaufman seem to be plotting a new trajectory for American cinema aesthetically and philosophically.[1] They are employing transformation as a discrete genre uniquely up to the task of describing the hyperallusive contemporary world and at the same time exploring our relationship to the recent past— both literal and textual.

Note

1. Jonze's 2009 transformation of Maurice Sendak's classic children's story *Where the Wild Things Are* may be another step in this direction, although this time his collaborators on the screenplay are Sendak and Dave Eggers.

Works Cited

Adaptation. Dir. Spike Jonze. Perf. Nicholas Cage, Chris Cooper, and Meryl Streep. Columbia Pictures, 2002.

Conover, Ted. "Flower Power." *New York Times* 3 Jan. 1999. 9 Apr. 2009. <http://www.nytimes.com/books/99/01/03/reviews/>.

Dayan, Daniel. "The Tudor-Code of Classical Cinema." *Film Theory and Criticism: Introductory Readings*. 5th ed. Ed. Leo Braudy and Marshall Cohen. New York: Oxford University Press, 1999. 118–29.

Kaufman, Charlie. *Adaptation: The Shooting Script*. New York: Newmarket, 2002.

Leigh, Danny. "Let's Make a Meta Movie." *Guardian*. 14 Feb. 2003. 30 Aug. 2008. <http://www.guardian.co.uk/film/2003/feb/14/artsfeatures>.

Mulvey, Laura. "Visual Pleasure and Narrative Cinema." *Film Theory and Criticism: Introductory Readings*. 5th ed. Ed. LeoBraudy and Marshall Cohen. New York: Oxford University Press, 1999. 833–44.

O'Hagan, Sean. "Who's the Proper Charlie." *Guardian* 9 Feb. 2003. 30 Apr. 2009. <http://www.guardian.co.uk/film/2003/feb/09/features.review>.

Orlean, Susan. Foreword. *Adaptation: The Shooting Script*. Screenplay by Charlie Kaufman. New York: Newmarket, 2002. vii–ix.

_____. *The Orchid Thief*. New York: Random House, 1998.

Studlar, Gaylyn. "Masochism and the Perverse Pleasures of the Cinema." *Movies and Methods: An Anthology*. Ed. Bill Nichols. Berkeley: University of California Press, 1985. 602–21.

Williams, Linda. "When the Woman Looks." *Re-Vision: Essays in Feminist Film Criticism*. Ed. Mary Ann Doane, Patricia Mellencamp, and Linda Williams. Frederick, MD: University Publications of America, 1983. 83–99.

3

Historical Figures Transformed: Free Enterprise *and* I, Tituba, Black Witch of Salem

MARNI GAUTHIER

Michelle Cliff's *Free Enterprise* (1993) and Maryse Condé's *I, Tituba, Black Witch of Salem* (1992) both transform little-known historical characters—Black women at the margins of mainstream U.S. history—into full-fledged narrators of their own vivid tales. *Free Enterprise* tells the remarkable story of Mary Ellen Pleasant, the successful San Francisco businesswoman and passionate freedom-fighter who allegedly financed John Brown's raid on Harper's Ferry. *I, Tituba* imagines the complete life of Tituba, Samuel Parris' slave whose testimony figured prominently in the Salem Witch Trials of 1692, which, in turn, Arthur Miller famously dramatized in his 1953 Tony award-winning play, *The Crucible*. Moreover, each novel transforms not only its protagonist, recovering her from the relative obscurity to which history has relegated her, but also modifies the genre of the historical novel itself that can be traced over the last two centuries to Sir Walter Scott.

While the traditional historical novel constructs a faithful historical "type," heroes who psychologically and politically embody the mainstream atmosphere of the age, postmodern historical fiction features "ex-centric" historical characters, transforming them from persons at the periphery of history to protagonists at the narrative center. *I, Tituba* exemplifies the postmodern historical novel that foregrounds the subjective nature of a history rife with omissions to provoke a critical view of it.[1] *Free Enterprise*, written seven years after Condé first issued *I, Tituba* in French as *Moi, Tituba, Sorcière ... Noire de Salem* (1986), likewise reflects a critical distance from history; it counters received versions of U.S. history through postmodern narrative innovations that moreover stake claim to counter-historical truths about the past. Drenched in archival research, this more recent historical novel form moves beyond problematizing the nature and status of our knowledge about the past to articulate a politics of truth.

Cliff's portrait of Pleasant transforms her from a figure known primarily through stereotypes to a complex historical actor. Cliff's concurrent acts of historical excavation and imagination are central to the politics of truth that the contemporary historical fiction represented by *Free Enterprise* asserts. Because subjugated historical subjects do not appear in the records and archives consulted by historians, historical novelists bring imagination to the facts that remain in order to more fully tell the truth of such subjects. In the case of *Free Enterprise* and *I, Tituba*, this brings a visibility not only to black women's lives, which have been invisible in traditional historical sources, but to a historically transnational America, different from the nationalistic sense that prevails in all but the most recent studies of the antebellum U.S. Yet to regard silences as an empty vessel for purely imaginative filling, with tenuous historical support, is to replace a history of silences with a fiction of contemporary desire—the project which Condé takes up in her novel. Where *Free Enterprise* transforms the virtually unknown Pleasant into a New World abolitionist who played a major role in a landmark event—Harpers Ferry—that led to the Civil War, *I, Tituba* transforms Tituba, whose fictional role in Miller's classic play is far better known than her actual history, into a self-proclaimed martyr for "the exploited and humiliated, whose name, language, and religion [are] imposed on them" (Condé 120).

Through their attention to the triangular slave commerce between Africa, the Caribbean, and the U.S., both *Free Enterprise* and *I, Tituba* exemplify an aspect of the contemporary historical novel germane to the recent key paradigm shift in the field of American studies towards a new "Americas studies." Recognizing the overlapping histories of colonialism within which the cultures of the Americas have been shaped, this hemispheric perspective questions modes of history that are delimited by the modern nation-state. Both novels re-write nationally delineated narratives of U.S. history that intersect in the Civil War and the Salem Witch trials, respectively, and in black resistance to slavery throughout the Americas, with particular attention to women's roles therein. In discussions of her novel, Cliff strategically moves between the terms "United States" and "America/n." Her profile suggests the transnational focus of American studies realized in the years subsequent to her writing *Free Enterprise*. Using "America" to mean "United

States" belies the fact that the rest of the Americas—Canada, Central and South America, the Caribbean—have histories and cultures independent of the U.S.; yet using the term "America" in a transnational context also broadens it, indicating that its traditional referent—the United States—shares overlapping histories and cultures with the rest of the Americas. As it has from its inception, American studies continues to examine U.S. culture; yet one facet of its recent transnationalization is the consideration of the relationship of the rest of the Americas (in particular) to the United States.[2] A transnational approach to U.S. literary studies calls attention to processes of displacement and dispersion within and between the Americas; the circulation of people and capital, languages and ideas; and the new cultural geographies affected by these mobilizations.

In their historical focus on the transatlantic slave trade, transnational alliances against it, and other forms of colonialism around the globe, *Free Enterprise* and *I, Tituba* underscore the fact that America has been implicated by a global economy from its inception—and it is the conditions of the United States' *emergence* as a nation-state that demands its consideration in a global context. I employ the term "transnational" throughout this essay to evoke the transatlantic circulation of slave labor and related capital central to the emergence of the U.S. as a neocolonial state, and the corresponding movement—of both slave traders and their cargo as well as of abolitionists—between multiple continents and countries figured by these novels. When I use "America/n," then, I use it in this multifaceted sense of a historically transnational United States.

Michelle Cliff's Free Enterprise

Free Enterprise is set both during and after the Civil War, yet it recontextualizes the War not as a nationalist narrative which consolidated the United States, but as a transnational slave revolt against imperialism in which black women, capital, and the discourse of "free enterprise" played a crucial role. The novel enacts this grand tale through the relatively obscure and enigmatic historical figure of Mary Ellen Pleasant. Pleasant was a black entrepreneur, civil- and human-rights activist, and abolitionist who made her primary home and extraordinary fortune in San Francisco through her luxuriant boarding houses and her savvy investments in mining and real estate between the 1850s and 1880s. Among her many abolitionist ventures, the one at the center of Cliff's novel, and the one of which the historical Pleasant was most proud, is her collaboration with John Brown.[3] An unapologetic and successful capitalist, Pleasant dedicated her talent for making profits within the system of free enterprise to abolition in a number of ways, including funding Brown's raid on Harpers Ferry.

Free Enterprise's first section, "Annie Christmas," immediately transnationalizes the Civil War by introducing Pleasant's Jamaican comrade, Annie, and Annie's Surinamese friend Rachel. As a young woman, Annie left her island home to join the abolitionist fight in the United States. Annie is now an old woman, for the year is 1920, and the place is Annie's provisional home, a rundown house near the Carville leper colony on the Louisiana banks of the Mississippi River. At their first meeting 62 years ago, Pleasant gave Annie a "*nom de guerre* fit for a woman," that of a "legendary African-American woman, a sort of female John Henry": Annie Christmas (Cliff, Letter). According to Pleasant, Annie's legendary namesake was born in Africa and "worked" the Mississippi during the revolutionary years; when she died, she and her sons "drifted down the river and out into the Caribbean" (25). The sparse details of Pleasant's tale imply that Christmas was an abolitionist, originally abducted from Africa, and perhaps, like Annie herself, she escaped captivity in the Caribbean by fleeing to the United States to work underground. Annie's singular visitor from the leper colony, Rachel, has a similar history: she has crossed continents before arriving in Carville. A Surinam Jew, Rachel is descended from the *marranos* (Spanish for swine), late medieval Spanish Jews who practiced in secret, having been forced to convert to Christianity. Moreover, she has lived among African slaves who escaped Dutch slavery by moving to the interior of Surinam, South America. Like Annie, Rachel has worked with "like-minded rebels, all focused on one thing, the cessation of the Trade" (182).

The overlapping histories of these three covert abolitionists—all women of color living and working in discrete periods at the geographic and political margins of national identity—foregrounds not only the transnational histories of U.S. inhabitants, but a historically deep inter–American resistance to slavery. A close reading of the first chapter shows that its portrait of Annie's home sets the stage for the novel's counternarrative of American slavery. The history of the Mississippi as the main waterway for the U.S. slave trade is evocative of the story's integral relation to the Civil War; at the same time, the marginal locale of Annie's house suggests the story's relegation to the margins of U.S. history. Annie's cabin is "Secluded," a place where her friends say she'd have "to be crazy to live," and "on the very edge— She and the house" (3). This setting also suggests the story's critical interrelation to other countries and cultures. Initially disorienting in its unindicated shifts between various times and places, Cliff's narrative organization in fact invites her readers to step back and connect this setting of the southern Mississippi and U.S. slavery to the international slave trade, and particularly to the triangular commerce between Africa, the Caribbean, and the U.S.

Yet *Free Enterprise*'s portrait of U.S. history informed by its transnationality is in dialectical relation to the traditional notions of "America" in which its protagonist (Pleasant), is earnestly invested, and which Pleasant's "tender comrade," Annie, foreshadows. Annie explains her flight from the subjugation of her Jamaican girlhood, her emigration to the States, and her joining the abolitionist cause "on the mainland": she believed "the island to be without hope" (10). Annie's "mainland / Island" description for the U.S. / Jamaican relationship intimates the transnational perspective shared by all the novel's characters—whose political activism, migrations, and rhetoric tend to substitute an essential interrelation and transnationality for discrete nations. And yet Annie's disclosure of her motive in leaving Jamaica for the U.S. betrays a faith in the pursuit of freedom and justice within the U.S. when that faith is elsewhere extinguished, connoting a distinctly "American" creed. It is thus fitting that the introduction of Annie—a native of the Caribbean and a U.S. abolitionist who lives among a community of transnational freedom-fighters—precedes and contextualizes the reader's introduction to Pleasant, an "American" in both the transnational and the traditional senses of the word.

Cliff's interpretation of a wealth of historical facts about Pleasant's life transforms a vague figure into a vivid historical personage. Pleasant was an entrepreneur, activist, and abolitionist who made her primary home and extraordinary fortune in San Francisco between the 1850s and 1880s. Whether she was born slave or free is one of the many mysteries of her life, but during her heyday she was one of the most influential, powerful, and respected women in San Francisco (Hudson 19–26). Pleasant furthermore figures at critical junctures in U.S. economic history including the Gold Rush and the urbanization of the west, having made her fortune in part by consistent savvy investment in the mining industry and real estate. In addition to her covert investments that undermined the slave trade and helped further her race—Pleasant employed blacks, backed them in business, and sponsored their legal representation; she harbored fugitive slaves and paid for their room, board, and escape fare; and she donated large parts of her fortune. During the Civil War, she led the Franchise League, a civil rights group she helped form in the 1850s to dispel secessionists from California, and waged several court cases to test new civil rights legislation.[4]

That historical materials on Pleasant are scarce is not surprising since it is only recently that historians have sought to study black women as serious historical subjects. Moreover, the traditional sources for such studies—church and city records, family and slave histories, female societies and clubs—are not the institutions where Pleasant is most visible. As historian Lynn Hudson explains, "Pleasant operated in movements and milieus traditionally known for their male hierarchies and cultures. As an abolitionist and businesswoman, much of Pleasant's work by its very nature remains secretive and hidden" (3). It is because, as Cliff declares, "Pleasant defeats every stereotype of an African-American woman in the nineteenth-century," that she was drawn to her as a subject. Pleasant was a successful capitalist and yet "always a revolutionary, and she never gave up the cause, even after the failure of Harper's [sic] Ferry" (Cliff, Interview 32).

When scant evidence fertilizes a legacy of power and influence from such an unconventional subject as a rich black woman in the nineteenth century, myth-making flourishes. Pleasant has been a subject of U.S. popular culture, including film, fiction, stage and television, yet she remains virtually unknown. (Most recently, *House on the Hill, Mammy Pleasant's Story* opened October 18, 2008, at the Playhouse Theatre Playhouse in Los Angeles). These posthumous dramatizations have represented her as a voodoo queen, mammy, and jezebel. Cliff is cognizant of the way that these stereotypes have overshadowed Pleasant's role in the abolitionist movement, and her novel endeavors to recuperate and recreate Pleasant's legacy. Her fictional Pleasant's reference to "[t]he official version [that] entertains" suggests the novel's deconstruction of these stock types in favor of its nuanced portrait of Pleasant.

Cliff's expression of Pleasant's claims to and her pride in her successful capitalist endeavors is rooted in Pleasant's history. In her autobiography, observes Hudson, Pleasant reflects on her successful decades of brokering deals, and "locates her knack for capitalist enterprise in her youth." As a girl, Pleasant worked in a shop that, she says, "very few people ever got by" without buying something from her. (Hudson 31). As an adult, Pleasant strived to protect her hard-earned capital, and firmly believed it to be fundamentally connected to her "rights as a free American citizen." A case that began in Superior Court in 1898, *Pleasant vs. Solomons*, particularly illuminated this. Pleasant charged that her former attorney, Lucius Solomons, had committed an act of fraud and tried to cheat her out of one of the lots she owned on Sutter Street; she brought the suit so that she could recover the real estate.

In a court statement, Pleasant explicitly links her free speech "rights as a free American citizen" to free enterprise and her wealth of private property (see Hudson 94), implicitly referring to the moral and material values inherent in the Declaration of Independence with its guarantee of "life, liberty, and the pursuit of happiness." An imagined conversation between Cliff's Pleasant and John Brown wherein Cliff justifies "slaves seizing" the properties "which they had been held responsible" resonates with the same principle:

"[I]n this world, Captain, property, ownership equals power [and] freedom
without the means to be self-supporting is a one-armed triumph....
[W]ithout my particular expertise at ownership, property, there would be
no thirty thousand dollars in gold, no rifles for our people. And that
money was made in disguise, in the dark, so to speak. I would like to step
into the open, for once."
... "So you see the profit motive as a measure of humanity."
"I would say instead self-sufficiency. Simple" [143–48].

Pleasant's emphasis on African-American ownership and the importance
of "self-sufficiency" echoes Emersonian "self-reliance," an expressly American creed that was at least as influential during Pleasant's lifetime as it is
today. Ralph Waldo Emerson's formulation of the self-reliant citizen sup-
plied currency to the Horatio Alger story with which Pleasant's own life
has been identified (Hudson 24–25). A contemporary of Pleasant, Emerson spoke in defense of John Brown—whom Pleasant aided—and in opposition to the Fugitive Slave Law—which Pleasant subverted. Pleasant's
articulation of Emersonian principles in this passage is both historically
congruous and quintessentially "American." Her story of making her fortune "in disguise, in the dark," and her desire to "step into the open" is
also unexceptionally a product of the United States in that it resembles
the experiences of other historically marginalized U.S. residents—both
native and immigrant groups—for whom access to good jobs in commerce,
business, and the public sphere has been limited. Consequently, members
of these groups often prosper in underground ways.

This fictional exchange between Pleasant and Brown also teases out
the conundrum of the title Cliff chooses for her novel. Cliff's portrait of the
slave trade reveals the irony of the phrase: the principle of free enterprise is
central to the discourse of an enterprise—the Trade-which depended upon
its product being un-free. *Free Enterprise* delineates the way in which, in the
nineteenth century, free enterprise—the development of industry and capitalism—relied upon slavery; yet the novel is foremost about the enterprise
of freedom, namely, abolition. Cliff's protagonist embodies the contradiction: Pleasant uses capitalism to undermine the Trade that thrived by it in
her time. Most significantly, Cliff represents Pleasant as a committed New
World abolitionist—a representation that is emblematic of the America
figured by *Free Enterprise*, in which the relation between the national and
the transnational is dialectical and constitutive. This key dialogue between
Pleasant and Brown is an important narrative moment that focuses this
conceptual territory. Though an indissoluble relationship of political and
economic freedom is vital to Cliff's heroine, here Pleasant locates African-
American apprehension of capitalist practices not with the U.S.—the nation

in which such values are most dominant—but with all the "New World." Similarly, although this conversation closes with an oblique reference to Brown's famous raid on Harpers Ferry ("thirty thousand dollars in gold [and] rifles for our people"), which Pleasant materially promoted and which is readily identified in historical imagination with the U.S. Civil War, *Free Enterprise* mentions neither the raid nor the War explicitly.

Furthermore, Pleasant rhetorically frames the slaves' battle as a New World struggle for abolition as well as for economic independence that involves slaves from all the Americas. Pleasant's transatlantic abolitionist sensibilities originally stem from her mother, Quasheba, who convinced the young Mary Ellen that, "On a clear day from the highest dune [of the Sea Islands] you could see the Guinea Coast, and all the traffic in between. The skin of the globe tightened and the over the curve ships came." Quasheba's frustration that the "transoceanic, African, eclipse-demanding, vengeance-hungry gods were helpless" to stop this traffic in African bodies is the seed that eventually blossoms into her escape from slavery, becoming an accomplished gunsmith and abolitionist, and passing down her ardent commitment to "the Cause" to her daughter (127–28). Pleasant's intimacy with the Jamaican-American Annie most clearly situates Pleasant's abolitionism within the contemporaneous transnational war for the Cause. Pouring over Mary Ellen's letters, Annie explains to Rachel that their "plan was very simple. Arm the slaves." But, "[t]here is a chasm between the [Civil] war and what we planned.... Our historical moment was lost, so our tapestry is dissembled.... Only with imagination [can] you draw it out" (191–93).

As the primary fictional character among this band of historical abolitionists, Annie functions to impel the imagination required to construct a politics of truth about transnational abolition. The dissembled historical tapestry to which she refers consists not only of Brown, Pleasant, and the Chatham Convention, but of global accounts of the movement that traditional modes of history have segregated from stories of U.S. abolition, and the Civil War.[5] Annie's story reflects such accounts. Her own role in Brown's raid is inextricable from her unrealized dream of "burning the great houses [of Jamaica] to the ground; along with Pleasant and Rachel, her conviction that "There is no 'someone else's fight'" for abolition and racial equality underscores the Cause as essentially transnational (199). While Cliff writes a constructive countermemory to the earlier one-dimensional narratives that have stood in for Pleasant, she also regards Pleasant as an American within a contemporary framework, where the U.S. is one member of the Americas. This portrait is truthful in that it is rooted in a traditionally neglected, yet historically valid transnational abolitionism.

Maryse Condé's I, Tituba, Black Witch of Salem

The publication history of Condé's novel itself reflects the circulation of people, capital, languages and ideas that informs the transnational context in which U.S. literary studies increasingly must be understood. Condé's novel has been claimed for the literature of Guadeloupe—Condé's native home where she lived before moving to Paris for college (and more recently, to London and then the United States). Condé, then, appropriates a figure embedded in the margins of U.S. history for Francophone Caribbean literature. At the same time, while her plot centers on the fictional Tituba's trials and transformation by her forced migration to mainland America, Tituba's placement in the Caribbean context transforms U.S. literary history. For Condé first and foremost brings Tituba's West Indian origins—about which the sparse historical record on Tituba merely speculates—into sharp focus. She locates Tituba in her native Barbados for nearly half of the novel, situating her there at the onset as she vividly imagines her childhood, her upbringing by native African parents, family, culture, and ancestry. Following her part in the Salem witch trials, Condé returns Tituba to Barbados where she lives the remainder of her life as a healer of slaves, eventually dying as a martyr for the abolitionist cause; even in her afterlife she uses her supernatural powers to advance the cause of abolition. In the middle portion of the text, Tituba is tried as a Salem witch and sold for the sum of her prison costs to a Jewish merchant, a bereaved widower with whom Tituba forms an intimate liaison.

In fact, from the first words of Tituba's tale to her time and trials in Salem, the novel emphasizes two unfamiliar aspects of Puritan cultural history: Puritan complicity in the atrocious African slave trade and the patriarchal oppression of women—in which Condé reads the engendering of female bonding. Condé also makes much of Tituba's essential Barbadian identity, for she is integrally bred and interwoven with island cultures and myth. "Abena, my mother, was raped by an English sailor on the deck of *Christ the King*," Tituba begins. "I was born from this act of aggression. From this act of hatred and contempt" (3). The tension implicit in the contradiction between the ship's name and the rank sins of its sailors produces a bitter irony that recurs in a decidedly Puritan vein when, twenty years later, Tituba and her husband John Indian board their first ship. They have been sold to an infamous Boston reverend, whose "ruthless violen[t] cutting words" greet them: "On your knees, dregs of hell! I am your new master! My name is Samuel Parris. Tomorrow ... we leav[e] aboard the brigantine *Blessing*" (36). Thus Condé graphically links the Puritans to the brutal Middle Passage and slave trade, and likewise roots the Salem witch trials to it as well.

Yet, through Tituba's foreign eyes and speech, Condé cleverly inverts the "evil" that the perpetrators of the witch trials later famously attribute to her. Her first night on the ship, Parris forces his slaves to pray along with his family. He "lifted his eyes to the ceiling and started to bray. I couldn't make much out of his speech, except the oft-heard words sin, evil, Satan, and demon" with which Salem village, Tituba soon discovers, is obsessed (41). The children's "favorites stories were about people in league with the devil"—yarns with which Tituba entertains them, out of her pity for the "coffin" their parents construct around their "youth," "so full of promise yet mutilated" (60).

Thus Condé foreshadows Tituba's ill-fated role of scapegoat in the forthcoming trials, while underscoring the trials' incipient causes in the culture particular to Salem village in 1692. To elicit her testimony, Tituba's inquisitors, four men wearing "black hoods, with holes for their eyes" bind, beat, and rape her, demanding that she "denounce [her] accomplices! Good and Osborne and the others!" (91). This vicious scene undermines Tituba's actual deposition, which Condé here inserts into the text. Because of this juxtaposition, the deposition appears as evidence of Tituba's manipulated—and thus silenced—voice:

> "And what would they have you do?"
> "Kill her with a knife."
> "How did you go?"
> "We rode upon sticks and were there presently."
> "Do you go through the trees or over them?"
> "We see nothing but are there presently."
>
> * * *
>
> It went on for hours. I confess I wasn't a good actress. The sight of all these white faces lapping at my feet looked to me like a sea in which I was about to drown [106].

The one-dimensional flatness of the "historical Tituba" contrasts so sharply to the fluent, passionate voice which sounds through the surrounding text that readers instinctively reject the historical Tituba's "confession" as forced by the Puritan judges, extracted from a hapless victim to serve as the scapegoat for the Salem witch hysteria.

To its scathing portrait of early America plagued by slavery, racism, and religiously inflected paranoia, the novel adds women who universally suffer in Puritan times. Like the wife of Abena's master, who "was not much older than my mother [and] hated this brute she had been forced to marry"—and who thus became close friends with Abena, Parris' wife and Tituba too form a sympathetic bond. "I soon realized that someone else shared my fear and aversion for Samuel Parris: Elizabeth, his wife" (38). This female bonding culminates with Condé's most flagrant anachronism: Tituba's influential encounter with Hester Prynne—of Nathaniel Hawthorne's *The Scarlet Letter*—in jail, following her conviction in the Salem witch trials. To achieve this encounter of the fictional Prynne and the historical-fictional Tituba, Condé not only shifts the setting of *The Scarlet Letter* from 1640s Boston to 1692 Salem, but also gives Hester a late twentieth-century feminist vocabulary and consciousness, which empowers both her and Tituba. Condé's bold re-writing of Hester and Tituba reveals the effacement inherent in both *The Scarlet Letter* and *The Crucible*. These historical-fictional portraits of Hester and Tituba are partly determined by their authors' fidelity to seventeenth-century social constructions of femininity. Consequently, each text simultaneously paints and punishes its heroine for transgressing those codes. At the same time, even in its self-consciously postmodern moment Condé's transformation of Hester is true to Hawthorne's. From her brazenly beautiful scarlet "A" to the evolution of the "A's" perceived meaning—from "Adulteress" to "Able" and "Angel"—Hester's quiet rebellion transforms the Puritan community's relegation of her to forlorn exile. In this literary-historical sense, Hester's 1850 triumph and survival begets Tituba's 1992 survival—that fate which her "invisible spirits" reiterate to her throughout the novel: "You'll survive" (9)—which stands in contrast to the historical Tituba, about whom little is known. That Condé's Hester hangs herself in prison only highlights Tituba's survival; Tituba is both paired to and a foil for Condé's short-lived Hester. *I, Tituba* portrays both women as martyrs—Hester for woman's rights; and Tituba for racism and, eventually, abolition.

While each chapter of Tituba's life further accentuates her Barbadian identity, Tituba's survival of the witch trials and eventual return to Barbados is the narrative vehicle through which Condé effectively re-contextualizes the Salem craze in terms of slavery and other contemporaneous oppression. Her first year in Boston, Tituba learns of the "slave trade intensifying," of the "thousands of our people [being] snatched form Africa," and that "the whites ... were also enslaving the Indians, the original inhabitants of both America and our beloved Barbados" (47). The Jewish merchant who buys Tituba from prison, Benjamin Cohen d'Azevedo, has fled with his family from Portugal to escape religious persecution. Like Rachel and Annie of *Free Enterprise*, Benjamin and Tituba's intimacy grows from mutual recognition of collective historical persecution. In each other they recognize their people "scattered throughout the world," lives lost "under the Inquisition" and "bled from the coast of Africa" (127). When, inevitably, a raging crowd stones Tituba in front of Benjamin's house, then burns his house and his nine children in it, the reader recognizes, with Tituba, the enveloping historical context of slavery and colonialism: "How many more stonings? Holocausts?

How much blood had yet to be shed? How much more submission?" From this moment on, Tituba "began to imagine another motive for life": "The Rebel has disappeared in a cloud of smoke. He has triumphed over death and his spirit remains. The frightened circle of slaves regains its courage" (136).

And thus, from Tituba's enslavement, which leads to her notorious part in the Salem witch trials and back to Barbados, the novel's urgent story becomes that of the Africa-Americas trade in human flesh and the violent struggle to vanquish it. Benjamin gives Tituba her freedom and passage home, and on the boat she laments "so many fevers and sicknesses [that] traveled between Africa, American and the West Indies, fostered by the dirt, the promiscuity and the bad food" (138). In returning to her hut at the outskirts of the plantation where she was born, Tituba learns that she has become a legend among the slaves, and devotes all her energy to deepening her art of healing them. When one of her patients joins the maroons to plot a major attack, Tituba is implicated in the second major revolt in three years; it ends in a bloodbath and her hanging. "My real story starts where this one leaves off and it has no end! ... I am hardening men's hearts to fight. I am nourishing them with dreams of liberty. Of victory. I have been behind every revolt. Every insurrection. Every act of disobedience" (175). In transforming history's muffled Tituba into a powerful healer and eternal abolitionist, Condé creates what she calls "an epic heroine" (Interview 201).

I, Tituba thus lends a potent voice not only to Tituba, but, along with *Free Enterprise*, to the muted transamerican struggle for abolition. Both novels ground their concerns with slavery in the Americas in a long historical sense of transnational struggles. But where Cliff attempts to show the "really complicated revolutionary movement prior to the Civil War," drawing on extensive personal research to counter "[t]he official version [that] has been printed, bound, and gagged, [that] resides in schools, libraries, the majority unconscious" (Cliff, "Art" 65; *Free Enterprise* 16), Condé employs flagrant anachronism to expose the subjectivity and contextualized nature of historical narrative and event. "*Tituba* is just the opposite of the historical novel," she asserts. "I was not interested at all in what her real life could have been ... I am not involved in any scholarly research" (Condé, Interview 201). In fact, where Cliff does not distinguish facts from inventions throughout *Free Enterprise*, Condé puts Tituba's deposition testimony—"the only historical part of the novel"—at *I, Tituba*'s center and marks it with a footnote that explains where to find the original document (*I, Tituba* 104). At the same time, she uses the deposition to call attention to the glaring omission of Tituba's authentic voice—not only from the deposition but elsewhere in history: "I can look for my story among those of the witches of Salem," says

Tituba, "but it isn't there" (*I, Tituba* 149). Ironically, the fully human, three-dimensional Tituba whom Condé invents effectively parodies the scant trace of Tituba that survives in the historical record. Likewise—and inversely—Cliff deconstructs the historical portraits of Mary Ellen Pleasant as a "Mammy" who ran a whorehouse and a voodoo queen to instead flesh out her "revolutionary" abolitionist work.[6] Both authors emphasize the relative inaccessibility of black women's history, foregrounding it as problematically "outside" national history. But while Condé uses her novel to remind her readers that silence in the historical record is not equivalent to absence, and to fill the gaps in the historical record with a compelling imaginative account of Tituba, Cliff's novel has much in common with Michel Foucault's notion of a genealogy that wrests truth from power through its excavation of the archival past and concomitant interpretation. By withholding its equation of research and imagination, it demands the reader's imagination of the history it writes and simultaneously invites the reader's investigation of historical remains. With their complementary articulations of complex transnational abolitionist history. *Free Enterprise* and *I, Tituba* are complementary critical projects that articulate a complex transnational abolitionism, transforming national(ist) conceptions of U.S. history.

Notes

1. Georg Lukács' renowned critical study *The Historical Novel* characterizes the historical novel popularized in the nineteenth century by Scott; Linda Hutcheon's *A Poetics of Postmodernism* fully characterizes postmodern fiction, which she famously coins "historiographic metafiction."

2. A decade ago, Patrica Wald stressed the clear "need to rethink the 'American' in American studies in the context of globalization [and] the effects and implications of the global economy and the decline of the form of the nation-state" (200–201). More recently, John Carlos Rowe clarifies the terms "transnationalism" and "transnational capitalism" as implying "a critical view of historically specific late modern or postmodern practices of globalizing [capitalism] for neocolonial ends" (78).

3. Hudson details several sources that validate Pleasant's testimony identifying herself as "the party who furnished John Brown with most of his money to start the fight at Harper's [sic] Ferry and who signed the letter found on him when he was arrested." Moreover, her "request that the words 'She was a friend of John Brown' be printed on her gravestone was honored in 1965 when the San Francisco Negro Historical and Cultural Society placed a marker bearing the phrase on her grave in Napa, California" (Hudson 60, 66). Elsewhere Pleasant asserts, "I never regretted what I did for John Brown and for the cause of freedom for my race" (qtd. in Bibbs 4). Since my original research for this essay, Hudson's dissertation has been published. All the citations to Hudson herein are from the dissertation as noted.

4. The title "The Mother of Civil Rights" appears in the official San Francisco memorial to Pleasant at the intersection of Bush and Octavia streets. The historical Pleasant seems most remembered by and in the city in which she became a sort of local celebrity. The African American newspapers *Pacific Appeal* and *The Elevator*, and the San Francisco mainstream press—*The Bulletin*, *Examiner*, and *Call*—chronicle her charity to African American churches and organizations of her day.

5. The 1791 Haitian slave revolt, for example, which began as a rebellion against slavery and French plantation owners but became a political revolution that lasted for 13 years and resulted in independence from France, inspired fear of similar revolts in other slave-holding areas of the Caribbean and the U.S. During the revolution years, refugees from Haiti settled in Louisiana, bringing accounts of revolution, revolt, and retribution with them. Slaveholders in the rest of the Americas attempted to isolate Haiti to keep the idea of emancipation from spreading.

6. Of the genesis of *Free Enterprise*, Cliff says: "I wanted to write a novel about Mary Ellen Pleasant because few know about her and she's a very important historical figure." In Cliff's words, she was "a revolutionary.... Most of my work has to do with revising: revising the written record, what passes as the official version of history, and inserting those lives that have been left out" ("Art" 65, 71).

Works Cited

Bibbs, Susheel. *Mary Ellen Pleasant 1817 to 1904: Mother of Human Rights in California.* San Francisco: MEP Enterprises, 1996.

Cliff, Michelle. "The Art of History: An Interview with Michelle Cliff," by Judith Raiskin. *The Kenyon Review.* 15:1 (1993): 57–71.

_____. *Free Enterprise.* New York: Plume, 1993.

_____. Interview with Renee Hausmann Shea. *Belle Lettres* 9 (Spring 1994): 32–33.

_____. Letter to the author. 6 June 1999.

Condé, Maryse. *I, Tituba, Black Witch of Salem.* Trans. Richard Philcox. Charlottesville: University Press of Virginia, 1992.

_____. Interview with Ann Armstrong Scarboro. Afterword. *I, Tituba, Black Witch of Salem.* By Maryse Condé. Charlottesville: University Press of Virginia, 1992: 198–213.

Foucault, Michel. "Nietzsche, Genealogy, History." *The Foucault Reader.* Ed. Paul Rainbow. New York: Pantheon, 1984. 76–100.

Hudson, Lynn M. *The Making of "Mammy Pleasant": A Black Entrepreneur in Nineteenth-Century.* San Francisco: University of Illinois Press, 2002.

_____. "When 'Mammy' Becomes a Millionaire: Mary Ellen Pleasant, an African-American Entrepreneur." Diss. Indiana University, 1996.

Hutcheon, Linda. *A Poetics of Postmodernism: History, Theory, Fiction.* New York: Routledge, 1988.

Lukacs, George. *The Historical Novel.* Trans. Hannah Mitchell and Stanley Mitchell. London: Merlin, 1962.

Rowe, John Carlos. "Nineteenth-Century United States Literary Culture and Transnationality." *PMLA.* 118:1 (2003): 78–89.

Wald, Priscilla. "Minefields and Meeting Grounds: Transnational Analyses and American Studies." *American Literary History.* 10:1 (1998): 199–218.

4

Post-Colonial Transformation: The Rejection of English in Gavin Hood's Tsotsi

ANNE M. REEF

"Tsotsi." The word sends shivers of fear down the spines of South Africans. Tsotsis rob, maim, rape, and kill; they are, according to Ernest Cole, "the scourge of the [black] townships" (qtd. in Coe and Metz 21). Tsotsis make strong stuff for texts of all kinds. Two especially lend themselves to juxtaposition: Athol Fugard's 1980 novel, *Tsotsi*, and Gavin Hood's 2005 film of the same name, which is based on the book. Both texts are set in South Africa, Fugard's just after the implementation of the notorious apartheid system, and Hood's in the early twenty-first century, the "post-apartheid" era.

Apartheid, Afrikaans for separateness, was a complex web of philosophies, practices, and laws designed to promote and to protect the Afrikaners—white descendants of the original European settlers—physically, politically, economically, and socially in the land they believed they were manifestly destined to rule. In practice, apartheid protected all whites from the loss of privilege that any kind of power-sharing with the 84 percent of the population known as "non-white" would entail. Afrikaner rule, which had been years in the planning, would last until apartheid's dismantling in 1994 and scar the country in ways reflected in its literature by writers like Alan Paton, Nadine Gordimer, J. M. Coetzee, and Fugard himself. Like his plays, *Tsotsi*, the author's only novel, critiques the horror and inhumanity of apartheid, and by doing so, resists and protests it. Younger writers, filmmakers, and artists like Hood need no longer struggle against apartheid; obviously aware of the system's legacy, their struggle is to represent the country's current constellation of concerns that include crime and HIV/AIDS.

Key to discussion of the two *Tsotsis* is the strategic question of language. Fugard wrote and published in English. Hood's text, which won the Academy Award for the Best Foreign Language film in 2006, rejects it in favor of Tsotsitaal, a hybrid patois that, while widely spoken in South African townships, has subversive, illegitimate connotations: Hood calls it "ghetto ... or gangster language ... the language of the streets" (Archibald). Tsotsitaal, the film shows, is the first language of its tsotsi protagonist; in the book, only the text's intonations reveal that his home tongue is not English. Hood's choice is thought-provoking. Why abandon the mainstream option of English, which would have been accessible to an international, primarily Anglo-American audience, in favor of Tsotsitaal, a mélange of many indigenous languages, smatterings of English, and a surprising amount of Afrikaans?

This paper argues that Hood's gesture is not just a realistic representation of post-apartheid South Africa's vibrantly multilingual society. By employing Tsotsitaal, Hood makes two simultaneous points that transcend post-apartheid preference and move his film beyond an adaptation of Fugard's book, transforming it into a potent post-colonial statement. First, in rejecting English, Hood stops one of the most imperial, imperious, and colonialist languages in its tracks, forcing audiences to mind a significant cultural gap between that of their own (perhaps) neo-colonialist societies and that of the class-stratified, crime-ridden, and HIV/AIDS-plagued, but still creatively competent post-apartheid South African society. Further, it makes a strong statement to Afrikaners, the colonizers during apartheid. Bill Ashcroft believes that a gesture like Hood's decision to use Tsotsitaal rather than English is equivalent to saying, "I am using [a form of] your language so that you will understand my world, but you will also know in the way that I use it that you cannot share my experience" (75). Ashcroft, Gareth Griffiths, and Helen Tiffin established themselves as important post-colonial theorists with their 1989 publication *The Empire Writes Back: Theory and Practice in Post-Colonial Literatures,* and Ashcroft especially has since participated in the discussion that has developed the ever-more complex field of post-colonialism. His *Post-Colonial Transformation* (2001), committed to foregrounding the creative energy of the colonized as a reaction to colonial oppression, is relevant to this study because it recognizes language as an important strategy for expressing such a robust response. Fugard's book takes a necessary first step toward post-colonial transformation by resisting apartheid and imperialism. As this paper shows, however, because the novel assumes English as the normative language, it does not adequately communicate the chasm between the colonial and colonized cultures and it may endorse aspects of imperialism. Hood's text represents the cultural rift more forcefully because of its rejection of English. And yet it also bears an unstable post-colonial message.

Thematically, both texts preoccupy themselves with the possibility of personal transformation more obviously than post-colonial transformation. As their titles suggest, both take a thug, indeed a gang leader, as their late-adolescent protagonist. "Tsotsi" is a moniker that the youth chose for himself—about ten years before, David Madondo repressed his real name along with the painful memories of the loss of his parents and pet. In the novel, apartheid brutality is the cause of David's parents' disappearance. In the film David's mother is dying of AIDS, and his father, frustrated and angry at her illness, becomes brutal, beats the dog, and alienates himself from his son. In both texts, the child takes to the streets as feral, adapting to violence by adopting it. Desperate to salvage dignity, and self-protectively wishing to indicate that he is fear-provoking, the boy goes by "Tsotsi."[1] In the book, Tsotsi attacks a hapless young woman who is on foot in a copse of trees, while the parallel event in the film is his carjacking of a woman in a BMW outside her home in an affluent, previously all-white suburb. The film foregrounds capitalist class inequities to an extent that Fugard's novel does not, as these parallel scenes demonstrate. In both, as a result of the attack, Tsotsi finds himself in possession of the woman's baby.[2] He soon sees something of himself in the infant's wizened vulnerability and improvises care for it. Along with other plot elements, the baby's presence jogs Tsotsi's memory of his suppressed childhood traumas. With these remembrances recovered, his humanity and capacity for self-confrontation, love, and compassion re-emerge to facilitate self-reformation. Both texts, then, empathetically emphasize a human capacity for transformation that may supersede adaptation.

But Hood's unmitigated endorsement of Fugard's overarching thematic preoccupations throws into more obvious relief his major strategic change, that of the text's language. During apartheid, South Africa's official languages were English and Afrikaans, while, paralleling apartheid politics, black African languages were marginalized. Since its post-apartheid constitution was implemented in 1994, the country has eleven official languages: nine black languages, and the two with imperial and colonial heritages, English and Afrikaans. English is spoken in South Africa because the country was ruled by Britain for three centuries. It is now a global language because the British Empire was, for over a century, so vast, and because

Anglo-American influence and power has remained extensive. Afrikaans has its origins in the Dutch spoken by the seventeenth-century European settlers of the Cape, who, paradoxically, became both colonizers and colonized.

Many South African novels explore this dual identity. As early as 1953, Alan Paton's *Too Late the Phalarope* investigated the Afrikaner mindset, and the works of authors like Mark Behr continue to do so. Surprisingly, few, if any South African films intended for international audiences challenge themselves with this theme. But while neither Hood's film nor Fugard's novel do, they are infused with a post-colonial ethos, a sense of being created as a direct or indirect response to imperialism and colonialism. In *Tsotsi*, Hood's refusal to use English for his soundtrack may be read as a rejoinder to those who believe that this imperial and global tongue is one of the few that merits international use; it suggests that English need not be the language of default in a film for a global audience.

The overt impulses governing imperialism and colonialism are the European/Western conviction of intellectual, cultural (including linguistic), and religious superiority, and self-entitling economic dominance. Strategies used by imperial powers from the sixteenth century onward were emulated by white South Africans in apartheid ideology, legislation, and practice. Even now, scholars agree, colonialism and imperialism endure. Despite their purported independence and freedom, many previously colonized societies are subject to new, sometimes subtle, forms of abuse and repression, including domination by multinational systems and corporations. This extant colonialism is called "neo-colonialism" and is one cause of the class inequities that trouble the globe. South Africans have not escaped the neo-colonialism that is the dual legacy of apartheid and globalization.

One South African problem that occurred as apartheid and neo-colonialism converged is, as Hood tells Archibald, "the elephant in the room" of this film: HIV/AIDS. AIDS became recognizable as such to the world medical community by the mid–1980s, which were also some of the darkest years of apartheid. The apartheid South African government was slow to educate its citizens about the disease and how it is communicated, and this delay allowed the virus to spread rapidly. By the time the first post-apartheid government assumed power in the mid–1990s, the country had been plunged into an HIV/AIDS crisis. It was also at this time, however, that antiretroviral "cocktails," potent combinations of drugs, were proven to reverse the course of the disease. But these medications were prohibitively expensive and thus out of the reach of almost all South African AIDS patients. Despite serious attempts by Nelson Mandela's post-apartheid government to persuade international pharmaceutical companies to lower their prices on these drugs, supply cheaper generics, or ease patents, the corporations were intransigent. As their opposition dragged on, President Thabo Mbeki's own tragic refusal to acknowledge the causes of HIV/AIDS and available treatment options complicated this dynamic. The situation was worsened by his government's fear that opposing the interests of multinational corporations would discourage essential foreign investment in the country. While these events played out, millions of South Africans, of whom Tsotsi's mother is fictionally one, became infected with HIV, and thousands died, thus revealing the extent to which powerful multinational companies still wield economic power—here to live or let die—over the lives of citizens in countries that are purportedly free from the yoke of outside control. South Africa's HIV/AIDS crisis, then, was exacerbated by apartheid, globalization, and neo-colonialism.[3]

Eliciting and articulating adequate, productive responses to recalcitrant, overarching oppressions like these is an ongoing challenge. The reactions—in impulses, in speech, and in texts of all kinds—to systems of imperialism, colonialism, and neo-colonialism, is termed "post-colonialism," and it is most usefully conceived as that which *results* from these oppressions. Post-colonial theory, like Ashcroft's, and literature broadly conceived, like Fugard's and Hood's, aim to identify, examine, and represent the dynamics of past and present colonial power, and their effect on identity, national belonging, and the process of globalization. In doing so, post-colonialism seeks to wear down the ideologies that promote Anglo-European superiority. The corollary of this is that colonized people should no longer be pushed, literally and metaphorically, either down or aside, nor should their voices be silenced. Because the ways in which cultures and individuals are depicted can reinforce or destabilize beliefs associated with imperialism, colonialism, and neo-colonialism, forms of representation become important tools of post-colonial thought. Ashcroft believes that they have the power to facilitate transformation. One effective way in which the colonized may take control of their identities in relation to their colonizers is through language. Using Tsotsitaal itself is an assertion of an identity, and Hood's employing it in his film makes a strong statement to those who oppressed its speakers— English and Afrikaners—that the identity being represented is not a pure European one, but a hybridized one that is unabashedly subversive of hegemonic structures.[4]

Although Ashcroft acknowledges the crises that colonialism has provoked, he refuses to focus only on these, and argues passionately that the colonized have rarely been oppressed into stasis and passivity. Though assumed to be limited by colonialism, they have often responded buoyantly and creatively within colonial structures to "resist" and protest them, and to halt or "interpolate" them, proving that their own cultures survive and are not stifled as servile. And, he holds, colonized cultures have gone a step further to achieve transformation: they have noticeably modified the colonizers' cultural tools in important ways, and in doing so, have exposed an unbridgeable gap between the colonial and their colonized cultures, often just as the cultures appear to blend. Language, Ashcroft explains, is a significant instrument for both establishing and representing this rupture because it is synecdochal or metonymic of—it stands in for—cultural difference and distance.[5] In Hood's film, language is one of the prime markers of the characters' cultural and class disparities, even those of the same race in the same society. The two brief scenes in the baby's mother's hospital room demonstrate this. Forcefully demanding that their baby be located, Pumla and her husband John engage in terse discussion with the two detectives, one of whom is black, and a policeman; the different language register in the dialogue here makes clear that these black characters are not of the street.

Language is also important to people who have been disempowered because it accords cultural capital. Though it often attends wealth, cultural capital describes abstract resources that buy social access, acceptance, and power, and thereby secures further opportunity and privilege. While Fugard's novel does not focus on it, the film pays attention to the concept by juxtaposing images of the teen and child Tsotsi, Pumla's purloined infant, and the baby of Miriam, the woman Tsotsi coerces into nursing the baby. In Hood's *Tsotsi*, Pumla, John, and their child enjoy an abundance of cultural capital. Not only their material wealth but their social and political position show that this family is of the post-apartheid élite class. Again, the brief hospital scenes are telling: Pumla's private, sterile, high-tech hospital room where three law enforcement officers convene to meet with her and John indicates not only sophisticated medical care but also her ability to command the time and attention of the state. Her fate is a marked contrast to that of another of Tsotsi's victims of the same evening, gang member Boston. After Tsotsi beats him brutally, Boston lies festering in the unsanitary conditions of Soekie's shebeen, with no recourse to the legal system.[6]

The ruling class always has more cultural capital in the area that it dominates than does the class over which it exercises power, and, through its control of ideology, it is able to promote its own culture as the most worthy one. Though intangible, cultural capital is, for Ashcroft, "a negotiable commodity" (41). Because "the colonized can enter into dialogue only when they acquire the cultural capital of imperial culture to make themselves heard" (107), language is, he insists, an important component of cultural capital.

Ashcroft's insistence on a link between cultural capital and language responds to and somewhat reconciles the polemical positions taken by two major post-colonial thinkers and writers on what it means to use a colonizer's language, especially English, in a post-colonial text. Chinua Achebe, Nigerian author of *Things Fall Apart*, realizing the necessity for the colonized to be comprehensible to their colonizers (when they choose to be), has advocated using English, while Kenyan writer Ngugi Wa Thiong'o vociferously advocates and models rejecting it in favor of a native tongue. In Ashcroft's view, the colonized can communicate that they have not been stifled by the ruling culture and can retain agency by appropriating the colonial language, then scrambling it so that it proves challenging for the colonizers to access; in this way, it is, paradoxically, both employed, as Achebe advised, and rejected, as Ngugi urged.

To achieve language transformation, according to Ashcroft, it is necessary to go beyond opposition to resistance and critique. Fugard's *Tsotsi* extensively models resistance in its critique of apartheid by exposing the destruction and misery that the imposition of apartheid brought about. He focuses especially on the problems precipitated by the Group Areas Act, the government decree that different races could not live in the same areas, and that only whites could live in areas that were the most fertile, mineral-rich, beautiful, and convenient to amenities. To achieve this separation, thousands of blacks were forcibly removed from their homes, which were razed to the ground, fracturing many vibrant communities. One of these notorious eviction projects was the 1950s destruction of Sophiatown, west of Johannesburg—Fugard's book is set in the midst of these events. Most of Sophiatown's inhabitants were then moved to the new location of Soweto, much of which lacked facilities such as electricity. The social and economic consequences of apartheid in such places produced slums, rife with crime. Serious violent transgressions, already a problem in South Africa by the late 1940s, became more frequent and more frightening, and the country is, as Hood's film indicates, still plagued by a high rate of pervasive and vicious crime.[7]

The novel also opposes imperialism, acerbically so. In a short but symbolic scene set in the churchyard late in the book, the rigid, imperious, "repellant," English-speaking Miss Marriot patronizes the black church janitor, Isaiah, who is frustrated and belittled by her as he futilely tries to plant seedlings according to her direction (154–62). The scene, perhaps metonymic of any relationship informed by the imperialist/colonialist's humiliation of the imperial/colonial subject, is pessimistic regarding a fertile outcome. When Isaiah appears in the book, he does not use Miss Marriot's English, but modifies it. However, his changes, like his calling the church that of "Christ the Dreamer" (159) rather than "Redeemer," are prompted by mistakes rather than the impulse to resist Miss Marriot by tweaking her tongue. Thus, while Fugard is taking a stand against imperialism by writing this scene, the imperial subject he inscribes offers ingenuous linguistic adaptation, and thus no resistance.

Representing the colonial subject as passive victim is problematic in a post-colonial context, and, as much as the ethos of Fugard's novel is anti-apartheid and anti-imperialist, aspects of the book's representational strategies, like Isaiah's use of English, destabilize its post-colonial message and may inadvertently support aspects of the colonialist systems Fugard obviously sought to resist. The end of the book is especially troubling. Tsotsi's recovered humanity is expressed when he tries to recover the baby, which he had hidden in the ruins of bulldozed buildings—this is partly precipitated by his growing awareness of the church in the slum, as well as his comforting encounter with Isaiah, who, in naïve terms, tells him about God and "Jesus Cries" (160). In the novel's last lines, both Tsotsi and the baby are crushed by a wall that is falling to an apartheid government bulldozer. Those who find Tsotsi's body see "a smile [that is] beautiful, and strange for a tsotsi" (167). This expression suggests Tsotsi's self-reconciliation and peaceful joy in death, in marked contrast to the anxious vigilance of the youth's adolescence. Fugard's final scene offers certainty, but his choice of ending is ambiguous in a post-colonial context. It clearly narrates the destructiveness of apartheid, but concomitantly suggests that the path to redemption is through Christianity. Such salvation is one of the grand narratives of European imperialism and colonialism, which promoted the "civilizing" mission of Western enlightenment and Christianity. For this reason, the novel's ending may undermine its own anti-imperialist and anti-colonialist sentiment.

This possibility is not mitigated by Fugard's overall linguistic approach in his novel. When his *Tsotsi* is juxtaposed with Hood's and examined in terms of Ashcroft's theory, his cleaving to standard English seems to comply with rather than to counter the demands of the imperial culture. Because English is Fugard's first language and it offers a wide audience for published work, it is a sensible choice. But, Ashcroft argues, if an act of resistance, like Fugard's plot, does not in some way interrupt and modify, that is, interpolate, the methods of the system against which it protests, it remains merely oppositional because the resister, while registering objection, repulsion, or refusal to comply, gains no power from the gesture. By co-opting and often deliberately dabbling with the modes of the colonizer, the colonized empower themselves.

Preceding transformation, but following the steps of critique and resistance, is interpolation. Characteristics of linguistic interpolation, according to Ashcroft, include "unglossed words, phrases or passages from a first language, or concepts, allusions or references which may be unknown to the reader. Such words become synecdochic of the writer's culture—the part that stands for the whole—rather than representations of the world, as the colonial language might [purport to be]" (75). Words or ideas selected by a writer from his or her first language that are strange to a reader, then, may, in a post-colonial text, be employed not simply to describe or "re-present," but to act as the proxy for a whole culture, which the author wants to communicate as foreign to the reader. The novel bears some recognizable instances of such a strategy in that it is lightly peppered with unexplained terms that are not English and would be unfamiliar to an English-speaking audience. For example, one of the gang members is always referred to as "Die Aap" ("The Ape/Monkey" in Afrikaans), with Fugard's only explanation being that the thug was "so called because of his long arms" (6). This may be a tentative, small-scale interpolation, an attempt to inscribe cultural difference through language, but its effect is mostly to situate the book in South Africa and to help establish atmosphere. In other places where Fugard might interpolate, he fails to do so by mediating, often by translating, as where he says that gang-member Butcher (aptly, considering his name) calls a woman "'Nyama,' which means meat" (52). Furthermore, the book is pervaded by a highbrow narrative tone that derives from its sophisticated word choices and educated, standard dialect. For example, as Tsotsi's disillusionment with his gang members grows, the narrator says that for Tsotsi, "theirs was a ponderous presence. In a subtle, ill-defined way it was intrusive, almost an incumbrance" (54). The use of such vocabulary and tone sanctions rather than questions the enduring supremacy of imperial British English. Fugard's text, then, does not seem to tender significant linguistic resistance, interpolation, or transformation. Despite its linguistic adaptations, it indicates no marked gap between the culture of the text and its creator, or between the text and its audience. In Fugard's novel, English still rules.

In contrast, Hood's rejection of English in the film is a sweeping act that functions to halt the assumption that English must continue to reign supreme in texts intended for an international audience. Hood's *Tsotsi* also intervenes in the common practice of offering the text's tongue as the one most familiar and accessible to its primary audience. Even when, rarely, English is used in the film, it is almost unidentifiable as such because of the extent to which alternative cadences and pronunciation substitute for standard ones. When the texts are juxtaposed, the most patent example is the almost incomprehensible English of the disabled miner, Moses Tshabalala, which is not notably challenging to understand in the novel. As such, Hood's deployment of English may be seen to constitute a linguistic interpolation.

For Ashcroft, the more creative, more sophisticated, and more permanent strategy is the next level of the colonized response to the colonizers: transformation. Hood achieves this in his text on an overarching level because his Tsotsitaal soundtrack is inaccessible to those who are not fluent in South African urban parlance and practice. While, like all films, its images are important, it relies on subtitles to convey its narrative. This establishes a gap between the text and the literate audience for whom it is intended—through language, the text exposes a significant fracture between township culture and that of the (presumably) more affluent cinemagoers. Approaching and connecting to post-apartheid South African black urban street life is thus symbolically denied to the film's audience at the very moment at which it may have seemed to them to be possible. For Ashcroft, this is a strong indicator of a linguistic post-colonial strategy of transformation.

By abandoning English in favor of Tsotsitaal, Hood achieves a second example of such a transformation. This is a result of the significant presence in Tsotsitaal of Afrikaans, the language of the Afrikaner. "Afrikaner" means "African" in Dutch and in Afrikaans. Because the original European settlers to South Africa had by the late 1800s become frustrated with both Dutch and British attempts to control them, they resisted by renaming themselves in order to signify that they wished to sever their link to the European metropole and associate instead with the continent of Africa, ironically co-opting one of their colonizers' tongues to do so. Afrikaners thereby signaled an ocean-wide space between themselves and those who had exerted hegemony over them.

But apartheid provoked a paradox for the Afrikaners in their self-identification as African. The Afrikaner colonized became the colonizers of the indigenous populations, a position these once–Europeans exacerbated by realigning with imagined European excellence. As Breyten Breytenbach, an Afrikaner intellectual and writer vociferously opposed to apartheid ideology explained, as Afrikaners segregated themselves from and elevated themselves above other South Africans, it became expedient to present Afrikaans as a pure(ly) European language, superior to any African one. But, Breytenbach asserts, "Afrikaans is a creole language" (353). This was a provocative statement because a cornerstone of apartheid was the prevention of miscegenation, literally and figuratively—in apartheid ideology, to confess to linguistic hybridity would be to admit, metonymically, to the failure of segregation of all kinds. By early 1976, Breytenbach, in traitorous sympathy with South Africans of color, claimed that, "Afrikaans is the language of oppression and of humiliation.... Official Afrikaans is the tool of the racist" (354). His perception was validated mid-year by the Soweto Riots which, as Leonard Thompson explains, began when "black schoolchildren ... demonstrated against the government's insistence that half of their subjects be taught in Afrikaans—as they saw it, the language of the oppressor" (207).

The Afrikaans-speaking oppressor and humiliator, represented as a racist policeman/detective/torturer, is an icon in South African texts set during apartheid. Fugard's *Tsotsi* and the films *Mapantsula* (1986) and *Catch a Fire* (2004) offer examples. It was to this Afrikaner and to official Afrikaans that Breytenbach objected, not to the language itself, which was, he noted, already widely spoken by South Africans of all colors and living in an array of circumstances. He thus makes an important distinction: "To be an Afrikaner is ... a blight and a provocation to humanity. Afrikaans, however, is a means of communication intimately interacting with the specific characteristics of South African life and history, and enriching the land in a dialectic of mutual shaping" (354). Thirty years later, it is this Afrikaans—flexible, productive, and accessible, a common, uncontrolled communication tool that is not context-specific, definable, or even predictable—that the Tsotsitaal of Hood's post-apartheid film foregrounds. In so doing, it draws attention to an irreversible hybridity that was anathema to the Afrikaners of apartheid and subverts any pretences that they had to colonial purity, superiority, and control.

But, as with Fugard's novel, the post-colonial ethos of Hood's text is not stable—it is mitigated by the film's reception, especially its Academy Award. The Academy Awards—synecdochically, the Oscars,—is transparently a competition and ceremony structured by the Academy of Motion Picture Arts and Sciences to promote and secure its own dominance in the movie industry. Through this contest, the Academy establishes itself as the most prestigious arbiter of aesthetic and technical excellence in film. Its endorsement doles out enviable and incalculable cultural capital to the recipients of its nominations and awards. By accepting the Oscar, is Hood endorsing the Academy's hegemony over Hollywood and Hollywood's ongoing dominance of the global film industry?[8] Another South African cultural and intellectual figure, J.M. Coetzee, refrained from full-fledged approval of a similar situation, indeed provocatively modeled resistance to it, when he famously declined to appear to receive either of his Booker Prizes.[9]

To further complicate this issue, Hood's text, though acclaimed, accepts relative marginalization within the Hollywood hegemony, because his rejection of English renders his text a "foreign language film" for the Academy. According to the Academy's Rule 14, a "foreign language film is defined as a feature-length motion picture produced outside the United States of America with a predominantly non–English dialogue track." In this context, the terms "foreign" and "non–English" are striking. Something "foreign" is unfamiliar or strange—while apparently used neutrally here, the word always refers to something from outside a place or culture, never with the cultural capital of the insider. Mild scrutiny of the prefix "non" supports this point: by definition, it identifies that which is negative about something. These terms, then, may be read as self-aggrandizingly restraining and separating. The Academy's instinct to categorize in this way, though perhaps pragmatic, subtly smacks of the separation mandated by apartheid and its linguistic accoutrements, with the term "non-white" an obvious example. Its definition is also suspiciously synecdochic of the (neo)colonialist practice of containing and marginalizing that which is not mainstream in the colonial metropole, and it is, therefore, inconsistent with the ethos and function of post-colonialism. Directors like Hood are, then, in a serious double bind— they are perhaps complicit in maintaining current colonialisms even as they achieve unparalleled recognition and cultural capital for their creative competence.

The extent to which Hood's *Tsotsi* might yet use its significant post–Oscar cultural capital to transform contemporary colonialisms cannot yet be determined. But, when read in conjunction with Ashcroft's theory, it is apparent that, through language, the film boldly rejects imperial and colonial cultures in a way that the book on which it was based does not. Fugard's only novel, though it critiques and protests apartheid and colonialism with integrity, suggests no significant, unspannable space between the culture of the writer and that of the reader. Hood, however, with his sweeping linguistic strategy, has taken Fugard's apartheid classic beyond adaptation, and has transformed it into a powerful post-apartheid and post-colonial film that also generates complex ironies and paradoxes.

Notes

1. Fugard and Hood may be using this name synecdochically to suggest that many township tsotsis are children forced by circumstance into criminality.
2. In both texts, the woman is black, but, though influenced by the larger context and legacy of racism, the crime does not appear to be racially motivated. Tsotsi attacks her impulsively, perhaps to release tension, after fellow gang member Boston's disturbing interrogation of his loss of "decency" and his subsequent beating of Boston. In the novel, "he didn't know what he was going to do [to her]" (34), and what he does do is unclear, but there are suggestions of rape. In the film, Tsotsi does not touch his victim (Pumla) before shooting her. The woman in the book appears to survive the attack; at the end of the film, Pumla is in a wheelchair and may be permanently disabled.
3. For a rich, theoretically informed discussion on the withholding of anti-retroviral drugs in South Africa, see Sitze.
4. "Hegemony" describes the constellation of forms of dominance and authority (including ideologies) that one culture exerts over others.
5. While Ashcroft, like most critics, uses these literary terms interchangeably, there is a difference. Metonymy is the more general one. It occurs when an object or concept is not called by its own name, but by the name of something closely associated with it. For example, in the phrase "she spoke in a tongue he did not recognize, "tongue" is a metonym of "language." Synecdoche is more specific; it describes a word or phrase in which part of something stands for the whole or the whole stands for the part—as when "mouths to feed" refers to hungry people.
6. A shebeen is a township drinking establishment. Until recently, most, run by intrepid

entrepreneurs like Soekie, were illicit and sold bootlegged liquor. Now, however, many are legal and serve mainstream beverages.

7. While the criminals in both texts are young black men, it is important to note that outside of the texts, criminality and the willingness to perform violence occur in people of all population groups and both sexes.

8. The term "Hollywood" refers not only to a place in California, but also functions as a metonym for the film industry and a collective noun for those who work in it. Even "Bollywood," the powerful emerging Indian film industry, is signified through obvious allusion to Hollywood—its identity is implicitly derivative.

9. Now known as the Man Booker, this prestigious prize is awarded annually to a full-length novel written by a citizen of the British Commonwealth or Ireland. Winning a Booker is a coup for the author and publisher, and even being shortlisted for the prize assures successful sales of a novel.

Works Cited

Academy of Motion Pictures Arts and Sciences. Rule Fourteen. *78th Academy Awards Rules for Distinguished Achievements in 2005.* 9 Oct 2007. <http://www.oscars.org/78 academyawards/rulesrule14html>.

Archibald, David. "Violence and Redemption: An Interview with Gavin Hood." *Cineaste* 21.2 (Spring 2006): 4pp. *Expanded Academic ASAP.* Gale. 8 Oct. 2007.

Ashcroft, Bill. *Post-Colonial Transformation.* London: Routledge, 2001.

Breytenbach, Breyten. "A Position on the Struggle for the *Taal* (Being Afrikaans)." 1976. *The True Confessions of an Albino Terrorist.* San Diego: Harcourt, 1983.

Coe, Sue, and Holly Metz. *How to Commit Suicide in South Africa.* New York: Raw One-Shot, 1983.

Fugard, Athol. *Tsotsi.* Jeppestown (Johannesburg): AD Donker, 1980.

Sitze, Adam. "Denialism." *South Atlantic Quarterly* 103.4 (2004): 769–811.

Thompson, Leonard. *A History of South Africa.* Jeppestown (Johannesburg): Jonathan Ball, 2006.

Tsotsi. Dir. Gavin Hood. Miramax, 2005.

5

Transforming Great Expectations: *Dickens, Cuarón, and the* Bildungsroman

ANTJE S. ANDERSON

Alfonso Cuarón's 1998 movie *Great Expectations*, based loosely on the 1861 novel by Charles Dickens, hovers between an adaptation and a transformation. On the one hand, Cuarón's movie is directly based on the plot and the characters of Dickens's novel and thus aligns itself with the many movie and television adaptations that have been made over the years.[1] On the other hand, Cuarón and his scriptwriter Mitch Glazer (who also transformed Dickens's *Christmas Carol* into the 1988 movie *Scrooged*) chose to deviate from the novel sufficiently for the movie to transcend adaptation. Not only does Cuarón relocate the plot, the language, and the environment from the 1820s and 1830s in England to the Florida and New York City of the 1980s and 1990s; he also uses his version of the story to draw our attention almost exclusively to the erotic tension between the main character, Finn (Pip in the novel), and the woman he has loved since childhood, Estella (whose name remains unchanged from the original). Admittedly, the hero's obsession with Estella is already powerfully present in Dickens's novel—even though the explicitly sexual element is new. But in Cuarón's movie, this all-encompassing obsession and its visual representation become the vehicle for transforming the entire plot of *Great Expectations*, typically categorized as a *Bildungsroman*, a novel of education and growth, into an anti–*Bildungsroman*—a narrative of circularity and stasis.

Although the idea of *Bildung*—education, growth, and change over time all rolled into one—strikes me as crucial to understanding Cuarón's movie in relation to his source, the term is virtually absent from most critical discussions of the film.[2] Ana Moya and Gemma Lopéz, who alone among the critics writing about Cuarón's film briefly evoke *Bildung*, conclude that Cuarón follows Dickens's lead in that he depicts a main character who changes and loses his innocence, and that especially the happy and coherent ending of the movie underscores the story's "Bildungsroman qualities" (182). Against this interpretation, I argue that Cuarón actually challenges Dickens's narrative of self-development and personal growth. His radical critique is achieved, first and foremost, by the cinematography—especially by the powerfully represented symbolically charged exterior shots, and by the inclusion of powerful visual imagery—especially of Finn's works of art. The director's decision to transform Dickens's storyline into an anti–*Bildungsroman* is both its most intriguing trait and its most striking achievement.[3]

In Dickens's 1861 novel *Great Expectations*, Pip tells the story of his growing up. Although he starts out as a penniless orphan living with his sister and her husband Joe, who is a blacksmith, he is told in his late teens that an anonymous donor (the novel's "benefactor") will bestow a fortune on him, and that he will be sent to London to become a gentleman worthy of such a fortune. Pip thinks that his benefactor is the eccentric Miss Havisham, at whose house he played once a week with a girl named Estella when he was a child. He assumes that Miss Havisham is making him a gentleman so that he can marry Estella, whom he has always admired and who has always very haughtily rejected him as a "coarse and common boy." He comes to find out that his fortune actually comes from an escaped convict named Abel Magwitch, whom, as a nine-year-old, he helped during an escape attempt described in the initial chapter of the novel. Pip is devastated when he finds out that a criminal (who became rich in Australia after completing his prison sentence, but whose secret return to England is punishable by death if he is discovered) is his benefactor. After a series of dramatic events, including both Magwitch's and Miss Havisham's deaths and Estella's marriage to another man, Pip goes abroad for many years. On the last pages of the novel, he returns for a visit to his hometown and runs into Estella on the grounds where Miss Havisham's house once stood. He finds out that she is no longer married; and although there is no formal declaration of mutual love, the ending, with the two of them leaving the grounds hand in hand, seems to imply that Pip and Estella will stay together.

Transformation is thus in many ways the theme of Dickens's *Great Expectations*—not in the sense of mythological shape-shifting or of objects changing from cars into weapon-wielding robots, but in the sense of changes that the main character's personality undergoes as he grows from a child into an adult, and especially as he traumatically loses his childhood illusions about his alleged expectations. A novel that tracks such growth and change is called a *Bildungsroman*, typically translated as "novel of education." The German term implies not just a story of someone's formal and informal education, but also one of growing and being shaped in a more organic sense.[4] Contemporary critics, among them Jerome Buckley and Franco Moretti, cite *Great Expectations* as one of the main British examples of the genre of the *Bildungsroman*. Like *David Copperfield, Jane Eyre*, or the twentieth-century *Catcher in the Rye*, it is a fictional autobiography in which the hero tells his own story of growing up.

However, while Buckley in his seminal study of the British *Bildungsroman, Season of Youth*, admires *Great Expectations* and claims that Dickens "gave the English *Bildungsroman* both personal intensity and objective power" (61), Moretti argues that British literature does not really have a *Bildungsroman* before George Eliot's novels are published. Novels like *David Copperfield* and *Great Expectations*, he claims, do *not* construct a character's growth into adulthood as an important, necessary, and ultimately positive process—they depict adulthood as a state of corruption and a loss of innocence: "[T]he most significant experiences are not those that alter but those which confirm the choices made by childhood 'innocence.' Rather than novels of 'initiation' one feels they should be called novels of 'preservation'" (182). The British novels, according to Moretti, inevitably end with the character's symbolic return to childhood and to a restored sense of order that hearkens back to the beginning of the story. For Charles Dickens's *David Copperfield*, Moretti's main example, his argument is fairly convincing. But for *Great Expectations*, his claim is harder to sustain because the ending of *Great Expectations* powerfully implies that Pip, the protagonist, has in fact grown into an adult, rather than returned on a circular pathway to his childhood. It is true that many of the experiences that lead to Pip's maturation are associated with disillusionment and loss, but Pip is clearly "altered" by the "significant experiences" (to use Moretti's words again), rather than intent on returning to his childhood self.

At first sight, it seems as if Cuarón retains Dickens's idea of the *Bildungsroman* and merely updates the story of *Great Expectations*, setting it in late twentieth-century America—so that it is not surprising that critics like Holt or Moya and Lopéz see Cuarón's adaptation in terms of his preservation of this theme. First of all, Cuarón, like Dickens, features a main character whom we first meet as a child and see transformed into a young adult in the course of the movie. Secondly, again like Dickens, Cuarón presents this character as someone with a specific but also somewhat difficult-to-define ambition: Whereas Pip wants to become a "gentleman"—he wants to move up into the British upper-middle or upper classes—Finn wants to become a successful artist and "make it" in New York City's elite art scene. In each case, the move from the provinces (Rochester in the southern marsh country near the English channel in Dickens's novel, the Florida Gulf coast in Cuarón's movie) to the big city (London, New York) signals simultaneously that the main character is moving up in society and that he is growing into an adult. Most importantly, however, in both versions of the story, the main character's social ambitions are directly connected to his fascination with a woman from the upper classes who represents his social aspirations and is socially and symbolically forever placed out of his reach.

However, a closer look at Cuarón's transformation of this story shows that the idea of growth and *Bildung* is undermined by the way he retells Dickens's story, but especially by the way he translates and reframes it visually. Instead of growth, we see stasis and regression as Finn makes his way in the world. Thus, while Franco Moretti overstates his case when he argues that Dickens's *Great Expectations* is regressive, his argument about its being a story of "preservation" would seem to fit Cuarón's movie very well. Unlike Pip, who discovers that he is ashamed to be a lowly blacksmith's apprentice and wants to become "a gentleman" as he comes into contact with Miss Havisham and Estella, Finn is represented as obsessed with art from childhood, and his adult dream of having his own art show and making a breakthrough in New York seems less of a realistic career goal than a child's regressive fantasy of an artist's career. Even the way in which the city is represented throughout the movie is relevant: the city locales do not form a contrast to the earlier Gulf Coast environment as much as they are a fantastic continuation of it.[5] More than anything else, however, it is the representation of Finn's obsession with Estella, at first sight so similar to that in Dickens's novel, that ultimately points to a new understanding of the relationship between the two main characters. Admittedly this is derived from the novel, but transformed radically by the refusal to see the characters as "growing up" or "growing into" becoming a couple.

Estella means "star" in Latin, and her name alone implies that she is a beautiful and desired but impossibly distant object. Given that she has been raised, in both the novel and the film, as her adoptive mother's instrument of revenge—i.e., to be a cold and distant beauty who attracts men but cannot return their feelings—her association with an ever-elusive object is very fitting. In both Dickens's novel and Cuarón's movie, Estella moves out of the main character's reach again and again, up to the very end of each story. Dickens's Estella, consistently associated with light sources such as candles, moves away from Pip bearing a candle in her hand, and is once referred to as a candle that attracts men like moths. Cuarón adds to the motif by linking Estella not only with stars, but also with birds in flight—while Finn himself is associated both verbally and visually with fish (and indeed a fish out of water when he tries to reach up to Estella and her sphere).

Both Dickens and Cuarón emphasize the hero's obsession with Estella by making her appear everywhere. I believe that Cuarón's visual representation of Estella takes its cue from Pip's passionate declaration of his love for Estella in Chapter 44 of the novel:

> You are part of my existence, part of myself. You have been in every line I have ever read since I first came here, the rough common boy whose poor heart you wounded even then. You have been in every prospect I have ever seen since—on the river, on the sails of the ships, on the marshes, in the clouds, in the light, in the darkness, in the wind, in the woods, in the sea, in the streets. You have been the embodiment of every graceful fancy that my mind has ever become acquainted with [364].

This description is the key to the way in which Cuarón visualizes Finn's obsession throughout the movie: Estella herself and the objects, animals, drawings, and colors that are associated with her appear everywhere in the movie, in virtually every scene.

Importantly, however, while his declaration locates Estella "in every prospect," Pip identifies a clear starting point for his obsession—the day when he first met Estella at Miss Havisham's house as a boy. Because Pip's obsession is a pivotal element of his character development and maturation, identifying this specific point of origin is crucial, as is the fact that his love for her grows and changes over time, especially once he realizes that Miss Havisham did not mean to bestow Estella on him. When he meets her again many years later, it is clear that the intervening years have brought further changes and disillusionments for both. By contrast, Cuarón presents Finn's obsession with Estella as an unchanging, ever-present element of Finn's life through scenes that are staged as a series of repetitions of the same narrative pattern—a close, intimate encounter between the two, followed by Estella's retreat into the distance, away from Finn. This unchanging obsession is reinforced by the ubiquitous visual allusions to Estella that are introduced as early as the opening sequence of the movie—before Finn has ever seen her or even become aware of her existence.

As the movie begins, we see Finn as a boy spending the day on his own in and out of his boat in the shallow waters of the Gulf coast of Florida, drawing what he sees in a sketchbook. The quiet of these lyrical establishing shots is dramatically interrupted when Finn is suddenly threatened by the escaped convict Arthur Lustig in a suspenseful scene that rivals the frightening and equally sudden appearance of Abel Magwitch in the first

chapter of Dickens's novel. Prior to this violent disruption, the dreamy, peaceful atmosphere in which Finn sketches a fish that swims around his feet
seems to indicate Finn's self-sufficiency, his innocence, and his bond with
nature. Coming as it does before the violent intrusion of the brutal adult
world in the form of the escaped convict, the opening scene creates the image
of a childhood paradise. Finn's artistic talent seems utterly natural; it belongs
organically to the peaceful coastal environment in which he draws and from
which he derives his subject matter. In fact, his name, which is revealed as
the convict asks for it, implies his connection with untouched nature; in
evoking a fish's fins, it refers us back to the very first object we see him draw.
Finn is also water-bound by his background as a boy growing up on the
shore in Florida, and his life before his departure for New York City links
him continually to water and to fish.[6]

Importantly, though, this idyllic childhood environment already
includes Finn's future obsession with Estella; she is symbolically present
both in his surroundings and in the sketch we see him working on. As Finn
stands in the water, focusing on water animals, he is surrounded by a flock
of coastal birds in flight, which anticipate the birds in Finn's art that are consistently associated with Estella and her constant move away from him.
Seemingly oblivious of their presence, he draws a fish—himself, not Estella,
if one wants to be simplistic. However, the fish in his sketch is surrounded
by stars that Finn *has already drawn*; when we first see a shot of the sketchbook page, the stars are already in place, as he slowly pencils in the fish in
the center. And while the fish is naturalistically sketched—shots of Finn's
drawing are intercut with shots of the fish in the water to imply that he is
"drawing from nature"—the stars in his sketch are not realistically drawn
starfish, but abstract five-pointed stars. In this fairly obvious foreshadowing
of Finn's obsession with images of Estella, the stars are thus already implicitly the work of Finn's imagination. They foreshadow not just Estella's presence, but also the way in which Finn will "create" Estella as an object of
desire in his portraits, in figure drawings, and in his many symbolic drawings of birds, stars, and airplanes.

Estella is thus a constant, static presence; she is not associated with
change in the positive sense of *Bildung*, but neither is she linked to the idea
of change as corruption, fall, or the loss of innocence. This emphasis on stasis and sameness is reinforced by the staging of the encounters between Finn
and Estella as a series of repetitions of the same moment, with frequent
visual allusions to this opening scene. Thus, when Estella is first introduced
as a girl, we see her in a setting that again associates childhood with a natural environment—namely Ms. Dinsmoor's unkempt and neglected garden,
complete with fountains and ponds. The garden is named "Lost Paradise"

("Paradiso Perduto" is inscribed on the arch over the garden gate) in a rather heavy-handed allusion to the theme of innocence and its loss; however, the loss of innocence seems to refer to Ms. Dinsmoor, whose abandonment by her lover many years ago is clearly associated with this site (the remnants of the wedding feast are not, as in Dickens's novel, left behind in a darkened dining room, but rot away in the garden). Although we learn later that Estella is inextricably linked to Ms. Dinsmoor's loss of innocence because she becomes her instrument of revenge, Estella is neither innocent nor corrupted, but rather seems to move outside of these categories altogether, an object beyond moral contemplation—a distant star, a bird in flight, a part of the natural environment that surround her. Thus, when we (and Finn) catch our first glimpse of the child Estella through the overgrown vegetation, this environment seems less like a paradise already lost than like a vast playground for playing hide-and-seek for a being who is as one with her environment. Estella, even more so than Finn in the earlier scene at the waterfront, blends into the brightly lit jungle-like environment with her blond hair and bright green dress.[7] Later encounters between the two also take place outdoors (several of them in Central Park), evoking again the linking of both characters with nature.[8]

These scenes all reiterate the dynamic relationship between Finn and Estella that is first hinted at when the birds scatter up and away from Finn in the opening scene. Estella's moving out of reach again and again takes the form of her being placed physically above Finn, looking down on him, or stooping to reach down to him or objects associated with him—only to vanish from sight just as Finn reaches her or touches her, literally or symbolically. Most striking is their last encounter as teenagers, just before Estella leaves for her schooling abroad. Finn is seated on his bed, looking up at her and fondling her legs and crotch as she stands in front of him. She is rendered imposing and powerful through several low-angle shots that align us with Finn's powerless position. At the end of this very close encounter, Estella again moves away from Finn, disappearing through receding doorways out of his reach.

Finn's attempt to move up to reach Estella is, as in Dickens's novel, also representative of his social ambitions, and Cuarón artfully links his dream of becoming a successful artist to his obsession with Estella. The link between his ambitions becomes explicit as he draws a portrait of Estella at Ms. Dinsmoor's behest when he first meets her as a child. In his retrospective voice-over, Finn contemplates that moment as the beginning of all his ambitions: "To paint for the rich. To have their freedom. To love Estella.... The things we cannot have." And, as in Dickens's *Great Expectations*, social and erotic ambitions do turn out to be equally impossible to fulfill. Estella keeps eluding Finn, and his success as an artist turns out to be an illusion: not only was his show bankrolled by his "secret benefactor," Arthur Lustig, but Lustig bought every painting in the exhibit, making him the manufacturer of Finn's career in art. Finn has not "made it" despite the buzz his show has created, just as eventually having sex with Estella does not bring her into his reach; she vanishes after a night spent with him just as she has after each previous encounter.

In the artwork that yokes Finn's infatuation with Estella to his passion for painting, Finn obsessively repeats the motifs associated with Estella's elusiveness, so that the movie's background sets are studded with even more visual allusions to Estella. Finn's sketches are intermittently visible throughout the movie—in his sketchbook, in his home in Florida, in his ratty hotel room and later in his snazzy warehouse-loft studio in New York, as well as in the gallery where his work is exhibited. The opening and closing credits also feature Finn's drawings, so that symbolic images of the relationship between Estella and Finn frame the entire story.[9] In Finn's art work, Estella and the relationship between the two characters appear repeatedly in drawings of birds and fish, or of water and sky—some in combinations that underscore the symbolic separation between the two. For example, we see a drawing of a fish chained with a heavy anchor to the sea. Another rather unsubtle sketch features the outline of a head filled with stars—easily readable as Finn's head filled with thoughts of Estella. Although we catch only brief glimpses of most of these images in the course of the movie, with many appearing only in the opening and closing credits, the common symbolic content is repeated over and over: Finn and Estella are creatures of different elements, and they meet only with difficulty, with Finn symbolically reaching up while Estella stoops down or swoops out of his reach.

Cuarón pushes the ubiquitous juxtaposition of Finn and Estella as water and air, below and above, fish and bird (or star) far beyond the novel. But his transformation lies less in the use of these images than in the fact that he introduces them so early, prior to Estella's first appearance on screen. The symbolic relationship between Estella and Finn is a constant that challenges Dickens's core narrative, implying that there is no *Bildung* for Finn as he moves from childhood to adulthood. However, Cuarón's insistence on stasis can be seen in a much less critical light than Moretti would see it— namely, not as a regression into childhood, but as a postmodern filmmaker's challenge to the idea that the self evolves, that progress and change are the only way to define one's identity.

The ending sequence of the film powerfully reinforces this sense of stasis and sameness as a sort of lyrical rebellion against the arc of the *Bildungsroman* and thus radically transforms Dickens's ending. In Dickens's novel, the last pages make very clear that things have changed. We learn that Pip has spent many years abroad, and upon his return to the marshes he runs into Estella at the site where Miss Havisham's mansion, Satis House, once stood. Estella asks him whether he can forgive her for her past cruelty, and when he says he does, she says she hopes they can be "friends apart." In response, Pip tells us:

> I took her hand in mine, and we went out of the ruined place; and, as the morning mists had risen long ago when I first left the forge, so, the evening mists were rising now, and in all the broad expanse of tranquil light they showed to me, I saw the shadow of no parting from her [484].

Although the two thus leave "the ruined place" hand in hand, I agree with the many critics who have argued that this ending is highly ambiguous and can be called a happy ending only with a hefty dose of wishful thinking.[10]

These ambiguities notwithstanding, however, the ending clearly implies that both Pip and Estella have been changed by their experience—they have each undergone a process of *Bildung* that has transformed them both. Estella, as she asks Pip for forgiveness, puts her own experience in words that would also describe Pip's disillusionment about his "great expectations" and his renunciation of his ambition to be a gentleman. She says that "suffering has been stronger than all other teaching, and has taught me to understand what your heart used to be. I have been bent and broken, but—I hope—into a better shape" (Dickens 484). As much as this form of *Bildung* is a negative, even violent process, it is constructed as an important, necessary condition for growing up and for the final union of Pip and Estella.

In contrast to this muted ending, Cuarón's movie wraps up with the lovers uniting as they hold hands and look out onto the ocean and into the sun.[11] But it is an ending that challenges the importance, even the possibility, of change; it effectively erases the story that has led up to this finale because Cuarón insists so aggressively on closing the circle by visually evoking the film's opening shots. As the movie's action moves directly, indeed with a certain facility, from the death scene of Arthur Lustig to Finn's return, many years later, to the Gulf Coast, Finn fills us in about the intervening years with his retrospective voice-over. He has become an artist (how, and whether with the use of Lustig's money, remain unanswered questions). "The years went by. And then one day, I went home," Finn says as we return to the settings of the film's very beginning. As he returns to the Gulf shore, we see shots of fish, starfish, and the shadows of birds, and then Finn himself wading through ankle-deep water—a clear visual flashback to the opening scene. A bridging shot of him entering his childhood home to visit Joe leads to the last scene of the movie—a return to Ms. Dinsmoor's estate.

The even more advanced decay of the garden (now that the owner has died and the house is about to be torn down) seems to indicate not so much that time has passed, but that everything has returned even more closely to its natural state since Finn first entered *Paradiso Perduto*. Finn seems to become his child self again as he catches sight of a little girl who looks like the young Estella flitting through the overgrown vegetation. When Finn finds the real, adult Estella herself on the decrepit mansion's waterfront terrace, the little girl—her daughter and, given her age, possibly his—is playing by the water, a visual reminder of childhood on the margins of the scene between the two adults. Like Dickens's Estella in the novel, Cuarón's Estella asks for forgiveness. Finn's answer to her question "Can you ever forgive me?" is vague: "Don't you know me at all?" he says. This question seems to imply, "Don't you know that of course, I will forgive you?" but the following voice-over implies that instead of forgiving, Finn simply wants to forget and thus erase all that has happened:

> She did know me, and I knew her; I always had, from the first instant. And the rest of it, it didn't matter. It was past.
> It was as if it had never been. There was just my memory of it.

Thus, in Cuarón's movie, forgetting, not forgiving—making the past not "matter," acting "as if it had never been"—seems necessary in order to make Finn and Estella a couple.

And not only does Finn's statement (the last words we hear in the movie) imply erasure or obliteration; so does the shot sequence that underlies it. Although we see the silhouettes of the two lovers coming close together until they stand hand in hand, the way the camera catches the refraction of the sunlight off the water results in an overexposure that keeps the two main characters visually separated by overly bright light in the center of the composition, even as they appear in the same frame. Cuarón uses overexposed and brightly lit exterior shots several times in the course of the movie, but here, in the last frame, the brightness is extreme, and radically at odds with the muted light that the rising "evening mists" evoke in the novel's last paragraph. The final shot overpowers the two characters visually, as if the very sunshine of their love made the lovers vanish along with their own past.

This verbal and visual erasure of the characters' story and history, of their growth and the possibility of their transformation, signals the culmination of Cuarón's anti-*Bildungsroman*. The ending accentuates the longing to return to one's beginnings and to forget the rest. But paradoxically, one's beginnings, as the movie insists by introducing Estella and Finn's desire for Estella in the opening scene, are never prelapsarian in the sense of being free of desire and longing. And prepubescent childhood, although associated with nature, in particular with the ocean as the primordial site of origin for all life (fish, birds, Finn, and all), is already inscribed with a desire that the movie constructs as unchanging, and unchangingly unfulfilled. If the desire for Estella, the desire to create art, and the desire to be one with nature are all one in the very beginning and do not undergo any change, the ending seems to imply that the only thing that can make these desires go away is not their fulfillment, but the obliteration of all desire in a vast ocean of nothingness: a brightly lit blank screen and then the fade to black that separates the movie's storyline from the final credits.

The transformation of Dickens's *Bildungsroman* into a story that virtually denies the possibility of (personal) transformation and growth is perhaps largely the result of the film's narrow focus on Finn's obsession with Estella, at the cost of other dimensions of Dickens's *Great Expectations*, in which the protagonist's growth, rather than his regression or stasis, are emphasized. For example, the relationship between Finn and the convict and also between Finn and Joe are strikingly underdeveloped in the movie. The emphasis on this sexual obsession may not have been all Cuarón's doing. As the director told critic Pamela Katz in a post-production interview, he was very interested in the question of social class, and especially in the relationship between Finn and Joe, but he was told by the producers to emphasize Estella's role, as she was played by Gwyneth Paltrow, a rising star at the time and the movie's main box-office draw (Katz 100).

However, Cuarón's emphasis on obliterating the past also echoes some of the thematics that he develops in several of his other films, in particular in his two children's movies, *Little Princess* (1995) and *Harry Potter and the Prisoner of Azkaban* (2004), both of which are also adaptations of famous novels, and neither one of which is exclusively a movie for children.[12] Of course, a happy return to the beginning is a common motif in children's fiction, but in the context of these movies "for children," one might say that in his transformation of *Great Expectations*, Cuarón creates a children's movie for adults—one in which the possibility of having everything return to the beginning, in a reassuring fairy-tale pattern, extends even to the undoing of sexual experience, commonly the hallmark of initiation into adulthood. As viewers, we may dismiss this insistence on the return to one's origins as a nostalgic and ultimately regressive denial of the validity of adulthood, including adult sexual experience, as Moretti would probably dismiss it. However, because Cuarón does not establish this blissful state of happiness as a "desire-free zone," but shows how Finn's desires are already part of this state, thus making it a natural, if static and essentialist, part of his self, one can also see his transformation as an intriguing resistance to the *Bildungsroman*. Cuarón's transformation of Dickens's story thus becomes a sort of postmodern—not to mention visually gorgeous—challenge to the idea that we need to see the self in terms of change, be it in terms of growth and progress (privileging experience) or of loss and fall (if we privilege innocence). Cuarón's early inscription of desire into the very fabric of Finn's identity, and his insistence on erasing him (and Estella) completely in the moment at which his desire is seemingly fulfilled in their reunion, refuses to portray Finn in terms of either experience through his *Bildung* or "preservation" of some earlier state of innocence. By that very refusal, Cuarón transforms and transcends Dickens's great *Bildungsroman, Great Expectations.*

Notes

1. For recent work on Dickens and film, and specifically *Great Expectations* and film, see Glavin; Smith; and Marsh's essay in *The Cambridge Companion to Charles Dickens.* The most-frequently analyzed adaptation of Dickens's novel is, of course, David Lean's 1946 movie, which would have to be discussed as a crucial subtext for Cuarón's film in a more fully developed analysis.

2. See the essays by Katz, Johnson, Antinucci, and Holt as well as Moya and Lopéz. Holt, although she does not use the term *Bildungsroman,* implies that the movie, like Dickens's novel, tells a "coming-of-age" story, revamped to show that Pip has strong affinities with the 1990s "Generation X" for which the movie was made. She also sees multiple allusions to various American variants of this story, such as Twain's *Huckleberry Finn* and the movie *The Graduate* (71).

3. I agree with one of the very few enthusiastic reviews of the movie, written by Charles Taylor for *Salon,* which praises Cuarón for not only successfully transforming the "gothic strangeness" of Dickens's novel, but also the film's stunning, lush cinematography. Antinucci's insightful analysis also notes the movie's "visual enjoyableness" (315). However, I would echo the general consensus of most other reviews that the script is at best mediocre. In particular, both Finn's voice-over and the dialogue are often painfully stilted and unimpressive.

4. Critics first used the term *Bildungsroman* in mid–nineteenth-century Germany to categorize German novels like Goethe's *Wilhelm Meisters Lehrjahre* (1795), but later on, the term was also applied to novels from other national literatures. Buckley and Moretti are major examples of the transfer of the term outside of German literary history; for an excellent introduction to the German critical tradition, see Sammons.

5. Compare Taylor's observations on the film's dreamlike images of Central Park, the Manhattan skyline, and SoHo interiors.

6. Joe, in the movie the boyfriend of Finn's sister, who raises Finn both before and after she vanishes, has been transformed from the blacksmith of the novel into a fisherman (when he can find work in his profession). Finn and Joe's first shared joke, right after the opening scenes, is about fish ("How do you smoke a swordfish?"), and the bridging shots that underlie Finn's voice-over explanation that he stayed on the coast for seven years after Estella's departure clearly imply that he and Joe now both make a living as fishermen.

7. The color green, which is used with disproportionate frequency for clothing, room décor, and other visual effects, so that it virtually drenches the film, always hearkens back to the pale greens of the shallow water and to Finn's clothing in the opening shots of the movie, and reinforces the link of the characters and their relationship to the natural world. For a different interpretation of Cuarón's "green tint" strategy, see Moya and Lopez 184–85.

8. These scenes frequently involve water—another allusion to the ocean beginning of the movie—in a highly eroticized way; for example, Estella kisses Finn twice under running water. In the sequence that introduces her as a child, they French kiss as they drink together

from a fountain in Ms. Dinsmoor's house; the scene is repeated as Estella kisses Finn as he takes a drink at a water fountain in Central Park. (Another important scene later on features a somewhat hackneyed kiss in the pouring rain, leading up to the movie's even more hackneyed bedroom scene.) For a slightly different, but beautifully detailed, analysis of the function of the ocean in the movie, see Holt 90n8.

9. The artwork was created by Francesco Clemente, an internationally renowned Italian artist who produced approximately 200 sketches for the movie ("Francesco Clemente: Biography").

10. The ambiguity of the novel's mutedly happy ending is reinforced by the fact that it is, famously, already a second version of the ending—Dickens initially wrote an altogether dysphoric ending in which Pip and Estella only catch a glimpse of each other and go their separate ways. For the most insightful discussions of the ending of Dickens's novel, see Falzon, the afterword to Miller, and Brooks's chapter on *Great Expectations* in *Reading for the Plot*. For an extensive comparison of the two different endings Dickens wrote, see especially Rosenberg as well as Kucich, Cloy, and Dunn.

11. This is the interpretation of the ending offered by both Moya and López (182) and Holt. While Holt discusses the use of brilliant light in the scene at some length, she concludes that the lovers looking out over a "brightly sunlit sea" suggests "the numerous, if uncertain, possibilities of their future," quite like Dickens's own ending with its "possibility of a future union" (87, 86).

12. Both of these films address the ideas of erasing the past and returning to an original state of bliss. The return of the father, believed to be dead, in *The Little Princess* and the use of the "Time Turner" in *Harry Potter* are in each case derived from the novelistic source, but both clearly fascinate Cuarón.

Works Cited

Allingham, Philip V. "Shadows of 'Things That Have Been and Will Be' in *Great Expectations.*" *English Language Notes* 41.3 (2004): 50–56.

Antinucci, Rafaella. "Alfonso Cuarón's 'Late Experimentations': Dickens and Post-Modernism." *Great Expectations: Nel laboratorio di Charles Dickens.* Ed. Francesco Marroni. Rome: Aracne, 2006. 293–319.

Brooks, Peter. *Reading for the Plot: Design and Intention in Narrative.* New York: Knopf, 1984.

Buckley, Jerome F. *Season of Youth: The Bildungsroman from Dickens to Golding.* Cambridge, MA: Harvard University Press, 1974.

Cloy, John. "Two Altered Endings—Dickens and Bulwer-Lytton." *University of Mississippi Studies in English* 10 (1992): 170–72.

Cuarón, Alfonso, dir. *Great Expectations.* Twentieth-Century–Fox, 1998.

Dickens, Charles. *Great Expectations.* 1861. London: Penguin, 1996.

Dunn, Albert A. "The Altered Endings of *Great Expectations*: A Note on Bibliography and First-Person Narration." *Dickens Studies Newsletter* 9 (1978): 40–42.

Falzon, Alex R., "All's Well, That Begins Well? True Starts and False Endings in *Great Expectations.*" *Great Expectations: Nel laboratorio di Charles Dickens.* Ed. Francesco Marroni. Rome: Aracne, 2006. 51–60.

"Francesco Clemente: Biography." *Guggenheim Museum: The Collection.* 28 Sept. 2008. <http://www.guggenheimcollection.org/site/artist_bio_31.html>.

Glavin, John, ed. *Dickens on Screen.* Cambridge: Cambridge University Press, 2003.

Holt, Shari H. "Dickens from a Postmodern Perspective: Alfonso Cuaron's *Great Expectations* for Generation X." *Dickens Studies Annual: Essays on Victorian Fiction* 38 (2007): 69–92.

Johnson, Michael K.: "Not Telling the Story the Way it Happened: Alfonso Cuarón's *Great Expectations.*" *Literature/Film Quarterly* 33.1 (2005): 62–78.

Katz, Pamela. "Directing Dickens: Alfonso Cuarón's 1998 *Great Expectations.*" *Dickens on Screen.* Ed. John Glavin. Cambridge: Cambridge University Press, 2003. 95–103.

Kucich, John. "Action in the Dickens Ending: *Bleak House* and *Great Expectations.*" *Nineteenth-Century Fiction* 33 (1978): 88–109.

Lean, David, dir. *Great Expectations.* 1946. DVD. Criterion, 1995.

Marroni, Francesco, ed. *Great Expectations: Nel laboratorio di Charles Dickens.* Rome: Aracne, 2006.

Marsh, Joss. "Dickens and Film." *The Cambridge Companion to Charles Dickens.* Ed. John Jordan. Cambridge, Eng.: Cambridge University Press, 2001. 204–23.

Miller, D. A. *Narrative and Its Discontents: Problems of Closure in the Traditional Novel.* Princeton: Princeton University Press, 1981.

Moretti, Franco. *The Way of the World: The Bildungsroman in European Culture.* 2nd ed. London: Verso, 2000.

Moya, Ana, and Gemma Lopéz. "'I'm a Wild Success': Postmodern Dickens / Victorian Cuarón." *Dickens Quarterly* 25 (Sept. 2008). 172–89.

Rosenberg, Edgar. "Putting an End to *Great Expectations.*" *Great Expectations* by Charles Dickens. Norton Critical Edition. New York: Norton, 1999. 491–527.

Sammons, Jeffrey. "The *Bildungsroman* for Nonspecialists." *Reflection and Action: Essays on the Bildungsroman.* Ed. James Hardin. Columbia: University of South Carolina Press, 1991. 26–45.

Smith, Grahame. *Dickens and the Dream of Cinema.* Manchester: Manchester University Press, 2003.

Taylor, Charles. Rev. of *Great Expectations*, dir. Alfonso Cuarón. *Salon* 30 Jan. 1998. 6 Jan. 2009. <http://www.salon.com/ent/movies/1998/01/cov_30great.html>.

6

A Fuller Statement of the Case: Mary Reilly *and* The Strange Case of Dr. Jekyll and Mr. Hyde

LAURIE F. LEACH

In the opening passage of Valerie Martin's novel *Mary Reilly* (1990), a retelling of Robert Louis Stevenson's short novel *The Strange Case of Dr. Jekyll and Mr. Hyde* (1886), the narrator describes being locked in a cupboard by a drunken, sadistic man who listens to her pleas with a "low, sick laugh" and then dumps a large rat inside with her (5). She was about ten years old at the time, and in the darkness, she was bitten by the rat until she fainted, while the man continued to drink until he passed out. When we encounter this opening passage we don't yet know the identity of the narrator (who turns out to be Mary Reilly, a young woman now employed as a housemaid by Dr. Henry Jekyll), but if we are aware that the book is a version of the Jekyll and Hyde story, we may immediately (and erroneously) assume that the cruel man is Hyde.

In Stevenson's novel, other than the trampling of a child and the murder of Sir Danvers Carew, Hyde's specific transgressions are left to the reader's imagination, but Jekyll describes Hyde as "drinking pleasure with bestial avidity from any degree of torture to another; relentless as a man of stone" (60). Mary describes her father similarly in Martin's novel. He sits quietly trying to invent new ways to torture her, laughs at her terror and pain, and does not relent though she "screamed and begged so that you would have thought a stone would be moved to pity" (7). This passage sets up a paral-

83

lel between Mary's father and Edward Hyde to which Martin frequently returns. Even though Mary's father is not Hyde, through the depiction of this character readers get a sense of what Hyde is like and the kinds of things he might have done, crimes that Henry Jekyll glosses over with a shudder in Stevenson's novel. While the two specific crimes Stevenson includes in his story are only alluded to in Martin's, she instead invents another horrifying crime that forces the reader to reconsider Jekyll's version of events and judge him in a harsher light.

Stevenson ended his novel with a chapter called "Henry Jekyll's Full Statement of the Case," which is a transcription of a document that falls into the hands of Jekyll's lawyer, Gabriel Utterson, upon Jekyll's death, and is meant to counter the condemnation of Jekyll in "Dr. Lanyon's Narrative," which constitutes the penultimate chapter of the novel. In that account Dr. Lanyon reveals that Jekyll can transform himself into Hyde by the means of a drug, and repudiates Jekyll because of the "moral turpitude" of his actions as Hyde (54). In the "Full Statement," Jekyll explains why he was drawn to these experiments, but cannot bring himself to dwell on the particulars of the evil he committed as Hyde. If he admits that he felt "no repugnance" but "a leap of welcome" when he looked upon the evil Hyde, a being so depraved that "none could come near [him] without a visible misgiving of flesh" (58), he also reminds the reader that "the evil side of my nature ... was less robust and less developed than the good" for he had lived "nine-tenths a life of effort, virtue and control" (58). His statement is a confession, but it is also a plea for sympathy which ends with Jekyll's insistence on the distinction between his true self and Hyde: "Will Hyde die upon the scaffold or will he find the courage to release himself at the last moment? God knows; I am careless; this is the true hour of my death and what is to follow concerns another than myself" (70). Jekyll's statement compels the reader's attention because it purports to solve the mystery and reveal what has been withheld. For most of the novel, the reader has merely glimpsed both Hyde and Jekyll through the eyes of Utterson, who mistakenly views Hyde as a separate, evil being who mysteriously controls Jekyll through blackmail. Lanyon holds Jekyll responsible for Hyde's deeds, but Stevenson lets Jekyll, who disowns Hyde and presents himself as a victim, have the last word.

Martin's novel reopens this strange case and manages, through the device of a working-class narrator, to present a sharply different picture of the man with a double life. The maid Mary Reilly replaces Utterson as the focal character. Marta Bryk notes the parallels between the two:

> Mary Reilly shares a number of characteristics with Gabriel Utterson....
> Equally loyal and devoted, she wants to shield her beloved "Master" from
> the bad influence of Hyde and, in doing so, she assumes all the roles that

Utterson also adopts. She becomes a baffled observer, an amateur detective and, occasionally, Jekyll's confidante [207].

Unlike Utterson, however, Mary is a member of Jekyll's household. She records her frequent encounters with him in her diary and later has memorable encounters with Hyde, giving the reader a much more intimate picture of both sides of the man.

It should be emphasized that as Bette Roberts maintains, "*Mary Reilly* goes well beyond a work totally dependent upon another" (39); that is, Martin's novel is a transformation rather than an adaptation of Stevenson's novella. I have called it a retelling of the Jekyll and Hyde story, yet Martin keeps that story in the background, foregrounding instead the story of Mary Reilly's life as a servant, especially her efforts to feel safe and content with her "good place" in Jekyll's household despite the long hours of manual labor, her traumatic past, and her unrequited longing for romantic attention from her master. The story is told exclusively through Mary's journals. A reader familiar with Stevenson's plot will recognize many references that allow us to understand that Martin's plot is unfolding at the same time as his and create the impression that Martin is revealing what was left out in Stevenson's telling. Utterson and Lanyon, friends of Doctor Jekyll and members of the upper class, become minor characters in her version. The servants, who with the exception of Poole were scarcely present in Stevenson's book, become major characters. The nameless housemaid who appears weeping and whimpering out of fear for her master in two sentences of Stevenson's novel becomes the heroine and narrator Mary Reilly. As a trusted servant, Mary has a window on to the upper-class world inhabited by Henry Jekyll, while knowing intimately the world of the servants, which he can afford to ignore. Furthermore she is a refugee from the streets, whose terrors she hopes to have escaped, while her master, in the guise of Hyde, seeks to make them his playground. Martin lays bare the labor and suffering of the servants that makes Jekyll's privileged life possible, and in so doing reveals the kindly Dr. Jekyll to be monstrously selfish.

A full appreciation of the scope of Martin's achievement involves recognizing two modes of transtextuality between her novel and Stevenson's and noting how these two modes work together. *Mary Reilly* is both a *hypertext* and a *metatext* as defined by Gerard Genette in *Palimpsests*. A hypertext is a text that "transforms, modifies, elaborates and extends" its predecessor, the hypotext (Stam 66). In composing *Mary Reilly* as a hypertext to Stevenson's *Strange Case*, Martin borrows Stevenson's characters, plot, and themes and even sometimes imitates his imagery and language. But she also transforms the novel by changing the perspective and making the original plot involving Jekyll and his experiments secondary to a larger narrative about the housemaid Mary's adjustment to life in Jekyll's service as she struggles to cope with a frightening past, her mother's death, the petty tyranny of Mr. Poole, and her confused feelings about her master. The novel is also what Genette calls a *metatext*—a text that offers a critical commentary on its predecessor (5). Bryk, emphasizing this aspect, argues that Martin's decision to make a housemaid the central figure in her tale brings issues of class and gender into focus (206). According to Bryk, "by focusing on power relations, as mediated by class, gender and sexuality, the novel presents a comprehensive view of late Victorian society, implicitly condemning the vision offered by Stevenson as inadequate" (207–08). I would argue as well that Jekyll's exploitative relationship to his servants and his indifference to their welfare, which Martin's novel highlights, has a parallel in Hyde's exploitation of the poor as victims of his crime sprees.

Bryk sees Martin as having an ambivalent relationship to Stevenson (208). She observes, "Rather than mounting a [direct] challenge to the precursor text, [Martin] reproduces it with almost reverential faithfulness" (206). Bryk's comments imply a contradiction between being faithful to the hypotext and "mounting a challenge" to that text, but these modes are not necessarily in conflict. Fidelity to Stevenson's plot is crucial to Martin's strategy of revision. It is precisely because we recognize the carefully constructed parallels that we can appreciate the different emphasis in the two novels and the ways in which Martin's text challenges Stevenson's presentation of Jekyll.

With the exception of condensing the time frame of Jekyll's experiments and one major alteration I will discuss later, Martin indeed remains faithful to Stevenson's plot and characters.[1] When Stevenson's characters appear in her tale, they behave in ways consistent with Stevenson's presentation; the events of his plot take place in the same order in hers, albeit in a shorter time frame; and numerous small details from Stevenson's novel, from the foggy atmosphere to the red baize door, are put to effective use in *Mary Reilly*. For example, both Mary and Utterson are oppressed by the nightmarish appearance of the Soho neighborhood where Hyde has his lodgings. Both comment on the heavy brown fog and the sinister and desperate appearance of the residents who are struggling to survive (Stevenson 23; Martin 125). Mary also observes that traveling in such a fog is dangerous "for one could be trampled as easily as seen, nor did I have a doubt that no carriage would stop, though its passengers were carried over a solid floor of broken bodies" (125). Though Mary knows nothing of the incident, her image recalls Enfield's account of Hyde carelessly trampling a child in Stevenson's novel, and it comes just before the point that Mary will witness the evidence of one of Hyde's crimes in Martin's.

This method of retelling a story from a new perspective and linking the two versions through the repetition of certain details is another way in which Martin imitates yet transforms the source. Stevenson tells his story first in a third-person narrative where Utterson is the central consciousness, then retells a small part of the story from Lanyon's perspective, and then finally goes over the whole plot from Jekyll's perspective in his "Full Statement." Items that appeared mysterious in the Utterson sections of the novel, such as the mirror in the doctor's laboratory, the will that left everything to Hyde, and the "pious work" covered with blasphemies written in Jekyll's own handwriting, are explained in the "Full Statement."

In Martin's retelling, however, the repeated details are not merely explained; they are viewed in an entirely new context. Take the example of the cheval glass. When Poole and Utterson break down the door of Dr. Jekyll's cabinet near the end of Stevenson's novel, they are startled by their own reflections in a large cheval glass, and Utterson wonders what it is doing in the middle of the laboratory. Jekyll later explains that on the first night he transformed himself, he had no mirror in his study and was forced to enter the house in order to view himself as Hyde. Therefore he ordered that the mirror be moved from his bedroom to the laboratory so he could witness future transformations. In Martin's novel, one of Mary's journal entries recounts an argument between two of the servants over how to move the heavy mirror:

> While they discussed the best method, I found myself puzzling on why Master would want a looking glass in his laboratory, but I didn't venture a guess as I knew Mr. Poole would be annoyed to have any of Master's wishes questioned and would tell me to mind my own concerns. They were having such a disagreement, though they spoke to one another most respectfully, [that] it was clear that Mr. Bradshaw thought Mr. Poole an unending, tiresome old crank and Mr. Poole though Bradshaw a brash upstart, and both were worried about the job for fear something would happen to the mirror and which one would get the blame if his method failed [44].

This passage is typical of the emphasis in the novel on the world below-stairs, the struggles among the servants to retain dignity and autonomy while serving in a hierarchal system where they must cater unquestioningly to the whims of their Master, no matter how inconvenient and nonsensical they may seem. When Mary takes Jekyll his breakfast later that morning, he playfully inquires, "Where is our Mr. Poole this morning, Mary, that you are sent on the breakfast mission?" Upon being told that both Poole and Bradshaw are busy moving the cheval glass, Jekyll then remarks that while he wishes them luck in moving the mirror, he will "avoid the scene of the struggle" (49). With that, Jekyll casually dismisses the labor of his servants just as he will later dismiss the consequences of Hyde's behavior to his victims. Ultimately he is the cause of the suffering, but he believes it has nothing to do with him.

Because Martin aligns her story with Stevenson's so carefully, the reader sees *Mary Reilly* as an expansion of Stevenson's fictive world rather than an alternative version. The reader is encouraged to believe that both stories are happening simultaneously and to correlate the events. Thus when Martin does deviate from Stevenson's plot, the discrepancies between the two works serve to undermine the credibility of Dr Jekyll in his "full statement of the case," where he attempts to establish his basic goodness.

In this statement Jekyll presents two reasons for beginning his fatal experiments. The first is his devotion to his scientific research, which tended "toward the mystic and the transcendental," and his desire to prove skeptics like Lanyon wrong (55). In Martin's novel, Jekyll also takes up this stance, depicting himself as wearily but determinedly pressing on with his demanding scientific work, sacrificing health and comfort for the sake of science. The second reason offered by Stevenson's Jekyll is his wish to pursue a long-cherished fantasy of separating the good and bad sides of himself so that the bad side can indulge in disreputable behavior freely rather than surreptitiously. Jekyll hastens to explain that the desires he longed to gratify were not really evil. He was merely tempted by his "impatient gaiety of disposition" to indulge in certain "undignified" pleasures (55, 60), presumably sex and drinking. Because he so valued his dignity and reputation, he felt constrained to hide and limit his escapades. While conceding that his impulses were not pure—if so he would have released an angelic rather than an evil version of himself—Jekyll insists that he sought another persona to indulge in pleasure, not to commit crime. He claims that he was horrified to discover that the Hyde persona was not after such innocent indulgences, but was in fact a sadistic monster.

Yet Martin's novel belies this defense by suggesting that Jekyll is aware of these sadistic impulses before he ever releases the Hyde persona. Fascinated by Mary's scars, Jekyll requests that she write about how she acquired them. After reading her account he wants to know how Mary feels about her father and is intrigued by her statement that he was not a monster but an ordinary man, transformed for the worse by drinking. Says Mary,

> "With my father, when he was drinking, it was as if he couldn't get
> enough of seeing suffering.... He was a different man then—as if the cruel
> man was always inside him and the drinking brought him out."
> "Or let him out," Master said softly [28].

With its emphasis on permission, the substitution of "let him out" for "brought him out" underscores Jekyll's awareness that by consuming alcohol, Mary's father gives himself permission to behave sadistically. Jekyll is musing on the potential consequences of using his drug, but he is not deterred from going forward by the tale of Mary's father's cruelty, nor does he seem concerned with Mary's psychological distress at being asked to recall such horrifying events. In fact, his vicarious enjoyment of Mary's tale prefigures his vicarious enjoyment of Hyde's behavior. Mary's thoughts are troubled for days, and she reflects "that somehow Master's kindness and interest has brought [my father] back to life for me" (41). On the night of Jekyll's first transformation she is awakened by Hyde's footsteps and thinks that they sound like her father's. While Mary is haunted by the fear that "something [is] amiss" and that her father could reappear to torment her (39), Jekyll is jubilant at having discovered a way to sin with impunity, as his conversation with Mary the following morning makes clear.

In a buoyant mood, Jekyll asks Mary a philosophical question: "If I told you there was a way to have a life in which you could act only as *you* please, *when* you please, with no consequences, no regrets, then wouldn't you say yes?" Mary replies that she doesn't believe that "there is any actions without consequences," and Dr. Jekyll seems annoyed with the failure of her imagination (48). Jekyll believes he has found a way to have such a life. There are no consequences to Jekyll for Hyde's actions because Jekyll stands apart and will not be recognized as Hyde. There are no consequences for Hyde because he does not really exist and can quickly vanish into the persona of Henry Jekyll if pursued. Jekyll displays the same attitude in his confession in Stevenson's novel:

> For me in my impenetrable mantle, the safety was complete.... Let me but escape into my laboratory door, give me a second or two to mix and swallow the draught I had always standing ready; and, whatever he had done, Edward Hyde would pass away like the stain of breath upon the mirror; and there in his stead, quietly at home ..., a man who could afford to laugh at suspicion, would be Henry Jekyll [59].

Jekyll eventually faces consequences because the mechanism for transformation fails, but Mary's answer points out that there were always consequences, only they were hitherto borne by Hyde's victims, who do not count in Jekyll's world. In fact, in a suggestive passage later in the novel, Mary describes the residents of a seedy section of London as living in "a place where no rules or manners need ever be applied and so they act exactly as they feel" (Martin 66). If it is Hyde who feels at home there and free to act on his murderous rages, it is Jekyll who assumes that his wealth and respectability will shield him from being called to account by Hyde's victims.

It is by adding a scene focused on Hyde's actions in this world that

Martin deviates from Stevenson's plot in order to emphasize the unacknowl-edged consequences of Jekyll's indulgence of his Hyde persona. The crucial incident that Martin adds to the story involves a bloody murder that took place in the Soho apartment of Edward Hyde no more than three weeks before the murder of Sir Danvers Carew. Martin prepares the reader for this scene by setting it in the context of a sequence of events that does align closely with the events in Stevenson's novel, beginning with Jekyll's decision to rent an apartment for Edward Hyde.

In the statement that closes Stevenson's novel, Jekyll explains that in order to give Hyde a place to indulge his pleasures, "I took and furnished that house in Soho, to which Hyde was tracked by the police; and engaged as a housekeeper a creature whom I knew well to be silent and unscrupu-lous" (59). In Stevenson's novel Jekyll does not bother to explain how he went about making these arrangements, but in Martin's novel he chooses Mary for the errand. Reluctant to enter such a bad neighborhood and annoyed that Jekyll expects her to give up her half-day to deliver his message, Mary reflects that "this is some business he don't want Mr. Poole to know of, which do lead again to the feeling that this is something no respectable gentleman mun engage upon" (63). Unwilling to think poorly of her master, she ignores her misgivings and concludes that he is only renting rooms for someone else, perhaps his new assistant, Edward Hyde.

Mary has not yet met Hyde herself, but one night she hears Hyde in the house and, after he leaves, finds Jekyll's checkbook lying open. Readers of Stevenson's novel will recognize the incident when Hyde is forced by Enfield to pay compensation to the family of the child he injured. Mary, meanwhile, is troubled by Hyde's intrusion in the house but is afraid to con-front him:

> I stepped back, leaning against the wall to hold myself up, feeling my mouth go dry and my knees give way.... In that moment he hurried down the stairs while I sank down on the carpet, my face in my hands. I heard the kitchen door open and then close. Wave after wave of fear flowed over me, and it was strange for I knew he was gone and I had nothing more to fear [97].

Mary's instinctive revulsion and fear are consistent with Stevenson's conception of the effect Hyde has on other people. In Utterson he inspires "disgust, loathing and fear"; to Enfield his appearance is marked by "some-thing displeasing, something downright detestable" (Stevenson 16, 10). But Mary's reaction is also influenced by her own past. As the passage contin-ues Mary begins to confuse her reaction to Hyde with her memories of her father. She crouches and tries not to cry: "I had the thought that came to me so often as a child ... if I kept myself small I hoped he would not notice me" (Martin 98). Mary knows nothing of the "act of cruelty to a child" (Stevenson 47) which has just been committed by Hyde, but she nevertheless intuits that he is a man like her father who delights in others' pain and tends to victimize the weak. In this way Martin uses Mary's suffering to represent the unacknowledged pain of Hyde's victims, who are also Jekyll's, as he willingly indulges Hyde's sadistic impulses.

Proof of Hyde's evil nature soon follows in the incident that Martin adds to Stevenson's plot. It begins with Dr. Jekyll sending Mary to Soho for the second time. Jekyll summons her abruptly and seems very angry: "His mouth was set and he looked at me so cold, I felt he hardly saw me, that I was some object to him, useful like his pen or his cheque, such as only exist to serve his will" (120–21). Indifferent to Mary's feelings, Jekyll tells her to deliver a check and a note to Mrs. Farraday. If we try to place this event into Stevenson's novel, it appears to be one of those incidents where, according to his statement, Jekyll "would make haste to undo the evil done by Hyde," yet not feel responsible because he considered that it was Hyde who was guilty (60). It is telling that, in Martin's version, Jekyll makes haste only indirectly, sending Mary to perform the delivery of the check that can supposedly "undo the evil."

When Mary arrives in Soho, Mrs. Farraday forces her to view a bloody crime scene. Hyde has apparently murdered a young prostitute in his quarters, which are covered in blood.[2] Mary delivers the check and a note requesting that the crime be hushed up. Mrs. Farraday promises to save Jekyll's reputation but demands that Mary return a bloody handkerchief bearing his initials to him with the message that "this is such linen [as even she] cannot clean for him" (134). When Mary returns, traumatized by what she has seen, to deliver the handkerchief to her master, she is amazed to find him relaxed and comfortable by the fire. He flinches when she gives him the handkerchief, but deflects the blame by implying that Mrs. Farraday's anger at him is misplaced. Mary says nothing but thinks, "I could not take this new picture Master made for me and fit it over what I knew" (136).

The same is true for the reader of *The Strange Case of Dr. Jekyll and Mr. Hyde* who now encounters *Mary Reilly*. Unlike most of the events in Martin's novel which match up neatly with those in Stevenson's, the Soho episode does not fit the account in Jekyll's "Full Statement." In Martin's novel the Soho murder is followed by a "quiet week" where Dr Jekyll stops going to his laboratory and socializes more, but this time of self-restraint is very brief. Soon Jekyll, bored with his "dry studies" in the library, makes the decision to become Hyde again. He tells Mary that his true "work is in the laboratory" and he resolves to return to it, even though he is frightened by what he might discover in himself (141). Shortly after this conversation, Hyde beats Carew to death. In the "Full Statement," by contrast, Jekyll explains the murder of Carew as the result of a period of voluntary abstinence prompted by his concern that the Hyde persona was becoming too strong. Jekyll laments that he didn't anticipate how much more evil Hyde would be after being "caged" for two months. When Jekyll finally indulges in the potion again, Hyde commits the brutal and senseless murder, prompting Jekyll in "gratitude and remorse" to renounce Hyde for good (Stevenson 64).

The sequence of events in Martin's novel appears to expose Jekyll's lies in his "Full Statement of the Case." He fails to confess the Soho murder, he falsely implies that the killing of Sir Danvers Carew represented new heights of depravity that finally awoke his conscience, and he claims more self-restraint than he actually showed, abstaining for a far shorter time and indulging again, not for the purpose of seeking an "undignified pleasure" without the possibility of detection but rather daring himself to see how far his dark side will go.

Admittedly, the shorter duration of Jekyll's abstinence may not be of major significance because it is consistent with the general pattern of Martin's novel in that the period of Jekyll's transformations is about half as long. More damning is the discrepancy between Jekyll's account of his behavior in the time period leading up to the Carew murder and Mary's account of that same period in her journals. Jekyll says that he found it difficult to give up "the liberty, the comparative youth, the light step, leaping pulses and secret pleasures of Hyde," and thus in an "hour of moral weakness," to reward himself for long weeks of abstinence, he deliberately became Hyde again (63). This description minimizes Jekyll's guilt by implying Jekyll was after some relatively innocent pleasure and could never have supposed that he would be capable of murder in his Hyde persona. If Hyde had just murdered a prostitute on the other hand, Jekyll could not have been so naïve. Furthermore, we know that Jekyll turned into Hyde at least twice in the days prior to the murder because Mary encounters him twice, which contradicts the claim that Jekyll's efforts to reform by giving up the Hyde persona for so long explain the ferocity of Hyde's unmotivated attack on Carew.

The Soho episode reveals that Jekyll did not stop his experiments because of moral repugnance toward Hyde's crimes—if so, the murder of the prostitute would have caused him to give up the Hyde persona permanently. No, he reforms only when his killing of a wealthy man brings the law upon him. To Mary's shock, he expresses grief and pity not for Carew but for Hyde (186–87). It is true that in both novels Jekyll does give up Hyde from this point, but Martin's changes cause us to reflect that he may be motivated more by the fear of being caught than by true repentance.

As a transformation, then, Martin's novel critiques the worldview held up by Jekyll and by Stevenson's novel, demonstrating that Jekyll is not a good man led tragically astray by overindulgence in pardonable human weaknesses but a dishonest, selfish, and ultimately abusive figure. Though Lanyon does condemn Jekyll, and Utterson seems disturbed by the idea that the doctor is willing to let Hyde go unpunished rather than risk any trouble for himself, Stevenson allows Jekyll the final word. Jekyll denies responsibility for Hyde's actions, but Martin undercuts Jekyll's credibility by adding an additional brutal crime that he apparently neglected to confess, one that did not have significant consequences because his victim was a poor prostitute. In Stevenson's novel, Hyde's victims are undescribed; Jekyll's servants are also mostly nameless and their work is invisible. Through the use of a working-class narrator and development of a plot that focuses on their lives, Martin calls our attention to the exploitation of the servant classes by the wealthy and shows us that even kindly Doctor Jekyll who seems to be especially fond of Mary Reilly is not above treating her as an "object [that] exists to serve his will" (121). Furthermore, Mary's suffering at the hands of her father, a character who is persistently linked to Edward Hyde, helps us to identify with Hyde's victims and recognize their pain even though Jekyll fails to do so. Martin's novel holds Jekyll morally responsible and suggests that Hyde's sprees were possible only because Jekyll lives in a world where the poor do not count and exist only to serve the wealthy.

Notes

1. In Stevenson's novel the time from Jekyll's first transformation to the murder of Sir Danvers Carew takes almost a year, from early winter or late fall until the next October. The book ends with Jekyll's death the following March. In *Mary Reilly* events happen in the same order but more quickly. Jekyll begins his transformations in the late spring while Carew is still murdered in the fall. The time of willingly transforming himself into Hyde is about five months rather than about ten. Martin condenses the time line in order to suit the immediacy of the diary format she uses for this period of the story.

2. Ann Heilmann and Mark Llewellyn suggest that once Jack the Ripper began terrorizing London with his serial attacks on East End prostitutes in 1888, "Stevenson's story seemed to take on even more sinister proportions" (399). They note that in unauthorized stage productions based on Stevenson's novel of the 1890s, Hyde was identified with sexual violence even though Stevenson never depicts such crimes in his novel. Bryk also discusses "Martin's presentation of Hyde as a monster of sexual violence" in the Soho incident and in the encounters between Mary and Hyde (213).

Works Cited

Bryk, Marta. "The Maidservant in the Attic: Rewriting Stevenson's *Strange Case of Dr. Jekyll and Mr. Hyde* in Valerie Martin's *Mary Reilly.*" *Women* 15.2 (2004): 204–216.

Genette, Gérard. *Palimpsests: Literature in the Second Degree.* Trans. Channa Newman and Claude Doubinsky. Lincoln: University of Nebraska Press, 1997.

Heilmann, Ann, and Mark Llewellyn. "What Kitty Knew: George Moore's John Norton,

Multiple Personality and the Psychology of Late Victorian Sex Crime." *Nineteenth-Century Literature* 59.3 (2004): 372–403.

Martin, Valerie. *Mary Reilly*. New York: Doubleday, 1990.

Roberts, Bette B. "The Strange Case of Mary Reilly." *Extrapolation* 34.1 (1993): 39–47.

Stam, Robert. "Beyond Fidelity: The Dialogics of Adaptation." *Film Adaptation*. Ed. James Naremore. New Brunswick, NJ: Rutgers University Press, 2000. 54–76.

Stevenson, Robert Louis. *The Strange Case of Dr. Jekyll and Mr. Hyde*. (1886). *The Strange Case of Dr. Jekyll and Mr. Hyde and Other Tales of Terror*. Ed. Robert Mighall. London: Penguin Classics, 2003. 5–70.

7

Transforming Shakespeare: Neil Gaiman and The Sandman

JULIA ROUND

William is new to comics, but we think he did a fantastic job helping Neil with our play-within-a-play's dialogue. We would ordinarily predict great things ahead for this hot British talent, but, unfortunately, he died over three centuries ago. Too bad; he might have written the definitive Batman story.
—Tom Peyer, Assistant Editor of *The Sandman*

William Shakespeare may be the most canonized name in English literature, providing both literary education and dramatic entertainment for over four hundred years. His plays remain a cornerstone of theater and modern media; film versions of the plays date from the earliest silent movies. Both cinema and theater have often sought to modernize and reinterpret his plays, and this interest has now extended into the alteration and adaptation of all things Shakespearean (as in films such as Gil Junger's *Ten Things I Hate About You* and John Madden's *Shakespeare in Love*). With such renewed interest feeding from popular culture back into literary scholarship, the man and his works live on in both spheres.

Alongside cinematic adaptations, Shakespearean plays have been recreated in comics, such as the Manga Shakespeare series (published by Self-MadeHero). However, perhaps their most interesting appearance within this medium was the incorporation of two plays into Neil Gaiman's award-winning fantasy series *The Sandman*, the flagship title used by American publishers DC Comics to launch its Vertigo imprint. The titular Sandman, Morpheus (also known as Dream of the Endless), is a member of the dysfunctional family of the Endless, deities older than gods who represent the functions of Death, Destiny, Dream, Destruction, Desire, Despair, and Delirium (who used to be Delight). On one level *The Sandman* is a *Bildungsroman* tale (referring to the formative years of Morpheus, whose humanization underlies the series), but on another the comic is simply one about storytelling: like dreaming itself, it is a vehicle for fantasy tales.

"A Midsummer Night's Dream" (*The Sandman* #19) and "The Tempest" (*The Sandman* #75) were two of three issues in the series to feature art by acclaimed fantasy artist Charles Vess.[1] "A Midsummer Night's Dream" follows on from *The Sandman* #13 ("Men of Good Fortune"), in which Shakespeare makes a Faustian bargain with Morpheus "TO GIVE MEN DREAMS, THAT WOULD LIVE ON LONG AFTER I AM DEAD" (Gaiman, "Men" 6.12.3).[2] In exchange for such a gift, Shakespeare agrees to write two plays specifically for Morpheus, *A Midsummer Night's Dream* and *The Tempest*. The former tells the story of four lovers lost in a wood outside Athens, whose misadventures over the course of one night are first complicated and then resolved by fairy interference. The latter is set on an island ruled by the exiled Duke Prospero, whose magical skills and fairy aides ultimately enable him to restore his kingdom and escape his island with his daughter Miranda when his usurpers are shipwrecked on his shores.[3]

Set in the Sussex countryside on 23 June 1593, *The Sandman* #19 tells the story of the first performance of *Dream* by Lord Strange's Men to an audience that includes Morpheus, Auberon, Titania, and the rest of the faerie folk.[4] This allows Gaiman to situate "real" versions of the play's characters and events alongside their actor counterparts. Despite their misgivings, Shakespeare's troupe perform for their strange audience, but during the course of the play Titania steals Shakespeare's son, Hamnet; the mischievous Puck takes over his role from the actor Dick Cowley; and the actors wake the next day with no more than dead leaves (rather than faerie gold) for their troubles.

The Sandman #75, the last issue of the series, returns us to an aged Shakespeare now living in Stratford and writing his final play, the plot of which draws upon literature, events from his life, and daily incidents. The poet Ben Jonson visits him and together the two compose the doggerel "Remember remember the fifth of November." Shakespeare falls asleep over the final pages of *The Tempest* and in so doing delivers the play to Morpheus in The Dreaming (Morpheus's realm), also sharing a glass of wine with him in his parlor to mark the end of his service. Shakespeare wakes with relief, saying he can now lay down what he calls "THE BURDEN OF WORDS" (Gaiman, "Tempest" 183.5), but realizes he must now write the play's epilogue alone, which he does.

Public perception of both the comic book medium and the genre of fantasy means that, like many contemporary cinematic productions, Gaiman's rewriting can be said to return these plays to the realm of popular culture. However, his versions do not simply modernize or update the plays; instead, many of their events and motifs are doubled in the framing story that Gaiman creates, such as Titania's theft of the Indian Boy/Hamnet or the commentary provided on *Pyramus and Thisbe/Dream* by their respective audiences. This not only sustains the plays' traditional interpretations and performance legacies (the subsequent body of work in all its various forms), but also incorporates them into a broad discussion of the nature of literary creation. In this sense *The Sandman* transforms Shakespeare's works into a metafiction that comments both on his life and on the nature of literary creation and storytelling as, for example, in "The Tempest" where the characters of Morpheus and Prospero are aligned with the island as sites of literary creation.

Shakespeare is a popular subject for appropriation and it first seems relevant to situate *The Sandman* with respect to other contemporary adaptations. While Shakespearean plays remain in the theater, and in this context may still attract an elitist label, it must be remembered that this medium was a popular entertainment venue for mass audiences in its day. As such, Shakespeare's adoption by popular culture is equally relevant to the performance legacy of these plays.

Early films offer an idyllic interpretation of *Dream*, for example, by featuring an entirely female fairy cast (the Vitagraph film of 1909, directed by Blackton and Kent) or an abundance of balletic fairies (in the 1935 adaptation by Reinhardt and Dieterle). This type of spectacle is traditionally associated with *Dream*, but it would not have been relevant at the time of the play's creation in the 1590s; Professor Christopher McCullough notes that these images owe more "to the imagination of a Victorian children's illustrator than they do to the Elizabethan mind" (108). Modernized productions of the play that are aimed at popular, contemporary audiences may have more in common with the original performances than do those perceived as "traditional." For example, rather than exploring the issues of patriarchy that were relevant in Elizabeth I's reign, the 2005 BBC series *Shakespeare Retold* follows this path by updating *Dream* to refer to today's divorce crisis (directed by Ed Fraiman, the story is set at a British holiday camp and focuses on saving the marriage of "Polly" and "Theo"). A similar theme is also apparent in *The Sandman*, which hints at an affair between Titania and Morpheus (Bender 79). While updates such as these may seem to separate modern versions from the Shakespearean text, in using the newest entertainment media and adopting contemporary dress and language, they actually bring the work closer to Shakespeare's tone than does the "traditional" Victorian model.

Similarly, Percy Stow's 1908 silent movie of *The Tempest* is easily the most visually imaginative and adventurous of the *Silent Shakespeare* collection, using location footage and elaborate tableaux. However, in locating Prospero's island as a literal rocky outcrop, the film bypasses the metaphorical value of the setting as either a peripheral space (dislocated from reality and geographically isolated from the world at large) or as the mental landscape of Prospero. By contrast, more radical interpretations such as *Forbidden Planet* (McLeod Wilcox 1956) do engage with the play's colonial themes by using a remote territory (the planet Altair-4), whose natives are extinct and upon which Dr. Morbius (Prospero) and his daughter have settled. Other films, such as Derek Jarman's *The Tempest* (1979), privilege the psychological subtext of authorial control by reinterpreting the events of the tale as Prospero's dream and characters such as Caliban as repressed elements of his personality. As noted, *The Sandman* similarly aligns the figures of Morpheus, Prospero, and the island, and metaphors such as these both invoke and comment on the play's content.

Period costume is often used in Shakespearean drama to comment extratextually—from outside the text—on the play in question: for example by indicating its Elizabethan origins. Visual coding thereby takes place both inside and outside the fiction of the play, as costume may indicate character function (for example, in *Dream* by contrasting a dowdy Helena with a glamorous Hermia) but also may allude to the play's cultural origins (since the dress, music, and setting used in versions of *Dream* are often Elizabethan rather than Grecian). Such productions therefore have an implicit frame of Elizabethan heritage, even though this is only referenced obliquely, for example, in Michael Hoffman's *Dream* (1999). This Hollywood version also offers a different set of intertextual relations around actors and their characters. Judith Buchanan has described this relationship as "textual penumbra," the attachment of an actor's reputation or body of work to her latest role; for example Calista Flockhart's famous role as Ally McBeal informs our reception of her role as the lovesick Helena in Hoffman's *Dream* (140). This type of coding can also be seen in films such as *Shakespeare in Love* (where Joseph Fiennes glamorizes the character of Shakespeare into a lover) and also makes up part of the intertextuality of *Dream*'s tradition. Although comics make no use of actors, *The Sandman* also uses the textual penumbra of literary figures such as Ben Jonson and Kit Marlowe to convey certain implications, as will be seen.

Textual penumbra and performance legacy are referenced both explicitly and implicitly in Peter Greenaway's *Prospero's Books* (1991). Greenaway amalgamates the figures of Shakespeare and Prospero by depicting Prospero as a scholar who is composing the action of the play and who initially speaks all the parts himself. John Gielgud brought a textual penumbra to the role that could be said to invoke both figures, as he was a well-established Shakespearean actor. Similarly, this film explicitly references the play's performance legacy. For example its opening credits show a book (presumably *The Tempest*) being passed from hand to hand. Buchanan recognizes this as an acknowledgement of the ongoing process of "textual transmission" that the text had undergone before Greenaway's version (174).

In recreating Prospero as the writer of his own play, Greenaway creates an alignment between Shakespeare the man and the protagonists of his work, a notion utilized by *The Sandman* and also employed in John Madden's *Shakespeare in Love* (1998). This film uses faction to create a frame that attempts to explain the creation of Shakespeare's plays.[5] *Shakespeare in Love* invents a doomed love affair between Shakespeare and Lady Viola de Lesseps, and relocates his writing of *Romeo and Juliet* as a response to this "star-crossed love." The play's scenes and even specific lines are drawn from the lovers' encounters. Words and motifs flow back and forth between the factional frame and the play itself. In this way the film provides motivations for many Shakespearean motifs (such as cross-dressing heroines), and redefines our understanding of Shakespeare by addressing the issue of his source material (as drawn from his life experience rather than from folktales or literature).

As such, the Shakespearean performance legacy has often drawn much of its impetus from current cultural conventions. However, many cinematic versions have nonetheless employed the language of his original texts to recreate the plays anew. In so doing, these interpretations have often commented upon the themes of the plays: such as *Dream*'s reality/illusion dichotomy and device of transformation, or *The Tempest*'s analysis of colonial space or authorial control. These productions have similarly used visual coding to create an implicit frame for the play that is both external to its fiction (referencing the play's origins and tradition) and internal (indicating character function and metaphorical meaning). Some later films have even gone one step further and added a more explicit frame that surrounds the plot with another level of fiction that can be used to explore the play's themes. Such variety testifies to the infinite adaptability of Shakespearean drama.

The Sandman #19 sustains various themes of *Dream*, the most obvious of which is its reality/illusion debate (see Girard for a full discussion).[6] Even the play's characters cannot agree on whether its events are real or fantastic (*Dream* V.i.1–27), and their disagreement draws attention to this dichotomy. Gaiman's frame of a fantastic audience blurs the lines between reality and illusion still further as events and characters are doubled. These include the outdoor setting, the mirroring of actor and role (Will Kemp(e)/Bottom), and specific linguistic quirks and events (see Round). As a consequence, the fiction with which Gaiman surrounds *Dream* begins to collapse into it, and in this way *The Sandman* replicates and comments not only upon many of the themes of the play, but also on its structure. For example, the Shakespearean play-within-a-play motif is employed, as *Dream* itself becomes the play within a play, and the breakdown of order that Gaiman's faerie audience create in his production ("*THAT* IS NOT COWLEY! WHAT'S HAPPENING? WHERE ARE THEY GOING?" [Gaiman, "Dream" 3.22.5]) mirrors the role of Shakespeare's fairies within *Dream*.

Although it appears to transform *Dream*, Gaiman's frame is in fact consistent with the play. While *Dream* is one of the few Shakespearean plays without obvious source material, Shakespeare drew on folklore and myth to create characters such as Titania and the Puck. Critics have concluded that "the names of fairies in *A Midsummer Night's Dream* convey their character and small scale" (Warner 173), and that other plays further reference their small size (for example *Romeo and Juliet*, I.iv.54–64). Yet, as Minor White Latham points out, except for a very few instances, previous to *Dream* "the fairies were never designated as little," and in other literature of the period they are similarly represented as adult-sized (79). By redefining the fey as diminutive, attendant sprites, Shakespeare's *Dream* departed from folk tradition in many ways and its fairies are "not of Shakespeare's time, but of his mind" (Latham 218). Keith Thomas adds, "The fairies of the Middle Ages were neither small nor particularly kindly" (724) and their origins were variously explained as fallen angels, dead souls, or as a third kingdom hidden underground, separate from both heaven and hell (Latham 41). They were shape-shifters (27) and might be aligned directly with ghosts, the devil, or evil beings from classical myth (45–55). They had few striking features (such as wings or similar) and in terms of size were compared to—and often disguised as—adult humans (68). Other legends similarly belie the diminutive and ethereal stereotype by describing the fey as bizarre and ugly (with the caveat that to call them so would result in a curse, hence providing an explanation for their ethereal depiction) (Morrow). Within *The Sandman* series Gaiman in fact supports both views by creating a magical glamour that is customarily worn by his faerie folk to disguise their true forms.

Shakespeare draws upon folk source material to create composite characters such as Puck and Titania; and while Peter Holland notes that "Robin Goodfellow, hobgoblins and pucks all belonged to ... a class of rough, hairy domestic spirits characterized by their mischievousness" (35), both he and Latham confirm that any authority Shakespeare might have had for identifying Robin Goodfellow as a puck, or the Puck, is unknown (Latham 226).

Gaiman accords with Shakespeare's composite, however, using the word "puck" in a generic sense (the character refers to himself as "A PUCK" and also speaks of "WE PUCKS" (Gaiman, *Kindly Ones* 10.2.7), and using phrasing (such as "ho ho ho") drawn from folk songs like "The Ballad of Robin Goodfellow" (Bender 79).[7] Charles Vess depicts the character as animalistic and demonic (red eyes, rough skin, and a grin that shows rather more teeth than is reassuring). In this way the Puck's appearance also accords with folklore—also named "Puck-hairy," he constantly rejects offers of clothes in English folktales and is frequently pictured with a thick pelt of hair (Latham 242–43).

Titania, Auberon, and the Puck, although humanoid, give off an alien air, subtly conveyed by the sidelong perspective and angular lines Vess uses to elongate their profiles (the Puck's head wisps off into nothingness, and the characters' extended ears, Auberon's horns, and Titania's long hair and jeweled headdress further emphasize this). The ethereal air Vess gives to these characters can therefore be viewed as a nod to Shakespeare's reinvention of the British folk fairies for *Dream*.[8] However, the rest of *The Sandman*'s fey are monstrous in both appearance and behavior and as such are visually more reminiscent of British folklore than the Victorian ethereal stereotype, a depiction that is supported by Gaiman's inclusion of Shakespearean quotations that reference this tradition (see Round for further details). Essentially, *The Sandman* #19 returns Shakespeare's fairies to their folkloric roots while remaining within the parameters set by *Dream*'s language.

The interpretation of *The Tempest* offered by *The Sandman* initially appears to transform the play in a similar way. For example, the setting of a peripheral space that is essential to a colonial reading of this play seems subverted by Gaiman's text, which takes as its setting Stratford-upon-Avon— one of the few known elements of the Shakespearean legend. In this sense the comic is located in a domestic space that seems almost antithetical to the play's content. However, by focusing on Shakespeare's day-to-day life, the representation of Stratford we are offered in fact privileges the unknown. Similarly, the introduction of Morpheus's realm (The Dreaming) in many senses provides an example of peripheral space (Gaiman, "Tempest" 176.6). In this way the setting, while initially appearing the most banal of realist scenarios, is shown to be a disputed territory of the type that underlies *The Tempest* and its performance legacy (such as *Forbidden Planet*), as noted.

Other elements of the play have parallels in Shakespeare's life. For example, he witnesses two sailors charging drinkers at the village pub for the sight of a dead Indian (Gaiman, "Tempest" 154–55), and later overhears these sailors singing drunkenly. These events are incorporated into *The*

Tempest as Stephano's song (II.ii.47–55) and a comment in Trinculo's speech: "when they will not give a doit to relieve a lame beggar, they will lay out ten to see a dead Indian" (II.ii.31–34). The locals comment that the dead savage "... SMELLS LIKE A *FISH!* LIKE A *SALTED COD'S HEAD!*" (Gaiman "Tempest" 154.4) and is a "FINE *CODFISH*" (155.4), and in this sense recalls the vocabulary of the same scene, where Trinculo comments of Caliban: "What have we here? a man or a fish? dead or alive? A fish: he smells like a fish..." (II.i.24–26), thereby aligning Caliban with the savage. The comic also situates the play's comments on Caliban and Miranda (I.ii.307–312) alongside Tom Quiney's courting of Shakespeare's daughter, Judith (Gaiman, "Tempest" 165), which it later reveals "WAS NOT A HAPPY MARRIAGE" (184.9). It also uses Caliban's comments on language ("You taught me language; and my profit on't / Is, I know how to curse") (I.ii.365–6) as Shakespeare's response to his wife's criticisms (Gaiman, "Tempest" 166.7). In this way the comic draws parallels that variously define Caliban as the savage, the unwanted suitor, and the maligned.

However, Gaiman's rewritten "Tempest" is achieved in quite a different manner. Whereas in "Dream" the play's events are mirrored by the drama that surrounds their performance, "The Tempest" instead demonstrates the ways in which fiction is life transformed, as we are first shown each "real" event, before an illustration of Shakespeare incorporating it into his play. As he comments: "THERE IS SOME OF ME IN IT ... THINGS I SAW, THINGS I THOUGHT" (181.5). Along similar lines, Shakespeare explains how he is all the characters in the play (175.6–176.2), referencing this type of interpretation from the performance legacy of the play. This also invokes the question of authorial control that underlies *The Tempest*. The play's performance legacy situates Prospero as ostensibly controlling the events on the island (although characters continue to plot against him), an interpretation that is emphasized by both Jarman's and Greenaway's productions. Paralleling the author with the magician also enables this play to be considered as a metafiction on the difficulties of literary creation.[9]

In this way, the framing device used to transform the texts reinforces interpretation of the epilogues of both plays. In the concluding pages of Gaiman's "Dream," the events both within and without the play merge. After showing Theseus' closing speech and the Puck's recital of the fairy blessing from Act V, Gaiman's Auberon (instead of Shakespeare's) then speaks, summoning the fey to leave the mortal plane (Gaiman, "Dream" 3.22.3). The blurring of story-level content in this way blends notions of reality and illusion completely, and the next page, which depicts the "real" Puck giving the epilogue, may as a result be read either as sheer reality or sheer illusion. This seems aptly suited to this type of Shakespearean epilogue where the actor both remains in character (in referring to himself as "an honest Puck" [V.i.421]) and also steps outside it (in acknowledging the play's fiction and asking for applause [V.i.428]) (Round 27). This technique is used similarly in "The Tempest," as Shakespeare awakes from his dream to find his play completed—except the epilogue, which he must write "WITH NO MAGIC BUT MINE OWN WORDS" (183.7). The first lines of the epilogue ("Now my charms are all o'erthrown, / And what strength I have's mine own, / Which is most faint") apply equally to both the fiction of the Shakespearean play and Gaiman's framing story. The final words ("… set me free") also recall Shakespeare's release from his pact with Morpheus.

The frame Gaiman uses also transforms the texts through the use of faction. Shakespeare's son says of his father, "IF I *DIED*, HE'D JUST WRITE A *PLAY* ABOUT IT. / '*HAMNET*'" (Gaiman, "Dream" 3.13.3), making extratextual reference to the existence of Shakespeare's famous tragedy and the historically documented death of his son in 1596. Although the link between the two is predominantly fictional (see Round) some scholars have theorized that *Hamlet* may in fact have autobiographical links with Shakespeare's life, for example with reference to marriage and infidelity. Similar extratextual comments run throughout Gaiman's "Dream," for example his use of the real setting of Wendel's Mound, the date of the performance, and the actors who make up his company.[10] "The Tempest" also makes similar use of the little we know about Shakespeare's life, such as his friendship with Ben Jonson (157.4), his work on church psalms (170.1), or his "shotgun" marriage to a pregnant Anne Hathaway (150.3). As such, even the factional elements of Gaiman's frame are not completely antithetical to our understanding of the Shakespearean canon.

However, prefiguring these stories are the events of *The Sandman* #13 ("Men of Good Fortune"), in which Gaiman rewrites the Shakespearean legend to include a Faustian bargain that practically makes Shakespeare into a Marlowe character. In this sense *The Sandman* can also be read as part of the long history of doubt surrounding Shakespeare's work, which dates from 1728 and includes both factional and fictional works.[11] These theories contain some persuasive arguments such as the educational limitations of the man from Stratford and his family, the dates ascribed to his named publications, his entry in the deaths register as merely a "gent" and the lack of elegies, memorials, or any literary possessions or bequests at this time. The Hoffman theory is one of the most striking of these arguments and credits Shakespeare's work to an exiled (rather than murdered) Kit Marlowe.[12] It has also been suggested that the two wrote in collaboration, with Marlowe providing the literary knowledge and Shakespeare the "common touch" (Rubbo). *Shakespeare in Love* also links the two writers creatively (showing Marlowe giving Shakespeare ideas for his script), and in fact goes one step further by having the character of Shakespeare pretend to be Marlowe at one point (Madden).

Although appearing to support bardolatry in his homage to Shakespeare, Gaiman's frame in fact may be said to subvert it by depicting the Bard as talentless prior to his pact with Morpheus ("Men of Good Fortune" 6.11–12, although this is later belied at "Tempest" 178.6) and providing a source for the two plays most commonly cited as "original" to Shakespeare.[13] In creating their pact, it may be that he is implicitly referencing (and supporting) the Hoffman theory, an observation that is emphasized by Marlowe's presence at the time of their bargain ("Men of Good Fortune" 6.12.1–6) and the alignment of this deal with the themes of his *Doctor Faustus*. However, Gaiman's purpose may be quite different. In naming Morpheus as Shakespeare's co-collaborator and the source for his rewrites of classical stories, perhaps Gaiman is merely offering a more pleasing alternative to the claims made by Hoffman and others and redefining Shakespeare as a divinely inspired genius.

A similar process is apparent in "The Tempest," which instead addresses the relationship between William Shakespeare and Ben Jonson. The two certainly knew each other, as Shakespeare's company produced some of Jonson's plays, and Jonson offered a number of critiques of Shakespeare's work, as reported by William Drummond (in the *Hawthornden Manuscripts*) and reiterated by Gaiman ("Tempest" 157.4). However, and although Jonson extolled Shakespeare as a natural genius, he had also commented of Shakespeare that he "wanted art" (Grady 266–67).[14] If this phrase is read (in the sense of *The Tempest*) as "desiring magic/talent" rather than "lacking education/skill," it may be that this comment inspired Gaiman's selection of Jonson to feature in *The Sandman* #75.

Obvious parallels are drawn between Morpheus and Shakespeare (as fathers whose estrangement from their sons leads, in both cases, to their loss), and this is further informed by their connection as storytellers. By approaching *The Sandman* as metafiction some critics have argued that the storytelling link can also be extended to Gaiman. This seems supported by Gaiman's comments on King Lear, which in 1789 is criticized by the character Hob: "THE IDIOTS HAD GIVEN IT A HAPPY ENDING" ("Men of Good Fortune" 6.18.1). However, Shakespeare was in fact the one to change the ending from his source material: both Holinshed and the Mirror for Magistrates restore Lear/Leir to his throne, with Cordelia as his heir (Castaldo). But Shakespeare's tragedy has now become the accepted version and its sources all but forgotten. A similar process can be observed in *The Sandman*, as the golden-age comic on which it was based has been completely eclipsed by Gaiman's reimagining.

In his introduction to *The Sandman: The Doll's House*, Clive Barker comments that "Mr. Gaiman is the Sandman." As a comic about stories and their telling, *The Sandman*'s alignment of protagonist and author (whether this function is represented by Gaiman or Shakespeare) allows Gaiman to talk about the creative process. These observations are further enhanced by the inclusion of *The Tempest*, whose alignment of Prospero and Shakespeare can be extended to Morpheus in a similar way. In answer to Shakespeare's question "SO WHY *THIS* PLAY?" he answers "because I shall never leave my island" and continues "I am ... in my fashion ... an island ..." ("Tempest" 181–82). Again, this refers to the performance legacy of *The Tempest*, which has defined the setting as Prospero's—or the author's—mental landscape.

In this way *The Tempest* can be read as metafiction about the nature of literary creation—Prospero's "art" can be taken as booklearning, and his magic be read as literary creation. Comics writers such as Alan Moore have noted the power of words and their ability to create, following Alistair Crowley in observing the dual meaning of "spelling" and approaching "grimoire" as another way of spelling grammar (Vylenz). This analysis of fiction is also referenced in Gaiman's *Dream*, as the Puck comments on the play, "IT NEVER *HAPPENED*; YET IT IS *STILL* TRUE. WHAT MAGIC ART IS THIS?" ("Dream" 3.13.9). In this light, Morpheus's statement "I am prince of stories, Will; but I have no story of my own" (Gaiman, "Tempest" 182.7), although patently false (as evidenced by the very existence of *The Sandman*), is fair comment on the author's role, whose legacy is the fictions he creates. This statement seems particularly suited to Shakespeare, of whose life we know so little.

As such, all three texts may be read as metafiction that deals not only with the creative process and the telling of stories, but also with the transforming power of fiction. Imagination makes impossible things into reality in Shakespeare's wood, where "fancy's images" are transformed into "something of great constancy" (*Dream* V.i.25–26). Prospero's "art" brings the events on the island to pass and restores his dukedom. Over the course of *The Sandman* the eternal and timeless Morpheus discovers he has changed and, although "ENDLESS," is even ultimately enabled to die.

In this way, popular culture versions of Shakespeare have used various framing devices to recreate the play anew. This performance legacy has had an effect on visualization, characterization, and interpretation, whether this has been achieved by foregrounding particular themes, providing the play with a strong historical context, or dislocating it completely from reality. *The Sandman*'s reinvention of Shakespeare is based around the plays' original themes, which are sustained by the blend of faction and outright fantasy that Gaiman uses to create his frame. In this way he also gives his versions metafictional status, and uses the text to explore the power of stories. In so doing *The Sandman* reinvents the plays anew, without the limitations of a themed modernization or contemporary updating. The elements Gaiman retains from their historical context are linked to the plays' themes and hence comment upon their origins and explore their content further, rather than being "factionalized" into a simple "explanation," as seen in metafictional films such as *Shakespeare in Love*.

Not only does this testify to Shakespeare's infinite adaptability, it may also be that *The Sandman* informs discussion of the idea of Shakespeare as literature. As the comic emphasizes, in Shakespeare's day his work was considered popular entertainment rather than elitist. That the same plays are now held in a completely different regard testifies that "literature" may best be defined not as an unchanging, eternal quality, but as a value held at a specific historical moment that is subject to constant change (Derrida 25). The adaptations discussed here have in many instances returned Shakespeare's work to its original context—the realm of popular culture—and in so doing have revived and recreated it for a new audience. *The Sandman* not only rewrites the Shakespearean canon in this way, but fictionalizes its historical background in order to comment on this redefinition. As such, it may be that the boundaries between literature and popular culture are more fragile than we might think.

Plot Summaries

A Midsummer Night's Dream is one of Shakespeare's best-loved plays, whose spectacle and comedy revolve around three interlinked plots. In Athens, the Duke Theseus is preparing to wed the Amazon queen Hippolyta and many festivities are being prepared for the wedding, including a play acted by some very unskilled but enthusiastic local tradesmen (the "rude mechanicals"). Meanwhile, patriarchal citizen Egeus is forcing his daughter Hermia to marry Demetrius, despite the fact that she loves another young man, Lysander, and her best friend Helena is in love with Demetrius. Hermia and Lysander elope, but Helena alerts Demetrius, who sets off in hot pursuit of his intended bride. Helena follows, and all four lovers end up lost in the forest outside the city.

They stumble into a dispute between the fairy king Oberon and his queen, Titania, whose refusal to give up a young pageboy to her husband leads him to plot to humiliate her. Oberon employs the Puck to anoint her eyes with the juice of a certain flower while she sleeps, which will result in her falling in love with the first thing she sees upon awakening. He also instructs the Puck to do the same to the Athenian man (Demetrius) he has seen berating Helena. Puck places the love-juice on Titania's eyes and arranges things so that she falls in love with Bottom (one of the mechanicals rehearsing in the forest), whose head he replaces with that of an ass. An adoring Titania takes Bottom to her bower and, while so distracted, is persuaded by Oberon to give him the pageboy he desires. However, the Puck mistakes Lysander for Demetrius and anoints both men's eyes—with the result that soon both are professing their love to Helena.

Despite the comedy of this situation, Oberon tells Puck to restore order to Titania, Bottom, and Lysander, although the charm is to remain on Demetrius who now loves Helena. The four lovers return to Athens the next morning with only hazy recollections of their night in the forest and, as there is no longer a dispute over Hermia's affections, Duke Theseus orders a triple wedding to take place; at which the mechanicals perform the unintentionally humorous play "Pyramus and Thisbe." *Dream* closes with Oberon and Titania's blessing on the house and its occupants and a final soliloquy from the Puck.

The Tempest is commonly believed to be Shakespeare's last sole-authored play. It tells the story of Prospero, rightful duke of Milan, who was exiled twelve years previously by his usurper brother, Antonio, who had plotted against him together with Alonso, the king of Naples. Prospero, who is extremely learned and a magician, has lived on the island with his daughter, Miranda, and two servants/slaves—the spirit Ariel and the deformed "monster" Caliban, son of the now-dead witch Sycorax, the only non-ethereal inhabitant of the island and, in many senses, its rightful owner.

At the start of the play Prospero summons a storm that causes his brother's ship to crash on the island and divides the passengers and crew so that each group believes the other dead. Three strands of plot then run through the play: in the first, Alonso's son, Ferdinand, meets and falls in love with Miranda, and works for Prospero to earn her love. Prospero eventually relents and allows the two lovers to be together, conjuring a fairy masque for their entertainment. Meanwhile, the slave Caliban encounters Trinculo and Stephano, two drunken crew members, and tries to raise a rebellion against Prospero, which ultimately fails. In the third subplot, the Duke Antonio and his brother Sebastian conspire to kill the King Alonso and his adviser Gonzalo, so that Sebastian can become King. Prospero uses Ariel to thwart this plan and manipulates their course across the island in order to bring them to him.

In the conclusion, all the main characters are brought together before Prospero, who forgives Alonso and Antonio and warns the characters against further wrongdoing. Alonso and Ferdinand are reunited, and all the characters plan to return together to Italy. Prospero then denounces his magic, breaks his staff, burns his books, pardons the slave Caliban, and finally gives Ariel the freedom he has promised him for so long. *The Tempest* ends with Prospero addressing the audience from this new position, and asking for their applause to "set him free."

Notes

1. "A Midsummer Night's Dream" was published in September 1990 and was the first and only comic ever to win the Word Fantasy Award for Best Short Story (in 1991, after which the rules were changed to exclude comics from this category).

2. In some trade paperbacks page numbering is retained from individual issues. In these instances I shall cite references as here, where 6.12.3 corresponds to part 6, page 12, panel 3. References given in a two-digit form (for example, 74.5) refers to trade paperbacks where the pages have been renumbered sequentially (page 74, panel 5). When quoting from comics I have used "/" to indicate divisions between speech balloons or narrative boxes and used small capital letters in order to avoid inflicting my own capitalization on the text.

3. Fuller summaries of the plots of these Shakespearean plays are printed at the end of the essay.

4. For the sake of clarity I shall retain the spelling Gaiman uses for his Auberon and other faerie folk (for Gaiman, "faerie" is the abode/adjective only, although the characters themselves are also known as the fey).

5. *Faction* is a blend of "fact" and "fiction" and refers to literature that treats real people or events as if they were fictional, or uses real people or events as essential elements in an otherwise fictional rendition.

6. Some of the following analysis of *Dream* and a fuller discussion of these points can be found in Round, "Subverting Shakespeare?"

7. Also named as "The Mad Merry Pranks of Robin Goodfellow" and popularly credited to Ben Jonson (Paster and Howard 309).

8. Mentions in other Shakespearean plays variously define the fairies as fiends, tempters, or familiars; focus on their powers of bewitchment; and include occurrences of mortal women being mistaken for them (see Latham 177–78 for a complete list).

9. A metafiction is self-referential fiction that deals with the writing of fiction, and thus draws attention to the relationship between fiction and reality.

10. The text is accurate in many respects. For example, Wendel's Mound is a chalk figure located near the village of Wilmington in East Sussex, and "Wilmington" may be derived from "Wendel's Mound Town." The figure is also known as the Long Man of Wilmington or the Wilmington Giant. Similarly, although the exact dates are uncertain, Burbage, Will Kemp(e), Thomas Pope, Henry Condell, and Robert Armin are thought to have worked with Shakespeare (British Library Board). Please see Round for a fuller discussion.

11. These early publications include Captain Goulding's *Essay against Too Much Reading* (1728) and anonymous allegories such as *The Life and Adventures of Common Sense* (1769) or *The Story of the Learned Pig* (1786). Many subsequent texts have theorized that Shakespeare was little more than a pseudonym and have accredited authorship of his plays to Kit Marlowe, Ben Jonson, Francis Bacon, William Stanley, or Edward de Vere. See http://www.shakespeare-oxford.com/histdoubt.htm for a complete list, and see Michael Rubbo's documentary *Much Ado About Something* for a more detailed discussion.

12. Although not the first to suggest it, American theater press agent and writer Calvin Hoffman popularized this idea in his 1955 book, *The Murder of the Man Who Was "Shakespeare,"* now out of print

13. The other two are *Love's Labour's Lost* (which may have been based on events and people contemporary to Shakespeare) and *The Merry Wives of Windsor*. These four texts are

the only Shakespearean plays where the plot does not directly reference an obvious literary or historical source.
14. For example in his poem introducing the First Folio of Shakespeare's plays.

Works Cited

Barker, Clive. Introduction. *The Sandman: The Doll's House.* New York: DC Comics, 1990.
Bender, Hy. *The Sandman Companion.* London: Titan, 1999.
Blackton, Stuart, and Charles Kent, dirs. *A Midsummer Night's Dream.* Vitagraph, 1909.
British Library Board. "Companies of Players." *British Library Resources.* 21 Sept. 2003. <http://www.bl.uk/treasures/shakespeare/companies.html>.
Buchanan, Judith. *Shakespeare on Film.* Harlow, Essex: Pearson, 2005.
Castaldo, Annalisa. "'No More Yielding Than a Dream': The Construction of Shakespeare in *The Sandman.*" *College Literature* 31.4 (2004): 94–110.
Derrida, Jacques. *Acts of Literature.* Ed. Derek Attridge. London: Routledge, 1992.
Forbidden Planet. Dir. Fred McLeod Wilcox. Perf. Walter Pidgeon, Anne Francis, and Leslie Nielsen. MGM, 1956.
Fraiman, Ed, dir. *A Midsummer Night's Dream.* BBC, 2005.
Gaiman, Neil. "Men of Good Fortune." Illus. Michael Zulli. *The Sandman: The Doll's House.* New York: DC Comics, 1990: 6.1–24.
_____. "A Midsummer Night's Dream." Illus. Charles Vess. *The Sandman: Dream Country.* New York: DC Comics, 1991: 3.1–24.
_____. "The Tempest." Illus. Charles Vess. *The Sandman: The Wake.* New York: DC Comics, 1996: 145–84.
Gaiman, Neil, et al. *The Sandman: The Kindly Ones,* 57–69. New York: DC Comics, 1996.
Girard, René. "Myth and Ritual in Shakespeare: *A Midsummer Night's Dream.*" *Textual Strategies: Perspectives in Post-Structuralist Criticism,* Ed. Josué V. Harari. Ithaca: Cornell University Press, 1979: 189–212.
Grady, Hugh. "Shakespeare Criticism, 1600–1900." *The Cambridge Companion to Shakespeare.* Eds. Margreta de Grazia and Stanley Wells. Cambridge: Cambridge University Press, 2001: 265–78.
Greenaway, Peter, dir. *Prospero's Books.* Perf. John Gielgud, Isabelle Pasco, and Kenneth Cranham. Cine Electra, 1991.
Hoffman, Calvin. *The Murder of the Man Who Was Shakespeare.* London: Max Parrish, 1955.
Hoffman, Michael, dir. *A Midsummer Night's Dream.* Perf. Kevin Kline, Michelle Pfeiffer, Stanley Tucci, and Calista Flockhart. Buena Vista & Fox Searchlight, 1999.
Holland, Peter. Introduction. *A Midsummer Night's Dream,* ed. Peter Holland. By William Shakespeare. Oxford World's Classics. Oxford: Oxford University Press, 1994. 1–117.
Jarman, Derek, dir. *The Tempest.* Perf. Heathcote Williams, Toyah Willcox, and David Meyer. Kino, 1979.
Junger, Gil, dir. *Ten Things I Hate About You.* Perf. Heath Ledger and Julia Stiles. Buena Vista, 1999.
Latham, Minor White. *The Elizabethan Fairies: The Fairies of Folklore and the Fairies of Shakespeare.* 1930. New York: Octagon, 1972.
Madden, John, dir. *Shakespeare in Love.* Perf. Joseph Fiennes, Gwyneth Paltrow, and Judi Dench. Miramax, 1998.
McCullough, Christopher. "Inner Stages: Levels of Illusion in *A Midsummer Night's Dream.*" *Longman Critical Essays:* A Midsummer Night's Dream. Ed. Linda Cookson and Bryan Loughrey. Harlow, Essex: Longman, 1991: 107–15.
Morrow, Greg. "Issue 19: *A Midsummer Night's Dream.*" *The Annotated Sandman.* 1993. 21 Sept. 2003. <http://theory.lcs.mit.edu/pub/people/wald/sandman/sandman.19>.
Paster, Gail Kern, and Skiles Howard, eds. *A Midsummer Night's Dream: Texts and Contexts.* London: Macmillan, 1999.

Peyer, Tom. Letters in the Sand. "A Midsummer Night's Dream," *The Sandman* #19. New York: DC Comics, 1990.

Reinhardt, Max, and William Dieterle, dirs. *A Midsummer Night's Dream*. Warner Brothers, 1935.

Round, Julia. "Subverting Shakespeare? *The Sandman #19: A Midsummer Night's Dream*." *Sub-Versions: Cultural Status, Genre and Critique*. Ed. Pauline MacPherson et al. Newcastle: Cambridge Scholars, 2008. 18–33.

Rubbo, Michael, dir. *Much Ado about Something*. Australian Broadcasting, 2001.

Shakespeare, William. *A Midsummer Night's Dream*. Ed. Peter Holland. Oxford World's Classics. Oxford: Oxford University Press, 1994.

_____. *The Tempest*. Arden Shakespeare. Ed. Frank Kermode. London: Methuen, 1954.

Silent Shakespeare. BFI Video, 2004.

Stow, Percy, dir. *The Tempest*. Clarendon, 1908.

Thomas, Keith. *Religion and the Decline of Magic: Studies in Popular Beliefs in Sixteenth and Seventeenth Century England*. 1971. London: Penguin, 1991.

Vylenz, Dez, dir. *The Mindscape of Alan Moore*. Shadowsnake, 2003.

Warner, Marina. *No Go the Bogeyman: Scaring, Lulling, and Making Mock*. London: Vintage, 2000.

8

On the Trail of the Butterfly:
D. H. Hwang and Transformation

DEBORAH L. ROSS

At some time in our lives, we all want to look or to be different: to transform. Transformation is liberating. It's what makes old cartoons so much fun to watch—objects mutating, boundaries dissolving, more like the world of dreams than of daytime reality. But dreams can also be nightmares, as many Disney cartoons remind us: the animated Alice can't wait to escape from Wonderland. Transformation has its dark side. It all depends on whose is the hand of the artist, who has control, and for what purpose.

Consider the butterfly, a perfect emblem of both the positive and negative potential of transformation. The butterfly is the culminating stage of an organism, not only far more beautiful to the observer than the worm it began as, but, probably, happier in itself, enjoying flight, able to choose which leaf to nibble on, where to light to get the best angle on the world. But the transformation to butterfly is a dangerous one. Despite protective coloration, moving up and out from its birth leaf, it is vulnerable to predators, including envious, greedy, scientific humans with their nets and pins and slides. Even if it escapes these, it is already in the final phase of its short life; immortality carries with it, by definition, a reminder of death.

Stories about butterflies, therefore, can't help commenting in some way about transformation. And when writers transform well-known butterfly stories into new stories of their own, they are in a sense capturing the butterfly, making it signify in accordance with their own vision. David Henry Hwang began writing his play *M. Butterfly* in 1986, after hearing about a French diplomat, Bernard Boursicot, who was on trial for espionage and who claimed to have lived in intimacy for twenty years with a Chinese spy, Shi Pei Pu, under the illusion that he was a woman. It occurred to Hwang that Boursicot had "probably thought he had found Madame Butterfly" (86), and he decided to take this occasion to expose Western attitudes towards Asians by making a "deconstructivist" transformation of Puccini's 1904 opera, *Madama Butterfly*.

Hwang achieved this transformation by constructing a new tale out of the French spy scandal, in which a Chinese opera singer, Song Liling, manipulates the diplomat, Rene Gallimard, by playing on the stereotype of the "lotus blossom pining away for a cruel Caucasian man, and dying for her love"—a stereotype that Hwang saw as originating in Puccini's opera (86). At first Song, who attracts Rene by singing an aria from the opera, is spying in hopes to avoid persecution by the Red Guard, who regard artists as enemies of the state. But gradually he warms to the role. Once Rene is arrested and Song's gender is exposed, Song offers to continue the affair, but Rene rejects him: he loved the fantasy they created together, not the reality. In prison, a disillusioned Rene concludes that the only way to have Butterfly is to become Butterfly, and so he acts out the death aria he had once heard Song perform and commits suicide. Thus, through this transformation of both the spy case and the opera, Hwang exposes the absurd unreality, and the potential dangers, of the "sexist and racist clichés" inherent in this common Western male fantasy of the Oriental woman (86).

Hwang undertook this project at first without even knowing the opera, but assuming that he already knew what it would contain. What he did not see is that many of his own insights about these "sexist and racist clichés" were already present in the opera. Furthermore, far from having "started it all," as Hwang assumed, Puccini was himself working from sources—a play by David Belasco (1900), adapted from a story by John Luther Long (1898)—that also show considerable awareness of the evils exposed in Hwang's play. Why then was a deconstruction of this butterfly plot necessary to transform audiences' ideas about race and gender? And does his transformation do the trick? Hwang's audiences sometimes come away from his play with ideas and feelings that contradict its ostensible thesis. Butterflies, it turns out, have quite a talent for eluding capture, for resisting saying what their authors want them to say. Looking at Hwang's play in light of its predecessors— retracing the flight path of the butterfly—may help us to see why.

Let us begin, however, at the end: with Hwang's *M.*—that is, *Monsieur—Butterfly*. For it is not at all necessary, to follow this play, to know any more about the opera than Hwang did when he first conceived it. Most of the plot is explained by the hero, Rene Gallimard, in the third scene, as he summarizes and re-enacts the opera for the audience's benefit. He assumes the role of Puccini's Lieutenant Pinkerton, the "Yankee vagobondo," and has his friend Marc play the American consul, Sharpless. Together, they explain the hero's (or villain's) intention to purchase Butterfly for the equivalent of sixty-six cents, to treat her badly (which is what Oriental girls want, he says), and then to leave her with a few nylons, happy to "know what it's like to have loved a real man" (12). Rene gets the chance to act out this fantasy of himself as the macho Yankee when he meets Song Liling, who soon becomes his Butterfly mistress. But here Hwang draws on the real-life case of Boursicot, for Song is, in fact, a man.

As the play goes on, the two main characters struggle for control of the story. Rene keeps trying to make it go his way: "Alone in this cell, I sit night after night, watching our story play through my head, always searching for a new ending, one which redeems my honor, where she returns at last to my arms. And I imagine you—my ideal audience—who come to understand and even, perhaps just a little, to envy me" (9–10). But Song keeps interrupting, moving center stage and talking to the audience, ignoring Rene's attempts to silence him, reminding everyone of Rene's mistake. Will it end as a comedy, with all of France laughing at Rene's stupidity, as we see them doing in the opening scene? Or will it end in tragedy, like the opera, in which a noble and dignified heroine dies for love? The only way for Rene to achieve this dignity is to switch from Pinkerton to Butterfly. Whether he in fact achieves the heroism he desires is partly up to the audience—on how much they sympathize with him or admire his sacrifice. Much in the play directs the audience not to do so.

M. Butterfly doesn't simply transform the plot of the opera by combining it with features of the Boursicot spy case. As befits a play about butterflies, it seems devoted to transformation on every level. It makes use of transformative theatrical devices to bring out transformations in the two main characters. Here, at climactic moments, characters sit before us putting on or taking off make-up, becoming someone else, reminding the audience that anyone can be anyone—that the judge in Act III, for example, is really just Ambassador Toulon from Act II in a wig. At the beginning of Act II, the stage direction specifies that "Song has completed the bulk of his transformation onstage" during the intermission, from a "she" back to a "he" (60), and in the last scene, Rene transforms on stage into Butterfly. We are thus always at least subliminally aware of how unstable personality is, how little we know of ourselves and others. This "disorientation," if I may be permitted a pun, may be necessary to set the stage for the audience's transformation, or moral and intellectual growth.

To bring about this new awareness, the play explores the dark side of human transformation, through the development of each of the two main characters. Rene, in the process of mutation, becomes trapped and suffocated in a hall of mirrors, whereas Song loses himself in a series of disguises. For both, opportunities for positive transformation, or growth, are available— but both choose to ignore them. As each in his own way falls victim to Western stereotypes, he exposes the unreality and the inhumanity of seeing the world in terms of the dualities of East/West and feminine/masculine.

The limitations of these dualities are mainly seen in Rene's constant failure to be what he thinks of as a real man. It was not himself but his friend Marc who resembled Pinkerton when they were youths together. To achieve the proper sense of masculine dominance, he needs an Asian woman, for "Orientals," he believes, both "fear" and desire to surrender to "foreign devils." (The opposite of this stereotype, the liberated Danish girl, Renee, with whom he has an affair, naturally strikes him as "masculine" [43].) Addressing the men in the audience, Rene asks them to acknowledge that they too would love the chance to be transformed from wimps into heroes, like Aesop's frog who wanted to be a bull—and who inflated himself till he burst.

During the play, Rene is given two opportunities to escape the frog's doom by moving beyond his narrow conception of masculinity. Up until Act II, he has respected Song's "modest" reluctance to be seen without clothes. Having been promoted, however, and gained a Pinkertonish swagger through an "extra-extra-marital affair," he orders Butterfly to strip. But then something comes over him:

> At the time, I only knew that I was seeing Pinkerton stalking towards his Butterfly, ready to reward her love with his lecherous hands. The image sickened me, pulled me to my knees, so I was crawling towards her like a worm. By the time I reached her, Pinkerton ... had vanished from my heart. To be replaced by something new, something unnatural, that flew in the face of all I'd learned in the world—something very close to love [47].

Unfortunately, instead of recognizing at this point that this tender emotion can be manly, Rene rather takes it as the first sign that he was meant to be a woman, the ideal feminine, the butterfly that Song only pretends to be.

Later, after the trial, Rene gets another chance to escape the paradigm when Song finally does strip, revealing his manhood, and then still offers him his love: "Under the robes"—under the gendered roles each was playing—"beneath everything, it was always me. Now open your eyes and admit it—you adore me" (66). But Rene is unwilling to acknowledge the real bond that had formed between them. Of course his reluctance to trust someone who has lied so often is understandable. But trust is now irrelevant to Rene, who no longer cares how Song really feels, as he considers the "real" Song about as interesting as "hamburger." "I've finally learned to tell fantasy from reality," Rene says. "And, knowing the difference, I choose fantasy" (67). Love won't work for Rene unless someone is Butterfly, and if it's not Song, than he must don the robes himself. The only way to transform his delusion into an ideal is through a beautiful death. Thus he deliberately turns away from the opportunity to grow—to recognize the happy fact that other people are in fact Other, clinging instead to an idea of "mysterious other" that, ironically, isn't Other at all, but the same old thing. He chooses, with open eyes, to remain a prisoner of his own closed mind.

Song, the Butterfly of the first two acts, is ostensibly free of these rigid gender definitions, as he flits between them seemingly at will; he expresses contempt for the Western males who are bound by them, and who try to bind others. During the trial in Act III, it is he who speaks what may be taken for the play's thesis: "The West thinks of itself as masculine—big guns, big industry, big money—so the East is feminine—weak, delicate, poor.... Being an Oriental, I could never be completely a man" (61–62). Song boasts of his ability to manipulate this male fantasy to his advantage—but he is not really in control. Song and Rene created Butterfly together, and Song admits to having put a great deal of himself into the character. Even if he is just acting—as he sometimes claims he is (48)—an actor playing too many roles can eventually lose his own identity.

Song appreciated the growing tenderness that Rene had seen as "unnatural" in himself, and hoped it was a sign that he had helped his lover to grow: "In the crush of your adoration, I thought you'd become something more." But "more" to Song, as to Rene, means "like a woman" (67). His criticism of Rene implies his own identification with the feminine, as he seems to forget that he himself is not a woman, and that in fact he rather dislikes women. His remarks about Comrade Chin, briskly competent in her unisex uniform, are particularly hostile: "What passes for a woman in modern China" (39), he says behind her back to the audience. He also insults her to her face, answering his own question to her about why men play women's roles in Chinese opera with the oft-quoted line: "because only a man knows how a woman is supposed to act" (49). Yet Chin has the last laugh, as in the end she is happily married, while Song winds up abandoned and alone. "You're now the nincompoop!" she tells him. "You're the blockhead, the harebrain, the nitwit!" (55).

The climactic scene in which Song forces Rene to look at his naked male body should be the ultimate demonstration of his power, hence his control of the story—yet it fizzles, embarrassingly, like a lost erection, when Rene laughs at him (66). For what is an actor without a costume? Having removed the Armani slacks, and refused to put on Butterfly's kimono, Song is nobody.

Or, rather, since now Rene is free to ignore the reality of Song, he can turn him into Pinkerton, and Rene can become Butterfly—dead, but a star. Yet neither man really wins, as no matter who plays which role, they are still caught up in the conflict of binaries, unable to escape the old "racist and sexist clichés."

An audience would have to very obtuse not to see that they are being asked to examine the stereotypes and see beyond them, particularly to see Rene and his delusions as ridiculous. Yet viewers do sometimes find themselves responding to the play in unauthorized ways. When I teach it, a small but steady subgroup of students sympathize strongly with Rene. His idea, that the perfect woman is submissive and "Oriental"—the very idea we are meant to deride—seems to them beautiful, especially when contrasted with the cheap, lounge-lizard reality of Song in his men's clothes. (Fewer respond in this way to David Cronenberg's film adaptation, in which the naked Song looks both attractive and sincere, his offered love an appealing alternative to suicide.)

This kind of transgressive response may be an unavoidable effect of Hwang's strategy: parodists are somewhat bound by the limitations of the work they are trying to subvert. The story Hwang inherited from Puccini, and Puccini from Belasco, is a tragedy, and tragedy by definition ennobles the sufferer. Thus what would be more readily seen as masochism in our next-door neighbor, in the theater can come to look like a beautiful sacrifice. The masculine power that so easily destroys so much beauty is also, in a way, glamorized: as Hwang has Rene say to his audience, "I suggest that, while we men may all want to kick Pinkerton, very few of us would pass up the opportunity to *be* Pinkerton" (35). Tragedy also carries with it a sense of inevitability, so that one cannot imagine a way for the protagonist's doom to be averted; the unwillingness to compromise is part of the definition of heroism. Simply reversing the plot and putting a man in Butterfly's robes does not necessarily destroy this powerful emotional dynamic.

In fact, casting a Frenchman as Butterfly may be seen as colonizing her even more thoroughly than the opera did. It is difficult to argue against the exploitation of women in a drama centering on the relationship between two men. And as Douglas Kerr, among others, has noted, it is similarly difficult to criticize Western hegemony in a drama centering on a Western male.[1] There is a Chinese "Story of the Butterfly" in which a girl raised as a boy in a society guilty of female infanticide grows up to fall tragically in love with a man. This, and not the Western opera, is the story Shi Pei Pu used to seduce Bernard Boursicot (Wadler 39–40). Of course, Hwang could hardly have included an allusion to this indigenous tale without hopelessly muddying the thematic waters. Yet its absence may remind us that in some ways

Rene's mistake is not so different from the artistic license that justified Hwang's determined lack of attention to both the opera and the espionage case that inspired his work. Both men preferred the purity of their own idea to an ambiguous, messy reality.

When we look at those transformed, subverted sources in the way Hwang purposely avoided doing, we may see why it is so difficult to pin down the butterfly to a single meaning—and also how the tragic plot may undermine a work's potentially transformative observations about social injustice. For both Puccini's opera and the Belasco play on which it was based contain ideas about the evils of Western machismo that are not so different from those found in Hwang's transformation. The audience's sympathy is firmly with the innocent, suffering heroine, who alone is capable of generosity and self-sacrifice, and who therefore suggests the moral superiority of women over men and East over West. Puccini's Pinkerton, especially, is a caricature of an American male from the foreign, critical perspective of Italians (that is, Puccini and his librettists). In the opera, his ship is named the *Abraham Lincoln* (changed from the *Connecticut* in Belasco's play) to emphasize the irony of Butterfly's enslavement by a citizen of the land of liberty, and thus to expose Pinkerton as not only a brute but a hypocrite. In the end, he also is a tragic figure, as Butterfly's death transforms and awakens his conscience, dooming him to live on in grief and self-recrimination: "In one sudden moment I see my heartless faults and I feel I will never have peace from this agony," he sings (49). Surely the audience too should be similarly schooled and transformed by his mistakes.

Yet clearly the opera's stronger emotional effect is in the contrary direction; Hwang had very good reason to blame it for perpetuating the negative stereotypes exposed in his play. For in the hands of Puccini, Butterfly's slow destruction is aestheticized, seducing the audience into a guilty, Pinkerton-like enjoyment of her ruin. Not that this Cio-Cio-San is truly a masochist. She does fear her story will end badly: that she will die if she speaks of her love, and that Pinkerton will pierce her heart with a needle, as one does with butterflies—and he does not deny that he will (27). But she surrenders to him not because she relishes this fate, but because he also promises to set her free, "guiding [her] wings to tender flights of love" (12). "Love," he tells her, "does not bring death, but life and the smiles of heavenly joy" (26). Up until the end of Act I, the mode is much more romantic comedy than tragedy, as the curtain comes down on the consummation of their vows.

Of course, from this point it is all downhill, but Cio-Cio-San keeps trying, in vain, to write her story differently, and to move towards a comic dénouement—much as Hwang's Rene keeps struggling to write his story as tragedy. At the opening of Act II, Pinkerton has been gone for two years, not knowing his Japanese "wife" has given birth to his child, but she is certain he will return as promised "when the robins nest again," despite what everyone else says—and in fact, the act ends with his ship in port, and with Butterfly laughing—though her maid, Suzuki, thinks she weeps (42). She remains so cheerful because she has planned a practical joke: she and the baby will hide so that when Pinkerton returns, he will be upset, and then she will rush out and yell "surprise!" The contrast between this expectation and the reality everyone can see looming pumps up the pathos: Pinkerton returns, but not to see her. He has married an American wife, whom he sends to Butterfly to take the baby away. As the reality dawns on the heroine, she kills herself, in the midst of one of the best loved arias in opera history.

Once again, despite the heroine's efforts—in part, because of them— tragedy engages our emotions against our judgment. Reason would extract from this drama the lesson that we should not waste love on shallow and selfish objects, and that if we destroy those who love us we will spend our lives in an agony of remorse. But feeling may tell us instead that Butterfly's sacrifice is not only noble but quintessentially feminine, and quintessentially Oriental, thus inciting Hwang's retaliation. Furthermore, the sense of inevitability that drives the tragic plot makes it nearly impossible for an audience to imagine a happier outcome. It doesn't do much good to have one's consciousness raised about a problem if there is nothing whatever to be done about it.

If *Madama Butterfly* perpetuates negative gender and racial stereotypes, then, the reason is not simply that Puccini believed in them, but that they don't automatically disappear when exposed as evil and dangerous. In fact, his other works reveal that these specific stereotypes had no particular hold on his imagination. In *Turandot*, for example (as Kerr notes in passing), it is the Chinese princess, not the Western man, who epitomizes heartless brutality, while the selfless devotee of love is male. The point of both these operas seems to be to explore what happens to civilizations and the people raised up in them when they overdevelop one aspect of their humanity and suppress all others. It seems highly possible, therefore, that Puccini, no less than Hwang, could see both Butterfly and Pinkerton as victims of a world that insists on exaggerated dualities, and that the tragedy for him was that neither is allowed to be a complete person. Unfortunately, when this potentially transformative insight is delivered by a tragic plot, the ending may leave us too emotionally drained, and too impressed by the power of destiny, to conceive of alternatives.

Puccini's *Madama Butterfly* derives both its sociopolitical awareness and the tragic plot that undermines it from American playwright David Belasco's turn-of-the-century drama of the same name. Belasco was the first to play up the Americanness of Pinkerton and thus to connect his personal exploitation of the heroine with colonialism. He made the American flag almost a character, seen first outside Butterfly's little Japanese house, and then, in the finale, in the baby's hand, waving as his mother dies. Belasco even made Butterfly's Japanese suitor a Japanese-American, as if to suggest that the home of the brave is also the home of all bad boyfriends. But in this "Tragedy of Japan," as the play is sub-titled—from which Puccini borrowed the heroine's touching surrender of her child to her American rival and her beautiful, decorous death—once again what is criticized is also glorified, making it difficult for the audience to imagine or want Butterfly to lose her beautiful illusion of her beloved, or of the idealized land of the free.

However, the play differs from the opera in several important respects. Puccini, like Hwang, did not make a deep study of his source and was untroubled by his inability to follow most of the English dialogue, preferring to simplify the downward trajectory of the plot and, along with it, Butterfly's character. There is much in the play that he chose to ignore—particularly elements Belasco retained from the original story by John Luther Long that do not harmonize with the opera's grandeur and pathos. Belasco's Pinkerton appears far less than Butterfly and is neither as evil nor as remorseful as in the opera. The only Pinkerton we hear much about in this version is the hero of Butterfly's own imagination, whom the self-effacing heroine bullies everyone around her into accepting as real. In this willful delusion she more closely resembles Hwang's Rene than one would expect from their having never met, suggesting there is something to be said for the accidents of literary heredity. The paradox of her shy persistence, exploited for pathos by Puccini, is here merely, like her broken English, an aspect of her cuteness. Belasco's audience was expected to laugh at her, as all France laughed at Rene—though in her case, with fondness. Today's audiences, as Kerr notes, would more likely find her embarrassing. Either way, she is hardly tragic. Thus the play draws a mixed, perhaps even confused, emotional response.

The humor that complicates the audience's response to Belasco's Butterfly derives from comic elements in the story on which it was based. John Luther Long's "Madame Butterfly" is the first work to bear that title, and it is therefore our butterfly's point of origin, and the end of our journey. Of course Long too had his sources—a piece of gossip his sister had heard while living in Japan with her missionary husband, according to a biographical note appended to the 1903 edition of the story. But like Hwang in his own preface, Long distances himself from any background facts that might distract him or his readers from his own vision, stating coyly that no artist really knows "what process of the mind produces such things" (Introd.).[2]

Long's story deliberately mixes tragic and comic elements, the words themselves arising frequently to direct readers to the appropriate mixed responses. "No comedy could succeed without its element of tragedy," the American consul says to himself, hinting that the author intends to wrap things up with a major triad (XI), though with a darkened atmosphere: the appearance of Pinkerton's ship is "tragically sudden" (XII); Butterfly's smile is "tragically bright" (XIV).[3] In romantic plots it is not only the ending that determines the genre. If, as Aristotle said, tragedy represents man as better than he is, comedy as worse than he is, it follows that in tragedy, the lover is unique, irreplaceable; in comedy, he is generic, something that happens to one in the spring. This is the season "when the robins nest again," a phrase of Pinkerton's that the American consul interprets as an "infernal joke" (XI). Comedy would remind us that, after all, Pinkertons, like robins, are more generic than individual, and that Pinkerton himself had fully expected to be replaced—"had probably not thought of her again—except as the prompt wife of another man" (XI). Only the heroine keeps a serious watch on the robins as harbingers of this pledge's fulfillment, thus placing herself in a tragic position. To her, this silly Pinkerton is a hero, "a god, perhaps" (XI)—definitely better than he is.

The question is, who is right? And who gets to decide? Long's Butterfly, like her successors, would love to be in a comedy, but of a particular kind: the kind where the lovers are reunited. This story is the origin of the practical joke she has planned for her dénouement (XII), transmitted to the opera through Belasco's play. However, Long's Butterfly is much less self-sacrificing than any of her later avatars. From beginning to end she is far more attached to her Japanese identity, giving up her family only with great reluctance when her husband insists (II), and never really believing a Christian god will be as effectual an aid as "Shaka" or "Kwannon" (VII, XV). Nor does she ever prostrate herself before her American replacement, but rather refuses the patronizing kiss of the woman who calls her a "pretty plaything" (XIV).

To the extent that Long's Pinkerton does transform Cho-Cho-San's character—his desire is to make her an "American refinement of a Japanese product" (IV)—the change is at least partly for the better, a form of growth. This may be difficult for an audience with today's post-colonial awareness to grasp, as it partly depends on the assumption, natural to Long and his readers, that even the temporary mistress of an American is better off than the wife of a Japanese man. Although Butterfly may be wrong in her belief that as an American Pinkerton can't divorce her without a lengthy trial and much expense, in Japan as Long presents it, a husband can divorce his wife at will. The Japanese suitor Yamadori—who in this first version is *not* from New York—has been married twice already (VII). Japanese women, we are told, must hide their feelings, and therefore become "accomplished actresses"—like Song Liling, perhaps—from a very young age (VIII). Under Pinkerton's regime, Cho-Cho-San for the first time has a room of her own (IV), her spirits are "unfettered" (IV), she expresses her passion, and even in the end, deserted and despairing, she affirms that falling in love with him was the source of the greatest happiness in her life (X).

This is the moment when, powerless to make her story a romantic comedy, Butterfly opts for tragedy and decides to end her life. However, as she presses the knife into her throat, she thinks about how love has attached her to life and changes her mind. When the American wife comes for the child the next day, instead of a weeping Butterfly willing to give up everything she loves most, she finds an empty house: Butterfly, along with baby and servant, has flown away (XV). The story is, finally, comic—not in the way the heroine had hoped, but in its suggestion that life, even with its suffering, is essentially good, offering possibilities for growth and renewal. Here, the false promise of Puccini's Pinkerton at the end of Act I—"love does not bring death, but life and the smiles of heavenly joy" (16)—is fulfilled.

Because this tragic-comic tale finally comes down on the comic side, it may enable us to see whether a butterfly "unfettered" by the demands of a tragic plot is better at pointing out a path beyond duality than the sadder heroines she inspired. Unfortunately, as we have seen, Long's story does not show the same interest in exposing racial and gender stereotypes that we have seen in its transformations, but is rather unapologetically ethnocentric. His Pinkerton is not a symbol of American boorishness, as we are often reminded that a more typical American man would have come back to Butterfly in the end. His Butterfly, clearly identifiable as the precursor of Belasco's, can be as cute as she likes without any authorial self-consciousness.

Nevertheless, there is something to be learned from a heroine who survives the death of her illusions instead of dying to preserve them. When Hwang's *M. Butterfly* has the desired transformative effect on an audience, it may be owing to comic elements inherited indirectly from Long's story, elements that lay dormant in the opera that was the only official literary source. The ending of the Cronenberg movie certainly plays up the ridiculous, or at least absurd, aspect of Rene's suicide, with the close-up shots of his clownish Butterfly make-up, the blood dripping grotesquely over the lipstick, the twitching, making it difficult to see this as anything like as dignified as the deaths of Belasco's and Puccini's heroines.

But perhaps the most enlightening, partly accidental source of comedy in Hwang's play is the true story of Boursicot and Shi—or at least what we know of the true story from Joyce Wadler's extended journalistic piece, *Liaison*. Boursicot too attempted suicide, like Long's heroine, but then decided he would rather live—with the male lover he had been involved with before, during, and after his affair with Shi—all the time persistently denying his homosexuality. Wadler presents the reader with two narcissistic, self-dramatizing protagonists who never had any relationship with anything as banal as facts (such as whether or not one has a penis); who engaged in silly acts of espionage that no one really minded, were briefly punished for it, and who then just went on living, and lying, more or less happily ever after in Paris. These two have none of the dignity of tragic figures nor the moral weight of role models. But their evasiveness—Shi's American lawyer said "he flows from one form to another—it's like trying to grab a cloud" (292)—may serve as a warning to the artist trying to capture the butterfly and write her dialogue. As D. H. Hwang and all the predecessors who have tried to capture her have found, she does tend to slip away, and may well be up there in her tree, looking down, oblivious of human intentions—or, perhaps, laughing at them.

Notes

1. The question of what position this play finally adopts on the subject of binaries has been much discussed. See Haedecke.
2. An undeclared source for Long's story, mentioned by Kerr, is a popular novel by Pierre Loti, *Madame Chrysanthème*.
3. The roman numerals in the citations refer to chapter numbers, not page numbers.

Works Cited

Aristotle. *Poetics*. New York: Hill & Wang, 1967.
Belasco, David. *Madame Butterfly*. New York: Little, Brown, and Company, 1928.
Cronenberg, David, dir. *M. Butterfly*. Warner Brothers, 1992.
Haedecke, Janet V. "David Henry Hwang's *M. Butterfly*: The Eye on the Wing." *Journal of Dramatic Theory and Criticism* 7.2 (Fall 1992): 27–44. *Literature Resource Center*. Gale. 30 Sept. 2008.
Hwang, David Henry. *M. Butterfly*. Dramatists' Play Service, 1988.
Kerr, Douglas. "David Henry Hwang and the Revenge of *Madame Butterfly*." *Asian Voices in English*. Ed. Mimi Chan and Roy Harris. Hong Kong: Hong Kong University Press, 1991. *Literature Resource Center*. Gale. 13 Nov. 2007.
Long, John Luther. "Madame Butterfly." New York: Grosset and Dunlap, 1903. *American Hypertext Project*. 30 Sep. 2008. <http://xroads.virginia.edu/~HYPER/LONG/contents.html>.
Puccini, Giacomo. *Madama Butterfly*. *Opera Journeys Libretto Series*. 2003. *ebrary ebooks*. 30 Sept. 2008.
Wadler, Joyce. *Liaison*. New York: Bantam, 1993.

9

Wicked and Wonderful Witches: Narrative and Gender Negotiations from The Wizard of Oz to Wicked

ALISSA BURGER

"Follow the Yellow Brick Road...." These words hold a privileged position within American popular consciousness, calling up images of adventure, self-discovery, and a journey, once more, into the fantastical land of Oz. However, as the familiar *Wizard of Oz* story is revisited and transformed, the women traveling this path and where the road itself may lead have become more complicated and compelling.

Since its inception, the 1900 children's book *The Wonderful Wizard of Oz* has gone through countless reinventions, including several more Oz books written by L. Frank Baum himself, additional books contributed by other "Royal Historians of Oz," and numerous adaptations for stage and screen. The 1939 MGM film version of *The Wizard of Oz* starring Judy Garland is undoubtedly the best-known film adaptation of Baum's American fairy tale. Famous for its narrative simplicity and recognizable character types, the film has been read from multiple perspectives, including as a psychoanalytic metaphor for self-discovery and a "Parable of Populism," as made famous by Henry Littlefield. In 1995, Dorothy was pushed to the periphery and a new leading lady took center stage. Elphaba, more commonly known as Oz's Wicked Witch of the West, is the unlikely and intriguing heroine of Gregory Maguire's best-selling novel *Wicked: The Life and Times of the Wicked Witch of the West*. *Wicked* stands out from other transformations of the Oz universe because it positions the familiar story from the perspective of the Wicked Witch, a character who had previously been read, and more or less dismissed, as monstrous and evil. Elphaba is revealed in Maguire's work as a flawed and fascinating woman, adding texture and a sinister undertone to Oz that had previously remained peripheral. Maguire's return to Oz enchanted readers, and with the opening of Stephen Schwartz and Winnie Holzman's Broadway musical *Wicked* in 2003, theater-goers too fell under the spell of Elphaba. Transforming the *Wizard of Oz* tale from text to performance, the Tony Award–winning *Wicked* continues to play to sold-out houses on Broadway and around the world.

There are multiple shifts in narrative form and gender representation in these transformations. Through a playful, intertextual critique of previous versions, these works reimagine and reinscribe female experience and expression, opening up new ways of looking at and thinking about the gendered body and self. The multiple revisionings of Baum's original Oz invite readers, viewers, and listeners to continually question the stories and structures of our culture in search of that which is truly wonderful or wicked. The narrative structure and range of gender representations in these versions of the *Wizard of Oz* narrative are intertwined, and the form of each transformation has a direct connection to its function. Baum's and MGM's versions of *The Wizard of Oz* generally follow a standard, linear structure, enacting a traditional journey or quest narrative, largely through identification with the heroine Dorothy. On the other hand, Maguire's *Wicked* in many ways rejects traditional narrative patterns, most notably in its lack of a resolution, by focusing on the subjective and personal experiences of Elphaba and situating the individual in relation to the larger culture and nation. Finally, the Broadway transformation of *Wicked* is more linear and tightly plotted than Maguire's novel, largely because stage performance requires a clear beginning, middle/intermission, and end, though Schwartz and Holzman nonetheless effectively bring political questions into the dialogue of the musical.

Negotiation of gender roles and representations also varies widely among these transformations, resulting in shifting notions of agency. Polarities of good and evil are central to Baum's and MGM's approach to the representation of female characters. For example, in *The Wizard of Oz* film, Dorothy and Glinda are "good girls," protected and blessed; conversely, the nameless Witches of the East and West are feared, despised, and thoroughly evil. Ozians celebrate the deaths of the Witches, while they revere Dorothy and Glinda. The two versions of *Wicked*, on the other hand, provide a number of flawed, imperfect, and sexual women, disrupting the gendered dichotomy of the earlier versions. While the casting of Judy Garland, a sixteen-year-old girl, in the role of a child problematizes the representation of MGM's Dorothy, the heroine remains firmly in the position of the "good girl," visibly adolescent though narratively desexualized. In contrast, in *Wicked*, sexuality and vice have profound narrative repercussions for its characters: Elphaba's green skin may be a side effect of her mother's drunkenness and debauchery, and Glinda is a materialistic social climber.

Maguire's *Wicked* shifts the narrative focus from Dorothy to Elphaba, following the unexpected heroine from her odd birth through rejection by her parents, discrimination because of her greenness, her struggle to fit in at Shiz University, and her adult life as an activist, instigator, and in the end, the self-proclaimed Wicked Witch of the West. Maguire transforms the familiar story by naming previously unnamed characters, turning previously marginalized figures into dynamic subjects, adding new people and creatures to a familiar story, and complicating the world of Oz through further narrative development and the addition of a sociocultural context overlooked in earlier versions. Focusing simultaneously on physical and behavioral deviations from an imagined feminine ideal, the transformations presented by Maguire and the Broadway stage draw attention to the constructed, normative nature of gender behavior and representations.

Baum's *The Wonderful Wizard of Oz* follows the pattern of a traditional quest story. Dorothy is a little girl who embodies the characteristics of the traditionally male mythic hero: she is independent and assumes an active leadership role. Because of this, Michael Patrick Hearn has argued that Baum's novel is "the earliest truly feminist children's book, because of spunky and tenacious Dorothy" (13). However, Dorothy is an accidental adventurer, which makes Hearn's argument that the tale is feminist difficult to sustain. Her desire to return home reaffirms her traditional gender role and moves the narrative continuously toward its inevitable resolution: Dorothy's return to Kansas. Furthermore, her desire to return home is another plot point that inhibits her status as a prototypical feminist. As Bonnie Friedman argues, "The boy's coming-of-age story is about leaving home to save the world" whereas the girl comes of age by "relinquishing the world beyond home" (9). The female adventurer must find "a way to sacrifice [her] yearning for the big world, the world of experience, and to be happy about it" (9). Joel D. Chaston reports that this single-minded insistence on Dorothy's return to Kansas is far from coincidental. During the writing of the film, *Wizard of Oz* screenwriter Noel Langley was instructed to "remember, at all times 'that Dorothy is only motivated by one object in Oz, that is, how to get back home to her Aunt Em, and *every situation should be related to this main drive*'" (41, emphasis added). Both book and film circumscribe the agency of their protagonist. While subsequent Dorothys refuse being drawn inexorably back into the domestic sphere and reject the limitations of such reincorporation, Dorothy is a remarkably independent heroine for Baum's time. Strong and independent, she is immediately recognizable as good, which is consistent for a traditional narrative like Baum's where good and bad women are clearly demarcated.

Through establishing a dichotomy that aligns good girls with selflessness and bad ones with ambition and desire, the Wicked Witch is automatically categorized as evil, and therefore worthy of destruction. As a result, every detail making up Baum's depiction of the Wicked Witch of the West speaks to her out-of-control thirst for power; for example, when the witch sees Dorothy and her friends making their way to her castle, even though "[t]hey were a long distance off ... the Wicked Witch was angry to find them in her country" (205), and she seeks to have them killed. Here the tyrannical nature of the witch is taken to its extreme: she is not attacking them when they besiege her, or even when they arrive at her doorstep, but rather for simply entering the boundaries of her country. The Wicked Witch can hardly suspect that Dorothy and her friends are coming to make a social call, and if she were to recognize their intent to destroy her, her anger at their approach and her subsequent retaliation would be much more sympathetic. But that is not a character construction allowed by Baum's text, which sketches the Wicked Witch in terms of her oversized ambitions.

MGM's *Wizard of Oz* makes Dorothy even more saccharinely sweet and innocent while further demonizing the Wicked Witch of the West, memorably played by Margaret Hamilton. Just as the single-minded narrative drive deprives Dorothy of agency, this representation of her gendered body and behavior neutralizes her activity, turning her into an even more passive subject. As Friedman argues of Dorothy's adventure, "[t]he drama of the daughter's journey is: who will control her? Will she capitulate to the Wicked Witch or will she make it home?" (24). Though she herself continues to be controlled by the Wizard's commands and her gendered role within her Kansas family, "Dorothy, who loves freedom, liberates as she goes" (Friedman 25). In the film even Dorothy's heroism is accidental. Though her dousing of the Witch in Baum's novel was the result of temper, it was at least an active performance of agency on Dorothy's part. However, in *The Wizard of Oz* film, Dorothy's melting of the Witch is altogether accidental: the Witch gets wet as Dorothy—ever the "good girl"—is putting out the Scarecrow, whom the Witch has set on fire. Not only is Dorothy's killing of the Witch validated by the Wicked Witch's treachery, as it was in Baum's version, but Dorothy is exonerated because she was acting to save the life of the Scarecrow.

The Wicked Witch of the West, on the other hand, is monstrous, and as Friedman points out, she is dangerous because she "is a woman who *wants*.... This depiction of an autonomous woman is of course a nightmare vision of feminine power, a grotesque of female appetite—as if to say that to be a woman who wants is to be a woman who can *only* want" (23–24, emphasis added). The Wicked Witch is defined by her desire alone, which makes her uncontrollable; she is the personification of excessive female power, terrifying and horrific. However, with the MGM transformation, viewers begin to get the first indications of the Wicked Witch of the West as a potentially sympathetic character. As Salman Rushdie has noted in his BFI Film Classics guide to the film:

> [T]he Wicked Witch is in a rage because of the death of her sister, demonstrating, one might say, a commendable sense of solidarity.... [J]ust as feminism has sought to rehabilitate pejorative old words such as hag, crone, witch, so the Wicked Witch of the West could be said to represent the more positive of the two images of powerful womanhood [the Wicked Witch and Glinda] on offer here [43].

While Rushdie admits that the Wicked Witch "may terrify us as children" (43), viewers begin to understand her rage because they get a glimpse of what motivates her to threaten Dorothy and her friends: she wants the ruby slippers, but perhaps even more she wants retribution for the death of her sister.

Dorothy and the Wicked Witch of the West are again depicted as polar opposites: while the Wicked Witch wants revenge, power, and the shoes, Dorothy wants nothing other than to be kind to others and to go home. She is free of the ambition and desire that characterize the Wicked Witch. Her passivity is confirmed when she wakes up to find her adventure has been only a dream, once again providing clean narrative resolution and setting all back as it should be. It is marginally acceptable, then, for "good girls" to unconsciously *dream* of adventure from the safety of their own homes and beds, as indicated by Dorothy's singing "Over the Rainbow" at the beginning of the film, but not to actually go on those adventures themselves, or—heaven forbid!—to even want to.

Though the independence of the Dorothy characters in Baum and MGM is remarkable for their time, both fall short in the context of contemporary feminism, in which a woman is not solely defined by her position within domestic structures of home and family. In contrast to its predecessors, Gregory Maguire's novel *Wicked: The Life and Times of the Wicked Witch of the West* creates a complicated heroine who lives outside the domestic sphere, creating a wider range of possibilities for his heroines than those offered by earlier versions of the *Wizard of Oz* tale. One key way he achieves this is by reframing his representation of Oz through the perspective of the Wicked Witch of the West, Elphaba. While in Baum's *The Wonderful Wizard of Oz* and MGM's *Wizard of Oz* the fantastical Oz was filtered predominantly through Dorothy's perspective and aims, Maguire's *Wicked* assumes a more national focus, framing Elphaba's life within the context of the political realities (racial and regional inequalities and the fight for sentient Animal rights),[1] and warring religious and pagan traditions of greater Oz, further complicating Elphaba's relation to and identity within the larger world around her. By reframing the narrative focus in his transformation, Maguire draws attention to perspectives and stories which have been omitted or occluded in the earlier versions, making a familiar story once again new and thought-provoking. Making the Wicked Witch of the West the protagonist of the novel calls attention to her marginalization in earlier versions and makes us wonder why this magical character was so vilified. Elphaba's story also asks readers to interrogate the gender framework employed by Baum's book and MGM's classic film. In addition, Maguire has drawn attention not only to the untold story of the Wicked Witch but also to the greater cultural and social realities of Oz.

Rather than perpetuating the good/evil dichotomy of female characters that distinguished the earlier versions of Baum and MGM, Maguire populates his novel with fragmented and flawed female characters, including Elphaba, Galinda/Glinda, and, tangentially, Dorothy. Elphaba attends to the needs of others, including aiding her sister Nessarose and fighting for the rights of sentient Animals. Elphaba's main motivation in heading to Kiamo Ko in the West of Oz is to seek forgiveness from her lover Fiyero's widow for Elphaba's role in his death; however, this forgiveness is continually deferred and denied altogether when the widow Sarima is kidnapped and presumed dead. In addition to the complexities of her private identity, Elphaba finds herself publicly labeled dangerous and wicked because of her refusal to remain complacent in the face of the Wizard's tyrannical rule; in challenging the Wizard, Elphaba ensures her own isolation and vilification.

In earlier versions, the Munchkins designated each witch as "good" or "wicked"; however, in *Wicked*, rather than being truly evil or even magically gifted, Elphaba simply names herself a "witch" in response to her position on the fringes of community, and for the freedom of movement and power the title affords her. As Elphaba tells her old classmates Boq and Milla, "I call myself a Witch now: the Wicked Witch of the West, if you want the full glory of it. As long as people are going to call you a lunatic anyway, why not get the benefit of it? It liberates you from convention" (Maguire 357). Elphaba understands the role of a constructed, public identity and its effect on individual acceptance and sociocultural power. Glinda, on the other hand, temporarily loses control of her own public image as she publicly performs altruistic acts while dressed at the height of fashion. She is rewarded for not challenging the Wizard's power, while Elphaba is punished for resisting. Maguire also complicates Glinda's character by making her a social climber as well as a do-gooder.

When Elphaba returns after her sister Nessarose has been killed, Glinda and Elphaba are reunited. It soon becomes clear that, while Glinda has a firm grasp of the significance of outside appearances, she is not as deft at manipulating her public identity as Elphaba is, for better or worse. Glinda approaches in a gown even more extravagant than those of their shared college days and Elphaba chides her old friend, telling Glinda, "[Y]ou look ridiculous in that getup. I thought you'd have developed some sense by now" (436). However, Glinda sees her appearance as playing a particular role in the social and political construction of her public identity, informing Elphaba that "[w]hen in the provinces ... you have to show them a little style" (436). Glinda has a point: her over-the-top resplendent appearance gains her popularity among the local people, affording her a certain measure of power and influence. Glinda's self-reflexive construction of her own identity does not extend to the social issues that preoccupy Elphaba; while Glinda makes "public charity" (437) a staple of her daily life, she remains unconcerned with the rights of sentient Animals and other structural abuses, such as the tyranny of the Wizard.

In contrast to the omnipresent and increasingly nuanced position of Glinda within these multiple adaptations of the Wizard of Oz narrative, Dorothy becomes a marginal character in Maguire's *Wicked*. She appears briefly in the prologue as an antagonist to the Wicked Witch to provide an entry point into the familiar story, though Maguire's description clearly marks a deviation from the figure of the young heroine depicted by Baum and MGM. The narrator says of Dorothy, "She was not a dainty thing but a good-size farm girl, dressed in blue-and-white checks and a pinafore. In her lap, a vile little dog cowered and whined" (3). The only other time Dorothy appears is at the end of the novel, when she arrives at Kiamo Ko and accidentally destroys Elphaba. Significantly, Dorothy's goodness is complicated as Maguire emphasizes the similarities between Dorothy and Elphaba rather than setting them against each other. As in the versions of Baum and MGM, in the novel Dorothy's arrival kills Elphaba's sister, as Nessarose is flattened by the Kansas girl's falling house. However, unlike the earlier versions, Dorothy feels remorse over this accidental killing. Arriving at Kiamo Ko, Dorothy pleads of the Witch,

> "Would you ever forgive me for that accident, for the death of your sister; would you ever forgive me, for I could never forgive myself!"
> The Witch shrieked in panic, in disbelief. That even now the world

should twist so, offending her once again. Elphaba, who had endured
Sarima's refusal to forgive, now begged by a gibbering child for the same
mercy always denied her? How could you give such a thing out of your
own hollowness? [402].

In Dorothy's search for forgiveness, Elphaba sees her own transgressions
reflected, namely her infidelity with Fiyero and the refusal of his widow,
Sarima, to hear Elphaba's confession and to absolve her. Although their
meeting is a site of violent conflict and terror in both the Baum and MGM
versions, in *Wicked*, Elphaba and Dorothy see their similarities rather than
their differences, with Dorothy repenting from her wickedness and Elphaba
mourning her own lost goodness.

Through these comparisons, Maguire is able to develop his characters
outside of their status as good or evil women. By complicating the female
characters as neither "wonderful" nor "wicked," Maguire prompts a critique
of the constructed nature of female identity. This reframing also allows
Maguire to leave the end of his novel largely unresolved; though the witch
is "melted," it is intimated that in some ways, Elphaba indeed lives on, echoed
by the storytelling trope that recurs throughout *Wicked* and serves as its closing lines:

> "And there the wicked old Witch stayed for a good long time."
> "And did she ever come out?"
> "Not yet" [406].

After all, as Maguire points out in the liner notes to the original cast
recording, "the Witch returns ... she always returns ..." (*Wicked* 5), emphasizing the pervasiveness of personal identity, power, and legend.

A key narrative revision of the Broadway musical version is a return to
Maguire's unresolved ending, though the theatrical production achieves this
irresolution in a dramatically different way. The musical resolves the romance
plot but leaves the characters up in the air, so to speak, thus deferring resolution. Where Maguire reinforces the idea of the timelessness of legend and
the individual, director Schwartz and his team opt instead to reveal Elphaba's
"melting" as an elaborate hoax, including an escape hatch in the floor which
allows Elphaba to slip away and be reunited with her lover Fiyero. This plot
revision, including Elphaba's survival, moves the debate beyond "good" and
"evil" or "wonderful" and "wicked." This version emphasizes the discrepancy
between representation and reality by calling such stock knowledge of the
Wicked Witch as "pure water will melt her" into serious question (Cote 165)
and revealing the ways in which these appearances are constructed and used.

In many ways, the Broadway production of *Wicked*, though compressed,
includes many of the narrative elements of Maguire's text, such as the key

issues of Animal rights and the constructed nature of identity. It retains elements of earlier versions as well, such as the musical structure of MGM's classic film. The live performance of *Wicked* allows for a more dramatic and visual embodiment of the differing femininities adopted by these two witches. For example, while Glinda's extravagant couture is repeatedly described in detail by Maguire, the good witch enters Broadway's *Wicked*, "resplendent and beautiful in her gown and tiara, [as she] descends from the sky on a mechanical device that spews soap bubbles" with the equally bubbly question "It's good to see me, isn't it?" (Cote 140). This entrance, coupled with Glinda's overwhelming visual presence, immediately positions Glinda as an effervescent, flighty beauty in the very opening scene of the production; as such, a significance that takes Maguire whole pages to establish is summed up in a matter of moments. The benefits of embodiment carry over into the understanding of character trajectory and development as well: Glinda holds herself and her body in dramatically different ways when she is descending gloriously upon the adoring Munchkins compared to when she is confronting Madame Morrible in the musical's final act. As such, the physical presence of her body on stage signals a change in personality and temperament with an immediacy that is difficult, if not impossible, to achieve outside of live performance.

Finally, central to issues of gender representation in the musical *Wicked* is the primary theme of Elphaba and Glinda's friendship, a female relationship missing altogether from earlier versions. Beginning as combative college roommates with nothing in common, Elphaba and Glinda discover the goodness and strength within each other. The foregrounding of the friendship between these two women takes precedence over their social differences and the more traditional romantic plot of each woman's love for Fiyero. While the Wizard acts to polarize these two friends by branding Elphaba as a dangerous fugitive while lifting "Glinda the Good" to celebrated visibility as a philanthropic socialite, nothing short of Elphaba's "death" can come between these women, each of whom is strong in her own unique way, largely because of what they have learned from each other. This depiction of women's strength in friendship further challenges the dichotomous positioning of female subjects by privileging the support they provide for one another over romantic competition, in addition to dismantling the good/bad dichotomy of Baum and MGM by showing the women as friends rather than enemies. Glinda's self-confidence and her performative, playful approach to public identity inform Elphaba's most powerful performance of her own agency in claiming the "Wicked Witch" title for herself. In the fluidity and fragmentation of these female identities, both versions of *Wicked* complicate traditional narrative patterns, disrupt the wonderful/wicked dichotomy, and create in-between spaces for these women to speak (or sing) from sites of negotiation and fluidity.

As these transformations demonstrate, repeated returns to this tale continue to create new spaces for imagining text and narrative, as well as innovative ways of addressing gendered bodies and expressions. At the time of this writing, the *Wizard of Oz* tale continues to flourish, and new and exciting transformations abound, from Gregory Maguire's additional books in his Oz story cycle, *Son of a Witch* (2005) and *A Lion Among Men* (2008), to the SciFi Channel's Emmy–nominated miniseries *Tin Man* (2007), a science fiction-fantasy reimagining of Oz that centers on Baum's iconic characters. More than one hundred years after the initial publication of Baum's generative children's book, audiences can look forward to new dramatic negotiations of narrative form and gender representation as this tale continues to be reinvented for new generations of audience members, viewers, and readers.

Note

1. Maguire distinguishes between sentient and non-sentient creatures through designation of upper and lower case: Animal versus animal. Sentient Animals are capable of intelligence, emotion, and higher-order thought; for example, Dr. Dillamond, a Goat central to Elphaba's tale in *Wicked*, is a professor of biological sciences at Shiz University.

Works Cited

Baum, Frank L. *The Annotated Wizard of Oz*, Centennial Ed. Ed. and Notes by Michael Patrick Hearn. New York: Norton, 2000.

Chaston, Joel D. "'If I Ever Go Looking for My Heart's Desire': 'Home' in Baum's Oz Books." *L. Frank Baum's World of Oz: A Classic Series at 100*. Children's Lit. Assoc. Centennial Studies 2. Ed. Suzanne Rahn. Lanham, MD: Scarecrow, 2003.

Cote, David. *Wicked: The Grimmerie (A Behind-the-Scenes Look at the Hit Broadway Musical)*. New York: Hyperion, 2005.

Friedman, Bonnie. "Relinquishing Oz: Every Girl's Anti-Adventure Story." *Michigan Quarterly Review* (Winter 1996): 9–28.

Hearn, Michael Patrick, ed. *The Annotated Wizard of Oz*, Centennial ed. New York: Norton, 2000.

Maguire, Gregory. *Wicked: The Life and Times of the Wicked Witch of the West*. New York: Regan, 1995.

Rushdie, Salman. *The Wizard of Oz*. BFI Film Classics. London: BFI, 1992.

Wicked: Original Cast Recording. Music and Lyrics by Stephen Schwartz. Book by Winnie Holzman. Perf. Idina Menzel, Kristin Chenoweth, Joel Gray. Decca Broadway, 2003.

The Wizard of Oz. Dir. Victor Fleming. Perf. Judy Garland, Margaret Hamilton, Frank Morgan, Ray Bolger, Bert Lahr, Jack Haley. MGM, 1939.

10

"Wonderland's become quite strange": From Lewis Carroll's Alice *to* American McGee's Alice

CATHLENA MARTIN

Digital media, especially video games, recall established children's classics that have captured our cultural imagination as source material for their narratives. Specifically, the golden age of children's literature, approximately 1865 to 1911, provides some of the best-known English children's stories: *The Wind in the Willows*, *The Secret Garden*, *The Tale of Peter Rabbit*, *Peter Pan*, and of course *Alice's Adventures in Wonderland*. At the same time on the American continent, writers such as L. Frank Baum, Louisa May Alcott, and Mark Twain were producing strong American fiction either specifically for children or later appropriated for children. Most of these golden era texts have been adapted in numerous forms, most often to film. Douglas Street explains that

> By the close of our century's second decade, while movies were still in their infancy, the neophyte filmgoer had already been treated to at least seven screen versions of Charles Dickens's *Christmas Carol*, four helpings of *Alice in Wonderland* beginning with Cecil Hopworth's 1903 print, three *Robinson Crusoes*, and three *David Copperfields*.... It is somehow fitting that the motion-picture industry in its own youth should turn for inspiration and development to the substantial literature of childhood [xix–xx].

As Hollywood came into its own, the obsession with adaptations did not wither. Golden era children's literature texts are predominant in Hollywood's golden age in films like Norman McLeod's *Alice in Wonderland*

(1933) and MGM's *Wizard of Oz* (1939) (Street xx). These films have remained in popular culture as classics, just as the books have, but some of these stories have retained their timelessness by being transformed into a digital medium.

It is the golden age triumvirate of books—Lewis Carroll's *Alice in Wonderland,* L. Frank Baum's *The Wonderful Wizard of Oz,* and James M. Barrie's *Peter Pan*—that show the most distinctive transformations from the print version into digital media, particularly video games. All these tales have gone through an intermediary stage of film and other forms of adaptation, so that multiple incarnations of each have placed these stories into cultural consciousness. Even those who have never read the original print text from the turn of the century are probably aware of the story's kernel, and know who Alice, Dorothy, and Peter are. As Cathy Lynn Preston notes of fairy tales, they "exist as fragments ... in the nebulous realm that we might most simply identify as cultural knowledge" (210), and these children's classics are beginning to acquire identifiable fragments (white rabbit, Wicked Witch of the West, lost boys) through these many adaptations. Examining the particular ways in which these stories have been translated into the interactive medium of video games offers the opportunity to analyze and revisit classic children's literature characters and tales, to explore new and additional facets of the story, and perhaps to gain a deeper appreciation of the original.

These three classic children's tales were easily adapted as video game narratives because they fit the basic narrative criteria of the games: they rely on a single hero or group of heroes who work with several outside helpers against a villain or group of villains, usually to save someone in need of rescue.[1] These stories also exist within a multitude of revisions, such as the Disney versions of *Alice* and *Peter Pan* and the MGM version of *Oz,* thus making the stories part of cultural knowledge. Widespread awareness of these tales makes them more immediately accessible for video-game players. At the same time the video games revise the stories and characters to present them from different perspectives. Besides, the verbal experience of reading and interpreting becomes a more graphically visual, interactive game—a different way of navigating the narrative. In a video game, certain interpretations of the source text are already fixed by the game's designer, but other decisions throughout the gameplay are left to the player. Thus a video game can create unique new viewable and executable worlds through which the player can examine and reinterpret the traditional tales. Players can potentially link to the characters and story in a more fully realized way because the characters become avatars for the player, and the story and setting provide an examinable space to navigate.

Video games that transform the *Alice* story, such as *America McGee's Alice*, exist not only against the backdrop of Carroll's work, but also against a great many adaptations including Walt Disney's animated film and video game. *Alice's Adventures in Wonderland*, first published in 1865, arguably has the widest reach into our culture of the three Golden Age texts. As popular cultural critic Will Brooker has described at length, Alice has become a prominent figure in popular culture, expanding beyond Dodgson's black-and-white photographs of Alice Liddell and the pages illustrated with John Tenniel's woodcuts. [2] Alice's story has been told many times, and as "character, text, and cultural concept" she has been referenced in locations as diverse as music videos and theme park rides (Brooker 201). A recent revision takes the form of a young adult fiction series *The Looking Glass Wars*, whose author attempts to explain the character dichotomy of a real Alyss of Wonderland who falls into our world and becomes the renamed Alice Liddell. Walt Disney, known for his animated features, creates a blonde cartoon Alice, while Jan Svankmajer's surrealist visions involve using a live Alice combined with stop-motion animated animals. Even iconic director Tim Burton is in production filming a live action and CGI version slated for release in 2010. The many techniques of film and image creation produce distinct versions of *Alice in Wonderland*, largely following their proven directorial patterns and auteur tendencies.

After using Carroll's work as a basis for his *Alice in Cartoonland* series, Walt Disney captured Alice in a full-length animated feature, transforming her into *Walt Disney's Alice in Wonderland* (1951). But the film did not do as well as his previous four animated films and was considered one of Disney's few box office flops. According to film historian Leonard Maltin, *Alice in Wonderland* did poorly because "critics resented Disney's tampering with the Lewis Carroll classic" (*Of Mice and Magic* 73). Apparently the viewing audience comprised many adults who had read the book as a child and brought their own children to the movie. The poor box office results may be one reason why the Disney film has not eclipsed Carroll's as *the* Alice. Yet, it is no surprise that Disney capitalized on the story with the release in 2000 of *Disney's Alice in Wonderland* for the Game Boy Color. [3] This video game brought the 1951 Disney film to life, for it even uses cut scenes from the movie.[4] In this side-scrolling adventure, Alice encounters key characters and helps them find their lost items. She, of course, finds magic mushrooms to alter her size as part of the game play. This game's visuals and storyline show a direct link to the Disney film.

America McGee's Alice (2000) revises the children's tale into a mature, dark and twisted journey that in many ways is closer to Lewis Carroll's original *Alice's Adventures in Wonderland* and *Through the Looking-Glass* than are

Disney's versions. McGee takes Carroll's structure and creates an action-adventure video game with melee and long distance fighting. While a good bit of the game involves combat, there are quite a few puzzles to solve along the way. Alice moves through a series of provinces, finding toys, fighting enemies, solving puzzles, and finally killing bosses. Some have classified *McGee's Alice* as a horror action-adventure game; it was even re-released in a box set titled *Vault of Darkness* in 2004, which included such horror games as *Dracula Resurrection* and *Dungeon Keeper 2*. The game was created on the *Quake III Arena* engine, which no doubt helped it earn a spot on Gamespot's ten "best-looking" games poll of 2001. *America McGee's Alice* provides a reinterpreted version of Alice and the whole of Wonderland that may have some players questioning which aspects are from Carroll and which are from McGee, thus potentially leading to a rereading of Carroll through the darker lens of McGee's *Alice*. This reinterpretation of *Alice* shows the versatility and mutability of the story across time and discourse.

The game follows Alice through a dark Wonderland, using a sleek, goth Cheshire Cat as a helper, in order to ultimately battle the Red Queen.[5] Charles Herold, who reviewed the game for the *New York Times*, claims that *American McGee's Alice* "is not an adaptation of these books but a sequel to them" because it has Alice return to Wonderland from the mental hospital in which she was placed after her parents died in a fire. But the game is more transformation than pure sequel because it pulls from the essence of Carroll's Alice, as well as popular culture idioms and medium-specific design alternatives, creating a new brand of Alice. This Alice is mature and darker, and she is provided with a purpose and weapons with which to traverse Wonderland in search of the Queen.

The two video games offer very different experiences, both defined in tone by the creator's name in the title. No longer is it Lewis Carroll's *Alice*; instead it is Walt Disney's or American McGee's. Each brand name brings along with it certain qualities. Disney brings the empire's history of successful feature-length films that incorporate the cutting-edge technology of the time to produce family cartoons with striking visuals and catchy songs. McGee's branding brings his quirky stylistic interpretations to the Alice world and his work from first-person shooter games like *Doom*, which helped initiate 3D immersive graphics. Both games pull scenes indiscriminately from *Adventures in Wonderland* and *Through the Looking Glass*. Visually, Disney imitates Tenniel's illustrations, but McGee seems more inspired by Carroll's own drawings in *Alice's Adventures Under Ground*, the original handwritten manuscript book presented to Alice Liddell on which the published typeset Macmillan version with Tenniel's illustrations was based. In general, McGee provides gamers with a more involved and intricate gameplay by openly accepting an older Alice who has changed over the last century and presenting her to a mature gaming audience.

Alice is largely successful as a video game because of Carroll's adherence to a gaming structure. Both *Alice in Wonderland* and *Through the Looking Glass*, as Walter De la Mare points out, "have a structural framework—in the one playing cards, in the other a game of chess" (61). This very specific structural framework coming from Carroll, a mathematician and logician, helps make *Alice in Wonderland* portable to a gaming situation: *Through the Looking Glass* is already based on a rule-bound situation of certain moves in the chess game, and computer programs must have parameters around which the code is built.

American McGee's Alice begins like most video games, with a cinematic opening cut scene that immediately sets up the relationship between Carroll's *Alice* and the game. An overhead long take scans the room showing Carrollian icons (clocks, playing cards, and a chess board) as well as black-and-white photographs of Alice, reminiscent of the photos Carroll himself took of Alice Liddell. The camera pans over a copy of Lewis Carroll's *Alice in Wonderland* lying open on the bed in Alice's lap. The player hears voices, presumably members of the Mad Tea Party, waking up the Dormouse and asking the famous riddle, "Why is a raven like a writing-desk?" At this, a black cat, supposedly Dinah, wakes up and knocks over a gas hurricane lamp which sets the room ablaze. Here, McGee visually declares his transformation of Alice. The camera gives a close-up of a page from the book with the chapter title "Smoke and Fire." This chapter is not in the original Carroll text, but the page has been recreated to match the layout of the original text and is illustrated in the style of Tenniel. A casual viewer may even assume that this is from the original text, but McGee is asserting his own revision of Alice, literally rewriting the print text to set up the game narrative.

As the fire burns, the same characters who were sharing riddles try to wake Alice to save her from the fire. The rest of the exposition is largely shown through black-and-white photographs and voice-overs of Alice's parents telling her to get out of the house and save herself. She survives the fire, but her family dies. Time passes and an older Alice is placed in a mental hospital, with bandages over her bleeding wrists and her spirit broken. In an act of kindness, a nurse places Alice's old stuffed rabbit in her arms, the same rabbit that she was snuggled next to in bed the night of the fire. Alice turns to cuddle the rabbit, who looks up at her. The shock in Alice's face is captured in a still frame, a black-and-white photograph of the moment. But the moment doesn't last; the camera cuts to an animated sequence of the stuffed rabbit falling down the rabbit hole. Also dropping down the hole is a pocket watch whose glass face has been broken, alluding to Carroll's shattering of the reality of time and space. Alice then follows down the hole, landing at the bottom to begin the game.

The game play begins in the Village of the Doomed, in a mine shaft where Alice lands after her fall. The white rabbit greets her, saying, "Please don't dawdle, Alice. We're very late indeed!" and then immediately bounds away. Alice is not alone for long, as the Cheshire Cat approaches her and they converse:

> "You've grown quite mangy, Cat, but your grin's a comfort."
> "And you've picked up a bit of an attitude. Still curious and willing to learn, I hope."
> "Wonderland's become quite strange. How is one to find her way?"

This initial dialogue and the characters' appearance set the tone of the game and place it in relation to Carroll's *Alice*. The player is at once experiencing Alice through the Carroll story of a white rabbit who is late and the transformed version through the dialogue and visual clues. Alice and Cat reference the passage of time, as well as the changes to Wonderland. The player is explicitly told not to expect the same Wonderland that Alice has visited previously, but a Wonderland that is "quite strange." This is a Wonderland that the player hasn't encountered before, one that has ties to the original, albeit strange in its own right.

Being a visual medium, the video game illustrates a strange Wonderland and immediately gives the player clues as to the transformation of Alice not only through her dialogue, but also through her appearance. She is recognizable in a blue dress and white pinafore, but a skull fastens her bow in the back and her front is blood-splattered.[6] She has exchanged Mary Jane shoes for knee-high boots and is usually depicted wielding a weapon. The Cheshire Cat has also been transformed. He still has a grin, but his teeth are rotting and are blood-specked. He is mangy and sports several decorative tattoos and an earring. His thin coat and visible ribs attest to the difficulties in Wonderland under the rule of the Queen of Hearts who harshly dictates life in Wonderland and enslaves its inhabitants. She has discarded the croquet games of Carroll in favor of a more fully realized execution predilection and dictatorship role, and Alice must defeat her in a one-woman coup.

To navigate Wonderland, the player moves Alice through various levels where she meets friends and fights enemies. The actual game space (the worlds in which the levels are played) has a basis in Carroll but is modified. For example, Alice must swim through a pool of tears and traverse Wonderland woods. Beside the pool of tears is a statue of a weeping girl. Throughout the game, McGee visually incorporates referential nods to Carroll. In addition to the Alice statue, he includes a portrait of Charles Dodgson hanging on a wall in the castle of the Pale Realm. McGee never lets the player forget where his inspiration comes from, but he doesn't allow the source text to restrict his creativity. Additionally, McGee could be forcing a comparison to Carroll by reminding the player of how different his version of Wonderland is. In this way, McGee keeps the economically advantageous tie-in to an established children's classic while still creating a game that popularizes him as a designer.

McGee freely picks and chooses what aspects of Carroll's tale to incorporate, for he is designing a video game, not another children's book. To effectively do this, he adds additional toys, creates new bosses and enemies, and places in the game geographical locations that are not found in Carroll's Wonderland. Some of the toys are taken from the toy chest and converted to a darker purpose, for example, demon dice, jack-in-the-box bombs, and jacks. Playing cards can be flung one at a time as projectile weapons or thrown as a whole deck for a stronger attack. Alice can use a croquet mallet for a melee attack at close range, or she can launch croquet balls to attack from long range. One toy, the jabberwock eyestaff, is constructed during the game and has a thematic basis in Carroll but no exact match. Other toy weapons are not part of Carroll's world at all, such as the ice wand and blunderbuss that McGee pulls from a larger gaming arsenal.

With these new toys Alice must fight new foes like Magma Man and the Centipede. The latter leads the Red Queen's army, which consists of various ants and ladybugs. But Alice is helped by newcomers like the Mayor and various downtrodden miners who labor under the Queen's rule. Additionally, bosses and enemies are pulled from the pages of Carroll and modified for the game. To defeat the game, Alice must beat the Queen of Hearts in a final boss battle. Leading up to the final battle, Alice engages in mini skirmishes with Wonderland characters such as the Jabberwock, the Red King, the Duchess, and the Mad Hatter, all altered similarly to Alice and the Cheshire Cat. Other modified Wonderland characters, such as card guards and red chess pieces, join the battle against Alice. Some Wonderland characters, such as the Caterpillar, Gryphon, and white chess pieces, are friendly and provide assistance. Old friends like the Cheshire Cat and the White Rabbit have to help Alice find her way around Wonderland because of the new territories, such as the lava fields in the Land of Fire and Brimstone and the Fortress of Doors. The game continues through this altered Wonderland, pulling allusions and references from Carroll while also adding entirely new material. The balance of childish influences merged with adult fancy turns *Alice* into a video game geared toward adults. It is in this transgressed space where we encounter the most creative transformations.

American McGee's Alice allows for a new audience to experience a transformed taste of Wonderland. It plays with the complexity of the audience question by drawing on a children's text but transforming it into a video game for adults. This is by no means an unusual occurrence. Children's texts have been crossing boundaries from before their classification as such. Historical border crossings include the ongoing debate between audience and purpose: is a book earmarked for a child or an adult audience? Does the book fulfill a didactic or an entertainment purpose for children? These debates can carry over from print text into electronic text. When asked in an interview if he believed the Alice books were really children's books, McGee answered,

> Technically, no. But that's not to say that I would withhold that book ... from the hands of a child.... [T]he Alice books may have been written for and about a child, but at the same time they contained commentary on politics that I doubt any child would comprehend or enjoy. Part of the beauty of the writing is that it can simultaneously serve two very different functions, and do both well [qtd. in Kramer 276].

Unlike the books, however, the video game doesn't seem to have as wide an audience with its ESRB rating. Quite clearly, *American McGee's Alice* wants to capitalize on the adult undertones in Carroll's *Alice*, transforming the print text into a video game for adults, rated M for Mature, which is the rating designated for material the ESRB board deems suitable for youth seventeen years old and older.

The relationship between adult and child, and between actual audience and intended audience, is a common point of discussion for children's literature. Perry Nodelman looks specifically at the case of Alice, pointing out story specifics that allow the adult reader to view the text not only as a children's story but also as it illuminates adult knowledge and experience hidden within the text, such as the preoccupation with death (73).[7] He explains, "[M]any adults now think of *Alice* as a children's book unsuitable for children" because "[i]f Wonderland is the world, then the fact that Alice, a mere child, experiences it in all its unsettling and dangerous uncertainty flies in the face of conventional wisdom about the simplicity, safety, and delight of childhood" (41).

Similarly, Carroll experimented with his own text, but transformed it for a child-only audience. Zohar Shavit describes Carroll's attempt to remove all adult content in *The Nursery "Alice"*:

> Carroll eliminated and deleted all the elements that he had elaborated in *Alice's Adventures in Wonderland* in order to make sure that his text would appeal to adults as well: He completely changed the tone of the text, omitting all its satirical and parodical elements, renouncing his previous attempt to blur the relations between reality and fantasy, thus transform-

ing *The Nursery Alice* into a simple fantasy story, based on the conventional model of the time [91].

The clear-cut distinctions eliminated the nuance and genius behind the *Alice* stories, reducing the text to an uncomplicated, simplistic story. Needless to say, the original books, which exhibit Carroll's playfulness toward reality and fantasy, time and space, size and proportion, provide the jumping-off point for McGee's *Alice*.

Video games, though they do involve learning, as James Paul Gee and Marc Prensky have discussed, are still largely seen as an entertainment medium. Yet this spirit of entertainment melds well with the original intent of Wonderland. Along with other Golden Age books *Alice in Wonderland* helped revolutionize children's literature, transforming mundane material with a pedagogical focus to books meant purely for enjoyment. Transferring Carroll's Alice stories into a well-designed, well-executed video game that is fun to play seems a high tribute to their original creator, whose goal was to amuse and entertain.

Alice has escaped from her bound pages and moved into a larger mythos, also escaping the nursery and complete Disneyfication. Because Alice has extended beyond the original source, and because of her numerous adaptations, she suits a video game adaptation such as *American McGee's Alice* that can take the essence and main characters of the story and easily transform them into a whole new genre.[8] With so many previous adaptations, it is no wonder that Alice stars in her own video games. This sort of transformation has also happened to other Golden Age characters like Peter Pan and Dorothy, but on a smaller scale.[9] No doubt, texts from the Golden Age will continue to be mined for high-quality stories to reinvent and reintroduce to today's children.

Notes

1. Vladimir Propp's term for these helpers is "donors."

2. Carolyn Sigler has explored the influence of Carroll's Alice books on contemporary female writers, examining transformed Alice texts in poetry and prose. She articulates authors' intimate relationship with Alice as evidenced through their own writing.

3. There was one *Alice in Wonderland* game before this one, produced for the Commodore 64.

4. Cut scenes are intended for viewing, not playing, and use conventional scenes from cinema to further plot or expand the narrative.

5. Brooker provides a chapter length walkthrough of the video game *American McGee's Alice* for a more complete reading of exactly what happens in the game (229–63).

6. The white pinafore has two pockets in front, just like Tenniel's illustrations, but on each is a symbol. The cover art on the box depicts the astrological symbol for Neptune and Jupiter on the pockets with Alice wearing an Omega necklace. In the game itself, the symbols are different and have not been deciphered to my satisfaction. The necklace is no longer an Omega but an A.

7. Alison Habens, herself influenced by Carroll enough to write her own transformation of Alice, the novel *Dreamhouse*, states, "In some places, the seamless joints between Carroll's text and my own shows how profound the influence of childhood reading was on adult writing" (147).

8. Electronic Arts announced in February of 2009 that there will be a follow-up to *American McGee's Alice*. The working title is *American McGee's Return of Alice*, and the potential release date is 2011.

9. Laurie Taylor and I explore in depth the transformation of Peter Pan into the video game realm and survey various video game versions using Peter Pan in "Playing in Neverland" (Martin and Taylor).

Works Cited

Alice in Wonderland. (Commodore 64). Prod. Dale Disharoon. Cambridge, MA: Windham Classics, 1985.

Alice in Wonderland. Dir. Clyde Geronimi, Wilfred Jackson, and Hamilton Luske. Walt Disney, 1951.

American McGee's Alice. (PC). Prod. Rogue Entertainment. Redmond, WA: Electronic Arts, 2000.

Beddor, Frank. *The Looking Glass Wars*. New York: Dial, 2006.

Brooker, Will. *Alice's Adventures: Lewis Carroll in Popular Culture*. New York: Continuum, 2004.

Carroll, Lewis. *Alice in Wonderland: Authoritative Texts of Alice's Adventures in Wonderland, Through the Looking-Glass, The Hunting of the Snark*. Ed. Donald Grey. New York: Norton, 1992.

_____. *Alice's Adventures Under Ground: Facsimile of the author's manuscript book with additional material from the facsimile edition of 1886*. New York: McGraw-Hill, 1966.

_____. *The Nursery "Alice": Containing Twenty Coloured Enlargements from Tenniel's Illustrations to "Alice's Adventures in Wonderland" with Test Adapted to Nursery Readers*. London: Macmillian, 1890.

De la Mare, Walter. "Lewis Carroll." *Children and Literature: Views and Reviews*. Ed. Virginia Haviland. Glenview, IL: Scott, Foresman, 1973. 57–63.

Disney's: Alice in Wonderland. (GameBoy Color). Prod. Digital Eclipse. Redmond, WA: Nintendo, 2000.

Electronic Arts. "EA and Spicy Horse Return to Wonderland for All-New Alice Title." *ea.com*. 19 Apr. 2009. <http://investor.ea.com/releasedetail.cfm?ReleaseID=366638>.

Gee, James Paul. *What Video Games Have to Teach Us About Learning and Literacy*. New York: Palgrave, 2003.

Habens, Alison. "*Dreamhouse* Revisited." *Twice-Told Children's Tales: The Influence of Childhood Reading on Writers for Adults*. Ed. Betty Greenway. New York: Routledge, 2005. 147–48.

Herold, Charles. "Game Theory; Down a Rabbit Hole to a Dark Wonderland." *New York Times*. 21 Dec. 2000: G9.

Kramer, Greg. "Interview with American McGee." Prima's *Official Strategy Guide: American McGee's Alice*. Roseville, CA: Prima, 2000. 276–78.

Maltin, Leonard. *The Disney Films*. New York: Crown, 1973.

_____. *Of Mice and Magic: A History of American Animated Cartoons*. New York: McGraw-Hill, 1980.

Martin, Cathlena, and Laurie Taylor. "Playing in Neverland: *Peter Pan* Video Game Revisions." *J.M. Barrie's Peter Pan In and Out of Time: A Children's Classic at 100*. Ed. Donna R. White and C. Anita Tarr. Lanham, MD: Scarecrow, 2006. 173–93.

Nodelman, Perry. *The Hidden Adult: Defining Children's Literature*. Baltimore: Johns Hopkins University Press, 2008.

Prensky, Mark. "Computer Games and Learning: Digital Game-Based Learning." *Hand-*

book of Computer Game Studies. Ed. Joost Raessens and Jeffrey Goldstein. Cambridge: MIT Press, 2005. 97–122.

Preston, Cathy Lynn. "Disrupting the Boundaries of Genre and Gender: Postmodernism and the Fairy Tale." *Fairy Tales and Feminism: New Approaches.* Ed. Donald Haase. Detroit: Wayne State University Press, 2004. 197–212.

Propp, Vladimir. *Morphology of the Folktale.* Austin: University of Texas Press, 1968.

Shavit, Zohar. "The Double Attribution of Texts for Children and How It Affects Writing for Children." *Transcending Boundaries: Writing for a Dual Audience of Children and Adults.* Ed. Sandra L. Beckett. New York: Garland, 1999. 83–97.

Sigler, Carolyn. "'Wonders Wild and New': Lewis Carroll's *Alice* books and Postmodern Women Writers." *Twice-Told Children's Tales: The Influence of Childhood Reading on Writers for Adults.* Ed. Betty Greenway. New York: Routledge, 2005. 133–45.

Street, Douglas, ed. *Children's Novels and the Movies.* New York: Ungar, 1983.

Svankmajer, Jan, dir. *Alice.* Channel Four Films, 1988.

11

Stories to Live By: Re-Framing Storytelling in the Arabian Nights Miniseries

Jennifer Orme

In its long and varied relationship with the *Arabian Nights*, Hollywood has not, on the whole, been overly concerned with fidelity either to the many stories within the ancient collection of tales or to the multi-layered complexity of its structure.[1] Rather, Hollywood has chosen to send audiences on "magic carpet rides of adventure," which are "fun for the whole family!" The 2000 television miniseries *Arabian Nights* marks a change in the cinematic approach to this most slippery and multifarious text. It does, of course, have "mind-blowing adventure and extraordinary special effects set against the backdrop of mysterious Arabia," as the DVD packaging unashamedly proclaims, but this version also tries, and mostly succeeds, in becoming more than a mere action-adventure romance. It is that, but like the textual *Nights* that it transforms, the miniseries is also very much concerned with narrative: how narrators shape their stories and how stories can shape their audiences. Indeed, this version goes so far as to argue that "stories can save us."

The basic plot of the frame tale of the *Nights* is simple. The powerful Sultan Schahriar is informed by his beloved brother Schahzenan that his wife is cheating on him with a house slave.[2] Schahriar is so outraged by this news that he decides that in order to escape the perfidy of women, he will marry a new woman every day and have her killed the next. After some time of this dangerous gynocide, which threatens not only the women of his nation but the royal line of succession and the stability of the nation itself, the famous character Scheherezade enters the picture. She marries the Sultan and is able to suspend her death sentence, and the death sentences of all Muslim women, by telling Schahriar stories that are so engrossing that he spares her life every day so that she can continue her storytelling the next night. This pattern continues for a thousand nights and a night, until Schahriar has learned his lessons about love, justice, and good governance from her stories. He then revokes his death sentence upon Scheherezade, thus reestablishing the political equilibrium of the nation and ending the tale.

Because it is a televised miniseries and it does not have a thousand and one nights to tell the tales, *Arabian Nights* embeds only five stories: "Ali Babba and the Forty Thieves," "BacPac, the Jester," "Aladdin and the Wonderful Lamp," "The Sultan and the Beggar," and "The Tale of the Three Brothers." The program originally aired over two nights in 2000 on the ABC network in the United States and has been released on DVD in a version that runs nearly three hours. Although she recounts only five tales, Scheherezade (Mili Avital) weaves action, adventure, comedy, romance, and tragedy into her tellings, and each tale contributes to the moral education of Schahriar (Dougray Scott) and enables both his eventual recovery from his madness and his transformation into a brave Sultan and good husband. The embedded tales are integral to the eventual reversal of Schahriar's decree and the happy ending of the program, but here I am primarily concerned with the famous frame tale of the wise and cunning storyteller Scheherezade and the mad Sultan Schahriar.

The *Arabian Nights* miniseries expands the frame tale by altering the relationships between the primary characters and by altering the characters' relationships to storytelling. In doing so, this transformation is able to claim a kind of authenticity while at the same time erasing the larger political implications of the frame tale in favor of a grand love story that meets the expectations of twenty-first-century viewers who just want to be entertained. The representation and expansion of the frame tale in *Arabian Nights* is an important development in Hollywood's long association with the *Nights*, for in allowing Scheherezade to reemerge as the teller of the tales, the film-makers are also ensuring that, in the minds of a mainstream Western audience who otherwise might only be vaguely acquainted with them, Scheherezade and Schahriar become once again, like Aladdin and Ali Babba, major figures in the *Nights*.[3]

The *Nights* is not a single text, but a textual matrix with a long and varied oral, literary, and cinematic history. The source text of the *Arabian Nights*, also known in English as the *Thousand and One Nights,* and *Alf layla wa-layla* in Arabic, is a composite text comprising the famous frame story of Scheherezade and the stories she tells. The stories in the *Nights* come from many cultures and have traveled throughout both East and West. They have been passed from the mouths and pens of so many storytellers over the last ten or so centuries that any attempt to trace the collection to an authentic original source is nearly impossible. We do know that many of the tales of the *Nights* were first compiled from oral sources around the tenth century and that these tales, along with their narrator Scheherezade, have gone through many manifestations ever since.

The *Nights* was first introduced to the West by the French translator and compiler Antoine Galland between 1704 and 1717; it became so popular that it was soon translated into other European languages, including English. Since then, the *Nights* has been through many transformations, a large number of them cinematic. As *Nights* scholar Robert Irwin points out, "the history of the *Thousand and One Nights* on film is nearly as old as the history of film itself," and this history includes "hundreds of films" (92). The legacy of the *Nights* is not only literary and cinematic. The tales have inspired plays and ballets; artists have depicted scenes from the tales, including the frame story of Scheherezade and Schahriar; and other characters from the stories, such as Aladdin, have been taken up by the Disney corporation and turned into commercial franchises. *Nights* characters turn up in British pantomime performances at Christmas time, and North American children wear *Nights*-inspired costumes on Halloween. Advertisers use scenes and images to sell products, and even pornographers have used the erotic reputation of the tales to sell sex. The figure of Scheherezade is so engaging and adaptable that feminist theorists and storytellers have also used her as a feminist icon; she is, after all, a woman who uses her wisdom and cunning to save herself, other women, and her nation from a dangerous madman. The richness and allure of Scheherezade and her stories, therefore, have meant that very few audience members come to any version of the *Nights* with no previous knowledge of some other version or image derived from the tales.

In addition to adapting and expanding the frame story for a contemporary audience, the producers are careful to present the miniseries as an "authentic" retelling but clearly do not feel bound to any specific previous version. One way the claim of authenticity is borne out is in paratextual information such as the blurbs on the DVD box, DVD extras, and other promotional materials that specifically link the new text to the old. In addition, *Arabian Nights* constructs a world that conforms to audience expectations of what the world of the *Nights* "should" look like. All transformations reflect the cultural and historical ideologies of the cultural context in which they are produced. In the West we tend to imagine the tales of the *Nights* as somehow exemplifying a strange and exotic Eastern past. *Arabian Nights* uses brilliant special effects, continuity editing, costuming, and set dressing to capture viewers' imaginations and keep them interested, not only in the embedded tales of Ali Babba, Aladdin, and the others, but in the frame story as well. The *Arabian Nights'* visual retelling employs state-of-the-art special effects to produce the iconic images we expect, such as flying carpets, magic lamps, and frightening beasts, as well as rich textures and a bold color palette, which produce what we have come to believe are "authentic" representations of the mysterious East. In fact, because the cultural conventions and stereotypes that spring out of the *Nights* are as old as the history of the translations of the tales themselves, many of these images come in large part from earlier cultural transformations of the *Nights* which, no matter how outrageous or exoticized, Westerners have used as models for understanding the Orient over hundreds of years.[4]

Arabian Nights makes gestures toward fidelity to the source texts that other cinematic transformations have not, for example, by emphasizing the importance of storytelling. Just as in the source texts, narrative and the act of narration take a central role which, as Arabic literature scholar Wen-chin Ouyang notes, is a first for cinematic renditions of the *Nights*. Although Ouyang praises this version for restoring "diversity to the *Nights* stories, the cultures they evoke, [and] the geographical span they cover" (404), in some ways *Arabian Nights* is really a form of visual cultural tourism. The mise-en-scène establishes an idealized imaginary Islamic culture, which, although it is long ago and far away, seems familiar, and where "they" seem more like "us."[5] As Ouyang suggests, this film is not about "them" at all, it is about "us," a globalized Western "us" positioned within the beautiful frame of a cultural mosaic that subordinates difference to a universalized romantic norm. All discourses relating to cultural difference in *Arabian Nights* are bounded by the grand narrative of monogamous heterosexual romantic love as the universal force that can conquer all. Further, the "timeless" love story of Scheherezade and Schahriar conceals the production's own political and gendered ideologies in the imaginary space of an ancient storytelling tradition that is more authentic to the Hollywood romance tradition than to the earlier ones from which the stories of the *Nights* spring.

In retaining the frame narrative but altering the content of that narrative in terms of characterization, central themes, and pivotal plot points, this transformation of the *Nights* also affects the ways the audience relates to the characters. The shorter and more traditional version of the frame tale has a distinct political element. The Sultan's overreaction to the betrayal of his first wife does more than put the lives of the women of the land in jeopardy: it puts the survival of the political configuration of the kingdom in danger of collapse. Scheherezade thus arrives as the figure who saves not only herself and other women from the Sultan's madness, but the kingdom as well.

In the miniseries though, Schahriar is not merely reacting to his first wife's affair with another man. As we learn in a series of flash-back sequences, her deception is much more egregious: she has taken his brother Schahzenan as her lover, and together the two of them have plotted to murder the Sultan so that Schahzenan can usurp the throne. Luckily for Schahriar, their plot fails. Unluckily for his wife, she is killed by a dagger thrown by Schahriar at his brother, which hits her instead. The action of the film begins five years later when Schahriar must marry again to prevent the throne from passing to his brother. Schahriar devises his own murderous plot in order to fulfill the edict that requires him to marry and at the same time keep himself safe from the "treachery" of women. In this version, Scheherezade learns of the Sultan's plan before he has ever put it in action; thus she is the only woman who is threatened by his madness. Moreover, there is no political unrest, for the people are entirely unaware of the Sultan's madness both before and after his marriage to Scheherezade because Scheherezade's father, the Vizier, has been able to hide it from them. The combination of these elements mean that Schahriar is no longer a brutal murdering mad king but a victim who has been betrayed and traumatized by his brother and wife, and he needs only to learn to love and trust again in order to be "cured." As a consequence, contemporary television viewers, who would normally have a hard time identifying with and rooting for a mad serial killer, are able to feel pity for Schahriar and to hope that he and Scheherezade will eventually come together to live happily ever after.

The film begins not with Scheherezade or Schahriar, but with a dream sequence. The dream quickly becomes a nightmare and when the dreamer awakes, we realize we have been watching Schahriar's dream with him. As a framing technique, this imaginative sequence establishes reading practice for the audience in relation to the later framed stories that will also be filtered or focalized through Schahriar's perspective. Character filtration, or point of view, is indicated by eyeline matches and a shot/reverse shot sequence of Schahriar and the things he sees in his dream. The smooth dissolve into his waking life also aligns the viewer with Schahriar. We "experience" the dream with him in these establishing shots, and have thus been led by the narration to align ourselves with him for the rest of the film. The consequences of this alignment are not insignificant, for although the embedded stories Scheherezade tells throughout the film are attributed to her, this sequence ensures that the audience is positioned to identify with Schahriar. As the cinematic filter through which we experience most of the frame story, he is our surrogate, and just as we view these imagined events from his perspective, the later tales will also be framed by his imagination and therefore primarily controlled by his narrative authority, rather than that of the storyteller, Scheherezade.

The expansion of the frame tale demands that the *Arabian Nights* allow Scheherezade and Schahriar's love story to emerge and reemerge often in order to keep audiences interested in their story and their fates. Narrative frames are structural and cognitive systems of organization; they create context, not only for the storytelling situation, but also for the discourses in action in a text. As in all other versions of the *Nights*, Scheherezade does not enter the story until Schahriar's story has been established and the dangers that Scheherezade will face are clearly set up. In the film, these opening scenes not only set up the situation but align the audience with Schahriar, make him pitiable, and provide him with excuses for his behavior. As it turns out, Scheherezade herself will also provide him with excuses.

The entrance of Scheherezade into the film immediately follows Schahriar's declaration that he will marry a woman from the harem and have her executed the next morning. Her father, the Vizier, who has been given the task of choosing a girl from the harem to be the victim of Schahriar's paranoid plan, discusses with Scheherezade the impossible position in which he has been put. Being the strong-willed girl she is, and recalling her childhood crush on the boy Schahriar, she determines to marry him herself. Her father tries to dissuade her from the idea. He begins by arguing that the Sultan has been made mad by power, and when this logic does not work, he begs her not to marry because he could not bear to lose her. She responds, "I'm not doing it for you, Father. I'm not even doing it for the girls in the harem. I'm doing it for Schahriar and myself." Scheherezade is determined to stick to her plan even though she has clearly not thought it all the way through: "I can save him from himself," she says, "I don't know how, but I've made up my mind. I know I can do it."

So here, an aspect of what has made Scheherezade such an endearing and enduring literary figure is entirely removed for Schahriar's sake. The political ramifications of the Sultan's gynocide have been elided by transforming the frame tale into a simple love story. Although her father's argument is based upon power politics, the claim that "power has made [Schahriar] mad," Scheherezade persists in her discourse of the power of idealized heterosexual love. This causes her father to change his tack, give up his politicized discourse, and appeal to her on the basis of filial love. But in this version, the story has become a romance in which love for one's man, even if he is dangerously mad, supersedes one's duty even to one's father. And further, a woman's status as member of the body politic is completely unimportant. In fact, as the failure of her father's political argument demonstrates, politics and the fate of a nation is not as important to Scheherezade as true love. Where the source texts clearly indicate that Scheherezade is a wise and educated woman who is aware of the political ramifications of the Sultan's madness and is willing to sacrifice herself in order to save the women and the nation, this Scheherezade is a naive young girl in love, and is only worried about saving Schahriar from himself.

In her discussion of narrative frames in her book *Narratology*, Mieke Bal notes that "[w]hen the embedded text presents a complete story ... we gradually forget ... the primary narrative" (53). In the literary versions of the *Nights*, she writes, "this forgetting is a sign that Scheherezade's goal has been accomplished. As long as we forget her life is at stake, the king will too, and that was her purpose" (53). In this version of the *Arabian Nights* however, Scheherezade's skill at entrancing the Sultan is rather less effective. Her confidence and skill as a storyteller are undercut by missteps that allow Schahriar to break the frame she is attempting to establish, thus also diminishing her narrative authority by indicating that he does not accept her story, that she has not provided enough information, or directly opposing her authority by insisting that she is "telling it wrong."[6] One of the effects of these interruptions is to continually bring Scheherezade and Schahriar's story back to the audience's attention and help develop tension and suspense about Scheherezade's fate as well as curiosity about the enframed story that has been interrupted. But another consequence is that these disruptions constantly put Scheherezade's storytelling powers into question.

In fact, her very first attempt to interest Schahriar in a story fails. This false start to Scheherezade's storytelling sets up a framework for the ways in which her narrations will be negotiated throughout the film. Her stories are not entirely her own; they are produced by inspiration from objects around her: a plate of grapes or a cockroach walking by, for example. Further, each morning after her life has been spared, she visits a master storyteller in the market who gives her advice on how to keep her royal audience's attention. Finally, the movement and the content of the stories themselves are dictated by the reaction of her audience. Scheherezade is no master storyteller herself, and Schahriar becomes a collaborator (or perhaps given his political position, dictator) in the storytelling. Each time he interrupts, rupturing the frame Scheherezade is attempting to construct, he demands and attains an amount of authority over the narrative just as he has authority over Scheherezade as husband and Sultan.

In all versions of the frame tale in the *Nights*, power relations and narrative authority are directly related. In the literary versions Scheherezade must fade into the background in order to be a successful narrator. In this version, although it is Scheherezade who is telling the story, it is Schahriar who dictates whether it will be told and even how it will be told; thus we are periodically reminded of her presence. Scheherezade tells her stories for her life; a wrong move does not mean only that the story will be abandoned, but that she will be killed. Schahriar's sinister threats and interruptions violently break the frame and force Scheherezade to navigate with more finesse. Thus Scheherezade also becomes a character who develops and grows by learning to tell stories that will entertain and distract Schahriar, and the television audience as well.

As the nights and the stories progress, Scheherezade becomes a better storyteller and Schahriar learns to be a better audience for the tales. He stops interrupting as often and begins to learn his lessons. He also gains personal insight, is cured of his madness, and falls in love with Scheherezade. He has realized through stories that align him with particular characters, just as the viewing audience is aligned with Schahriar, that Scheherezade truly loves him. At this point the viewing audience expects that he will rescind Scheherezade's death sentence and that they will live happily ever after, but Schahriar's evil brother still lives and is at this moment marching on Baghdad.

The relationship between the brothers is another key to the recuperation of Schahriar that converts him from the two-dimensional villain of the source text into the fallible but lovable hero of the miniseries. The loving relationship between the two brothers in the source material is now a relationship of sibling rivalry based upon competition, distrust, and betrayal. Because of his usurping brother, Schahriar can be pitied further, for not only has Schahzenan betrayed him with his first wife, but the politics of the nation are completely changed: it is the evil Schahzenan who threatens the nation, not the Sultan. The danger is from without rather than from within the power structure, and Schahriar can be seen as the savior of his people rather than as their doom.

As the threat from Schahzenan's army looms, the frame narrative seems to leave the embedded stories behind. But there is one more story to be told. Just as Schahriar has learned to be a better man, Scheherezade has learned to be a better storyteller and she is no longer interrupted in her tale telling. In the narration of the last story, which is the story of Schahriar's final conflict with his brother, Scheherezade continually reemerges in voice-over as the audience watches the battle in progress. It is during the battle between the brothers' armies that the audience discovers one more thing Schahriar has learned from Scheherezade's stories: how to wage war.

The arrival of Schahzenan's army into the frame narrative changes the purpose of Scheherezade's storytelling. Until this point she has told the tales to save her life and to instruct Schahriar in becoming a better man and a wiser ruler, but the earlier embedded stories are now also key to helping

Schahriar vanquish Schahzenan and his army. Rather than teaching him lessons about the responsibilities of great power, the evils of violence and domination, and the importance of diplomacy and cooperation to a wise ruler,
Scheherezade's ultimate triumph is in preparing her husband to become a
warrior king. Schahriar has learned from her tales, not to dispel conflict
peacefully, but cunning battle strategies and imaginative ways to dispense
death in order to retain his kingdom and prove his supremacy over his
brother.

As we watch the various ways in which Schahriar employs important
plot points from Scheherezade's stories to wage war on his brother, it would
seem that Scheherezade finally has taken narrative authority upon herself.
She is now a war queen who watches the battle from the sidelines and is
united with her victorious husband with a kiss. However, *Arabian Nights* has
one more narrative twist. Rather than ending with the happily ever after of
a battle won and the lovers' kiss, we learn that the story of the battle that
Scheherezade has been narrating is framed yet again. The story we have
been watching was being told by Scheherezade, not to her husband, the Sultan Schahriar, but to her two young sons many years after the events took
place.

Neither the narration of the battle nor the addition of yet another narrative frame in which Scheherezade is discovered to have been telling the
whole thing to her two sons appears in the source material. These embell-
ishments not only add further layers of narrative complexity but they affect
the story in numerous ways. Schahriar has been freed from his madness, his
loneliness, and, as a result of these additions, from the tale itself. He is no
longer contained by the frame at all, for he does not appear in the last shot
of Scheherezade and their children. Having been freed from his madness he
apparently no longer needs the stories that saved him. But Scheherezade
must continue to tell them. She is significantly less free even than she was
at the beginning of the film when she was able to roam around the palace
at will or go to the marketplace whenever she chose. Now it would seem she
is bound to repeat the stories she once used to save her life to entertain the
sons of the man who threatened it. The frame and the film close with
Scheherezade having transformed her mad Sultan into a warrior king, and
herself from a naïve young girl and novice storyteller into a mother and an
entertainer of children. Significantly, the two little boys look remarkably like
younger versions of Schahriar and Schahzenan. This resemblance, revealed
as it is immediately after the scene in which Schahriar kills Schahzenan,
raises some troubling questions. If Scheherezade's earlier stories were meant
to save both her life and Schahriar from himself, what is this story about
deadly rivalry and fratricide meant to teach her young sons?

This closing scene re-frames the whole program and causes the audience to rethink the context of the stories they have been watching so far. Ironically, the battle between brothers, in conjunction with the closing frame, works to doubly negate Scheherezade's thesis that stories can save us. Rather than teaching her sons, and her television viewing audience, that storytelling can be a diplomatic, nonviolent means of problem resolution, the battle in which Schahriar employs her stories to wage war and to murder his brother overrides the original purpose of the stories entirely: in the end they are used to bring death rather than to preserve life. Not only does the battle scene privilege violence as a means of problem solving, but the final shot of Scheherezade with her sons works to dismiss the whole adventure, from Schahriar's dream to the couple's loving kiss. For, although Scheherezade explicitly claims that "stories can save us," this ending sequence seems to indicate that, after all, it was *just* a story.

In reintroducing the tale of Scheherezade and Schahriar to this contemporary transformation of the *Nights,* and in focusing upon the importance and power of storytelling to shape the way we see the world and affect how we act within it, *Arabian Nights* performs an important service to its viewing audience and contributes to the history of the text itself. However, by trying to make the story of Schahriar and Scheherezade more palatable and entertaining to contemporary Western audiences, *Arabian Nights* also does it a disservice. It is not the fact that the filmmakers attempt to make the film seem authentic and relevant to contemporary audiences that is the root of the problem, but the choices they make in doing so. By altering the fundamental relationships of characters to each other and to the story, presenting the tale of the two protagonists as first and foremost a love story, and shifting the political threat away from the Sultan and to his brother, the film undercuts its own message about the power of storytelling. *Arabian Nights* creates in its portrayal of Scheherezade a young girl who is not only willing but eager to enter into a relationship with an abusive mad man. Furthermore, her most redeeming quality, her power as a storyteller, is constantly undermined by the man who is threatening her life. At the same time, *Arabian Nights* excuses Schahriar's villainy and madness by making him a pitiable victim of an egregious crime. In this version, Schahriar needs only the unconditional and self-sacrificing love of a good woman in order to be "cured" of an understandable but misdirected anger for which he is not actually responsible. This victimization of Schahriar shifts the political implications of the frame tale by making Schahzenan and Schahriar's first wife irredeemably evil and the cause of Schahriar's suffering. And in adding the battle between the brothers' armies, *Arabian Nights* subordinates the lessons of cooperation, negotiation, and nonviolence to the excitement and adventure of a seemingly inevitable war. Finally, the insertion of another narrative frame of Scheherezade and the two little boys ultimately reframes all the other stories, including her own, and reduces them to mere infantile entertainment, which is not really very important after all.

And that is what is most troubling about this transformation of the *Nights*. It is a beautiful film, full of action, adventure, magic, and mayhem. The stories it adapts within the frame tale are entertaining and a great deal of fun. But its entertainment value creates a strange irony. Although *Arabian Nights* claims that storytelling is important, that it shapes how we see the world and can help us cope with and solve real-life problems, the final frame shot of Scheherezade telling her sons these stories at bedtime overthrows that claim. The *Arabian Nights* miniseries in DVD format is likely to become the introduction to the *Nights* for many North Americans in the near future. These audiences are in for a wonderful experience in many ways, but if we listen to Scheherezade's claim that "stories can save us," we must also recognize that they can trick us into underestimating their power. We must listen to our stories carefully to hear what they are telling us under the surface, listen to what is hidden between the frames, and consider the contradictions as well as the truths embedded within them. In other words, we must not dismiss them as mere entertainments.

Notes

1. In order to minimize confusion, from this point on I will use *Nights* to refer to the long-standing tradition of the *Arabian Nights* or *A Thousand and One Nights* or *A Thousand Nights and a Night* (all different and accepted English-language titles used for the collection of stories), and I will refer to the specific version with which this essay is concerned by its title, *Arabian Nights*.

2. The spellings of names of the characters in the *Nights* in print are not stable. They often change between translations and from version to version. I have chosen to use the spellings used by the producers of the miniseries in this paper because it is my primary source. Spellings in quotations are consistent with their sources.

3. The storyteller framing technique is popular in contemporary fairy-tale films. It appears in many feature films and television programs based on fairy tales such as *The Princess Bride* (1987), *Ever After* (1998), and Jim Henson's *The Storyteller* (1988) series, in which, like *Arabian Nights*, each episode is introduced by a storyteller sitting by a fire telling the embedded stories to his audience, who in this case is a dog. *Pan's Labyrinth* (2006), the *Shrek* series (2001–2007), and many Disney fairy tales begin with a voice-over narrator speaking a typical fairy-tale opening phrase such as "Once upon a time...."

4. To learn more about Orientalism, or the ways in which the West has discursively produced and "naturalized" these models, see the introduction to Edward Said's book *Orientalism* (1978).

5. Mise-en-scène is a cinematic term used to refer to all the elements placed before the camera including sets, costumes, and the "look" of the actors, as well as the way they are lit, framed, and shot.

6. This situation may also bring to mind another cinematic transformation of a fairy-tale novel, *The Princess Bride*. At one point in the film when the young boy being told the story does not like the way the plot is progressing he tells his storytelling grandfather to "Get it

right!" The grandfather threatens to stop reading the story altogether if the grandson does not stop interrupting. Unlike the relationship between Scheherezade and Schahriar, in *The Princess Bride* it is the storyteller who holds the narrative authority and has all the power over the telling of the tales.

Works Cited

Arabian Nights. Perf. Mili Avital, Dougray Scott. ABC, 2000.
Bal, Mieke. *Narratology: Introduction to the Theory of Narrative.* Toronto: University of Toronto Press, 1997.
Ever After. Dir. Andy Tennant. Twentieth Century Fox, 1998.
Haddawy, Husain, trans. *The Arabian Nights: Based on the Text of the Fourteenth-Century Syrian Manuscript edited by Muhsin Mahdi.* New York: Norton, 1990.
Irwin, Robert. "A Thousand and One Nights at the Movies." *New Perspectives on Arabian Nights: Ideological Variations and Narrative Horizons.* Ed. Wen-chin Ouyang and Geert Jan van Gelder. New York: Routledge, 2005. 91–102.
Jim Henson's The Storyteller. HBO, 1988.
Ouyang, Wen-chin. "Metamorphoses of Scheherazade in Literature and Film." *Bulletin of School of Oriental and African Studies.* 66.3 (2003): 402–18.
Pan's Labyrinth. Dir. Guillermo del Toro. Paradiso, 2006.
The Princess Bride. Dir. Rob Reiner. Twentieth Century–Fox, 1987.
Said, Edward W. "Introduction to *Orientalism*" (1978). *The Norton Anthology of Theory and Criticism.* Ed. Vincent B. Leitch. New York: Norton, 2001. 1991–2012.
Shrek. Dir. Andrew Adamson and Vicky Jenson. Dreamworks Animation, 2001.
Shrek 2. Dir. Andrew Adamson, Kelly Asbury, and Conrad Vernon. Dreamworks Animation, 2004.
Shrek the Third. Dir. Chris Miller and Raman Hui. Dreamworks Animation, 2007.

12

Mulan: Disney's Hybrid Heroine

LAN DONG

In 1998 the Disney Studio released its first animated feature film with a Chinese lead character, *Mulan*. The film tells the story of a legendary young woman who pretended to be a man in order to fight in her father's place and achieved great honor as a heroine after her female identity was revealed in the midst of warfare. As Disney Company's effort to expand the market in Asia and to broaden the subject matter of its production, *Mulan* soon became a hit not only in the United States, but also around the world.[1] Critical reaction, however, was mixed. In their article published shortly after *Mulan*'s release, Corie Brown and Laura Shapiro praise the film's empowering of women in portraying a strong-willed heroine who takes action and successfully saves the day (64). Reviewer Mimi Nguyen admires the Asian heroine as a "girl of action and intelligence" who "defies convention, hoodwinks patriarchal authority and goes on to save the masses"—which she calls the "dominant fantasy" of her childhood. In a scholarly analysis of the animated film as a Disneyfied and globalized legend, Joseph Chan claims that its influence is so significant that thereafter "it will be difficult for a re-invention of Mulan not to have a dialogue with the Disney version" (241).

Not all critics of *Mulan* are approving, of course. Nadya Labi, Jeanne McDowell, and Alice Park argue that the necessity for Mulan to adopt a male disguise sabotages the film's theme of female heroism and confirms male rule (60). Asian American scholar Sheng-mei Ma criticizes the film for the way it exoticizes and re-orientalizes China and Chinese sources for American viewers to consume and projects American longings onto the Other (126). Dolores de Manuel and Rocío Davis consider the film a "total-

156

izing and homogenizing" version that exploits the martial arts caricature and reverts to the stereotypical Fu Manchu-like villains despite its claim of cultural authenticity (viii, xi). These observations are quite polarized; the critics either valorize the film for its overtures to feminism or demonize it for its cultural appropriation. By examining both the feminist and transnational interventions made by the Disney Studio in transforming a classic Chinese folk story into a Western, family-oriented animated feature film, the reader will gain a fuller picture of the hybrid nature of *Mulan*.

The first point to make is that *Mulan* is a homogenized version that emphasizes the story's universal themes and values of love, courage, and independence (Wang and Yeh 182). Despite the Disney production team's efforts to make the artistic design, characters, and storyline culturally authentic, and the film's success in globalizing the heroine's fame and providing a transcultural version of her tale, the film is at best a hybrid—an artifact of global culture, that is, "not genuinely Chinese, nor ... all American" (Chan 241). Combining different elements results in a mélange of cultures designed to appeal to a wide range of audiences, and this represents the very process of Disneyfication.

The character of Mulan has had a long history and remains well known within almost every household in China. It is believed that the poem titled "Ballad of Mulan," which appeared about the fourth to sixth century, is the earliest written account of Mulan's legend.[2] In Chinese culture during later periods, there have been many adaptations and transformations of Mulan's tale in different genres that re-imagine the heroine's deeds as well as her characteristics. These stories by and large maintain essential narrative elements of the 300-odd-word "Ballad" and collectively contribute to the character's long-lasting fame—in modern China the name "Mulan" is a synonym of "heroine." The film *Mulan* retains the basic storyline of the renowned Chinese folk story: in order to save her aged father from going to war, the daughter Mulan impersonates a young man to join the army and serves her country for years. After her troops' triumph, Mulan turns down the official rank and welfare bestowed on her, re-dresses in feminine clothes, and returns home to her womanly life.

The film narrative develops these elements for theatrical effect, filling the old tale of Mulan with many new Disney features. Besides the talking animal sidekick (Mushu the dragon), these include Mulan's interview with the matchmaker, the training sequence, the shifted timing of the reveal of her female identity, and the culmination in the form of the Emperor's approval and praise. In order to produce a transcultural product that could appeal to American viewers as well as audiences worldwide, the Disney Studio used what has become its production formula to transform the story and

reconfigure the few brief episodes found in the "Ballad." In retelling a culturally specific fairy tale, folk tale, or story such as *Aladdin* (1993) or *Pocahontas* (1996), a typical Disney production features an adolescent protagonist
who is disappointed by his or her present life and thus embarks on a journey or process in search of a true self. After a confrontation with an embodiment of evil or a challenge as the climax, the hero or heroine finally achieves
individual fulfillment and proves his or her value to the world. He or she
then is rewarded with a promising coupling that closes the film narrative
(Zipes 110–12; McCallum 118). In the past, such a formula has proved successful for Disney's entertainment enterprise, which is aimed at a predominantly white, middle-class American family audience.

Opening the film narrative with a desperate protagonist who is trapped
in a disappointing or boring reality and thus longs for adventure is not unique
for the Disney production of *Mulan*. According to Eleanor Byrne and Martin McQuillan, "Disney's renaissance in the 1980s was marked by the birth
of a new breed of newly born women" who have desires to escape the pris-
ons of domesticity (66). Embarking on her unusual adventure with courage,
young Ariel (*The Little Mermaid*, 1989) trades her voice to Ursula the Sea
Witch for a pair of legs and is determined to make her dreams come true.
Princess Jasmine (*Aladdin*) and Pocahontas are similarly bright, beautiful,
free-spirited, and adventurous. Like them, Mulan is shown to have a mischievous side. Even before going on an adventure, she is strong, smart, and
skillful at horse riding. Clearly, neither does she dream about a prince or
wait to be rescued. Instead, she takes up action to save the day. Hence, *Mulan*
belongs to the group of Disney animated features that recasts a culturally
specific traditional tale into a story of adolescent struggle. And, it is different from the Disney pre-feminist Alice (*Alice in Wonderland*, 1951) in that
the heroine Mulan does not simply fantasize about a young woman's life
that is full of freedom and excitement (after all, Alice's adventure was only
a dream).[3] Rather, she moves to the level of action to protect her family's
honor, achieving extraordinary success and outshining her male contemporaries in the process.

The opening scene of the film *Mulan* is set on the Great Wall, the
defense system at the Chinese border where the Huns undertake a surprise
night attack. Then they march rapidly, crossing the northern borders and
impeding an imminent threat to the capital city as well as to the vast interior land of China that is identified as "the Middle Kingdom." The film then
crosscuts to the Imperial Palace. To protect his Empire and his people, the
Emperor issues an order to recruit one man from each family to reinforce
the defense army. The opening sequence poses an emergency for the nation's
security as well as for the Fa family's well being, for the imperial order enlists

Fa Zhou, Mulan's disabled veteran father. The next transition leads the audience to the Fa family house on the day of Mulan's interview with the matchmaker. Mulan, the only child and daughter, has to impress the matchmaker by presenting herself as a well-groomed maiden so that she can be properly betrothed, thus bringing honor to her family. The protagonist's first appearance on screen indicates that it would be a challenge for her to accomplish the task of "upholding the family honor" through obtaining a marriage proposal. Not only does she trick her dog, "Little Brother," into helping her feed the hens, which results in much disorder at the family temple, but she also rushes into town on horseback and arrives late for the dressing-up preparation before her interview.

The film stresses the protagonist's personal dilemma by demonstrating the gap between her individuality and her society's expectation of a young woman. As articulated by the song in the film "Honor to Us All," Mulan can bring honor to her family only by receiving a marriage proposal that matches her social standing. The song also makes it clear that the only way she can fulfill her duty is by serving her in-laws and extending her husband's family line by producing a son. But Mulan is intelligent and outspoken, and therefore doomed to fail as an obedient bride. The expectation articulated to Mulan is that she can bring honor to her family only through marriage. Regardless of the painstaking process of bathing, dressing-up, and making-up arranged by her mother and grandmother and her efforts to be passive and demure, Mulan's meeting with the matchmaker ends in disaster. Infuriated, the matchmaker declares the devastating failure of the young heroine: "You are a disgrace. You may look like a bride, but you will never bring your family honor." As has been made clear in the song, men and women have different positions in the society and different duties to fulfill: a man fights for his country, whereas a woman gives birth to sons. Feeling humiliated and frustrated, Mulan cannot even face her father after returning home.

These plot details in the film make it quite clear that Mulan was born with a free spirit and behaves accordingly. Such traits are absent in the original Chinese "Ballad," which says little about Mulan's personality and reveals few details about her life as a daughter before her enlistment in disguise. Later transformations have added such a thread and enriched the image of the character. For example, the same year the film was released Robert San Souci, one of the authors of the film story for Disney's *Mulan*, published a picture book, *Fa Mulan: The Story of a Woman Warrior*. It portrays Mulan as a tomboy. He begins his book with Mulan slicing the air with a bamboo stake pretending to be a swordswoman and her elder sister scolding her and reminding her, "Proper young women do not play with swords" (San Souci). The re-imagination of Mulan as tomboyish that appears not only in San Souci's book but also in Disney's film is of particular significance in the transformation of her tale. Since tomboyism for a girl is oftentimes associated with the heroine's desire for freedom and mobility, it is considered "a sign of independence and self-motivation" as long as it is linked to "a stable sense of a girl identity" (Halberstam 6). In the film Mulan's tomboyism, harbored within safe boundaries, enables her female masculinity to be tolerable and non-threatening, as her motivation emphasizes (to save her father and to honor her family) and the ending confirms (to bring home not only honor but also a love interest).

Before Mulan can assume her role as heroine, she runs into another conflict between social expectations for females and her strong personality. The enlistment order calling Mulan's father Fa Zhou to join the defensive war provides her the opportunity to gain honor for her family and to prove her worth by taking an unusual path. Thus, in her father's place Mulan dresses in his armor, runs away from home, and joins the army. Her actions unmistakably show her love for her father and her dedication to her family. Yet at the same time her stealing away from home is also a daring personal adventure for the young heroine. Now she has new hope, founded on the opportunity to make her father proud and in the process to escape from a disappointing reality in which the family honor is in danger and in which she is identified as a misfit and a "disgrace." In contrast to the "Ballad," which describes the heroine's military career in only a few lines with hardly any detail, the film goes on to portray Mulan's success in the military expedition in terms of her wisdom, courage, persistence, and skills acquired through intensive training.

Mulan's military adventures are important innovations of the film. In particular, the production team designs the new feature of the training sequence. The need for inexperienced young men to go through rigorous training results in a sequence common to many films with a cross-dressing heroine. Mulan must hide her female body, adopt a new gender-neutral name, Ping, and toughen up. Together with other new recruits she gains new combat skills such as fighting with staves, archery, artillery, and hand-to-hand combat. The film shows Ping/Mulan's transformation into a "tough-looking warrior" in a series of fast-paced crosscuts. On the first day Mulan not only sleeps in and comes to the morning assembly late, but she also forgets to bring her sword. Together with the unprepared cadets, Ping/Mulan meets Captain Li Shang, the General's son, whose goal is expressed clearly in the song, "I'll Make a Man Out of You." The film shows the challenges Ping/Mulan faces due to her lack of skills, strength, and military experience before displaying her innate characteristics such as persistence and sound judgment.

At the military camp it is Ping/Mulan who refuses to give up, rises above adversity, and retrieves the arrow from the top of the pole while carrying two heavy weights that represent discipline and strength. Toward the end of the training sequence, the chorus of "I'll Make a Man Out of You" points to the promising result of all of that practice. The soldiers show their quick moves and strength, which the song compares to a mighty river. The lyrics also add a hint of darkness as they celebrate male prowess, for the man who has acquired fiery strength is also as untamed as the moon's dark side. Interspersed with these comparisons to nature is a phrase so common it has become a cliché: "be a man." The chorus clearly equates masculinity with physical strength coded as natural, which makes it even more remarkable that Mulan, a girl, becomes one of the best "men" in the company.

The visuals emphasize the impressive martial arts skills Ping/Mulan and her fellow recruits have acquired. These scenes, to some degree, resemble the martial arts montage in other films showing physical strength, skill practice, and competition to prove who is the best. Ping's triumph in military training poses a contrast to Mulan's failure at her interview with the matchmaker. Here her determination and strong will no longer make her a misfit; rather, she thrives as a young "man" in military service. The training episodes are also of particular significance in the film's narrative because they introduce Mulan's love interest, Captain Li Shang. During the course of intensive training Mulan develops respect and liking for Li Shang who, despite the initial appearance of being tough and proud, cares about the cadets, guides them with knowledge and patience, and successfully trains them into capable and confident soldiers.

After the new recruits complete their field lessons guided by Captain Li Shang, Ping/Mulan and her fellow combatants march into the battlefield full of energy and confidence, only to find out that the main strength of the imperial army led by General Li, Li Shang's father, has been completely wiped out by the Huns. In an unanticipated confrontation with the Hun troops, who overwhelmingly outnumber the remaining cohort of the imperial soldiers, Ping/Mulan shows extraordinary courage and wisdom in defeating the enemy. The juxtaposition of the computer-generated image of the Hun horse cavalry spreading out everywhere and pressing forward and Li Shang's orders that Yao aim the last canon at the Hun chieftain Shan-yu and that his soldiers prepare for combat and die in honor reveals a dire situation.

Upon seeing the reflection of an overhanging snow-covered mountain peak, Mulan takes the last cannon and runs toward the Hun troops single-handedly. She blows up the mountain peak when Shan-Yu is just a few feet in front of her, causing an avalanche that buries the entire Hun army, and thus saves the imperial soldiers miraculously. Ping/Mulan's exceptional military performance also provides an opportunity for the film to plant the seed of a love affair by showing the attraction of Ping/Mulan to Li Shang and thus to imply the possibility of the future development of their relationship. When Li Shang drifts away in the snowstorm, without hesitating Ping/Mulan rushes to his rescue at the risk of losing her own life. When the soldiers praise Ping/Mulan as their hero, "the bravest of us all," and cheer about her victory, she not only wins the battle but also the Captain's trust and, as the audience will find out later, his heart. Yet, Ping/Mulan's glorious triumph also leads to the revealing of her secret. Ping/Mulan, who has been slashed by Shan-Yu's sword, passes out from her injury; when she is treated by the military doctor, her female identity is exposed.

Disney's film is the first version to reveal the protagonist's gender identity before the end of the war, and thus breaks new ground. The revelation at first threatens Mulan's safety, for dressing as a man is underscored as a fatal crime that is strictly forbidden. Mulan again is thrown into a desperate situation in which she could not only let her family down once more but lose her life. The image of Mulan kneeling down on the snow-covered ground, hunching her female body under a thin blanket, is a sharp contrast to the previous celebration in which everybody is cheering for the military success attributed to Ping. Suddenly, the war hero Ping, admired by other soldiers and officers, has turned into Mulan, a condemned "treacherous snake" who has committed "high treason," to use the counsel's words.

More importantly, this early revelation of the character's sex enables Mulan to achieve ultimate success at the climax as a woman, instead of in male disguise. In other variations of Mulan's story beginning with the "Ballad," the heroic and the female features of the character are separated. When Mulan is a woman, she is not heroic; when she is a hero, she is dressed in a man's clothes and therefore appears to be male. In this sense the military achievement and honor Mulan receives still belong to a hero. In contrast, Mulan confronts the foe and wins the final victory as a heroine. The turnaround for Mulan's desperate situation as a young woman begins when she learns of the plans of the recently defeated Hun army. The surviving Huns break through the snow-covered ground and gather around Shan-yu. The Hun leader, surrounded by a handful of his henchmen, marches to the capital city with a new scheme to capture the Emperor and to overthrow his rule. They will attack while the Chinese people are intoxicated by their military victory, enjoying a magnificent celebration to welcome the heroes home, blissfully unaware of their enemies' existence. Instead of going home and facing her father with yet another failure and dishonor, Mulan-as-woman single-handedly launches a journey to the Imperial Palace to save the Emperor and the Empire, which also restores honor to her family and proves her worth.

In the film three fellow soldiers, Ling, Yao, and Chien-po, follow Mulan's lead and rescue the Emperor as a team; furthermore, they dress as women so that they can catch the Huns off-guard. This episode is another invention of Disney's production team and has no trace in the "Ballad" or any of the aforementioned versions. In contrast to Mulan's disguise, the three soldiers' cross-dressing appears to be a device for comic effect in the film. The men look like "ugly concubines," in the words of the Hun soldiers. Their attacks with watermelons, apples, bananas, and oranges, all fake breasts pulled out of their dresses, enable the potentially violent fighting to appear comical and entertaining. The soldiers' cross-dressing also accentuates how daring and impressive Mulan's disguise is because hers is dangerous and institutionally forbidden while theirs is acceptable, constituting merely a distraction. As Victoria Flanagan has argued, male cross-dressing in children's literature is mostly depicted in superficial ways and diverges sharply from female cross-dressing in that "the issue of gender performance is seldom raised as a serious concern" (53). Male cross-dressers are typically portrayed in a comic mode that emphasizes their inability to behave convincingly as women (Flanagan 53). This episode, together with the fireworks that destroy Shan-Yu, turns violence into festival entertainment, which helps make the film suitable for its target audience, children and their families.

After rescuing the Emperor from the Huns' confinement and winning the one-on-one combat against Shan-Yu in the Imperial Palace, Mulan stands in front of the Emperor, who affirms Mulan's victory as a woman. He speaks to her: "I've heard a great deal about you, Fa Mulan. You stole your father's armor, ran away from home, impersonated a soldier, deceived your commanding officer, dishonored the Chinese army, destroyed my palace, and you have saved us all." These words are an apt summary of what the maiden has gone through, but they take the form of an official approval for her unusual conduct. Given the Emperor's position as the symbol of supreme authority, his judgment represents society's reaction to the female protagonist's unconventional behavior. When the Emperor bows to Mulan to show his gratitude for saving him and his Middle Kingdom, his people have no choice but to acquiesce and approve of her behavior. It is acceptable for Mulan to adopt a masculine persona when it is in the service of her country. Because of her success, Mulan is perceived as a heroine instead of an offender. Moreover, the counsel, Captain Li Shang, and Mulan's fellow soldiers inside the Palace as well as the huge mass of Chinese people outside the Palace prostrate themselves to her, a woman, to show respect and gratitude. This approval of Mulan's unusual behavior on different levels is a unique aspect of Disney's version.

Commenting on this specific scene as the confirmation of Mulan's achievement in the "Bonus Features" of *Mulan* DVD, the producer Pam Coats remarks, "[Mulan] has changed the way society thinks about the role of women. This is made very clear in that final sequence where the Emperor bows. And then she turns around and you see this entire sea of people bowing to her." The film's portrayal of a successful able-minded and able-bodied protagonist cannot help but remind readers of Maxine Hong Kingston's "White Tiger" chapter in her acclaimed *The Woman Warrior: Memoirs of a Girlhood among Ghosts* (1976), which transforms Mulan from a Chinese folk heroine to an Asian American woman warrior.[4] Due to its popularity among general readers as well as its far-reaching influence on a number of scholarly fields, Kingston's text not only has made Mulan a familiar name to many English-speakers but also has prepared the ground for the reading of this character from a feminist perspective.[5] Another example that re-imagines Mulan's story with a feminist spin is Jeanne M. Lee's bilingual picture book, *The Song of Mu Lan* (1995), which is dedicated to "all women, young and old."[6] Kingston, and Lee's works may not have influenced Disney's film directly, but they were available to the Disney Studio's production team to draw on and react to.

Despite the feminist elements featured in the Disney film, Mulan does not represent a feminist character in everyone's eyes since her adventure and accomplishment are motivated by filial duty to her father and family rather than righting a wrong or seeking female empowerment and glory. In fact, Brenda Ayres argues that Mulan is respected *because* she is "prepared to give up her life in order to save the life of her father and later the life of her lover. Ultimately, her demonstrated feats of bravery, fighting skill, and intelligence serve to bring honor to her father and prove her worthy of the captain's love" (48). After all, like many of its Disney predecessors the film ends with a promising marriage for the protagonist. In the closing scene, Mulan returns home with the sword of Shan-Yu and the crest of the Emperor and meets her father in the family garden. Fa Zhou's words, "The greatest gift and honor is having you for a daughter," ultimately join together the family honor with the heroine's personal achievement. Not all the family members are satisfied, however. Mulan's grandmother remarks, "Great. She brings home a sword. If you ask me, she should've brought home a man," trivializing Mulan's heroic experience and signaling that the rest of the film is pure Disney. Getting a hint from the Emperor that "a flower that blooms in adversity is the most rare and beautiful of all.... You don't meet a girl like that every dynasty," Captain Li Shang shows up at the Fa home to hand over Mulan's helmet. Mulan, now bashful, but obviously pleased, asks him, "Would you like to stay for dinner?" Her grandmother's line, "Would you like to stay forever," puts closure on Mulan's adventure away from home and emphasizes her return to the appropriate social position for a young woman, marriage.

Regardless of Mulan's daring spirit and skills, it is noteworthy that "one of Disney's most vigorous heroines literally has to disguise herself as a boy" (Labi, McDowell, and Park 60). Even though Mulan achieves success after she resumes her female self, her victory as a woman is portrayed as a one-time measure to save the day. Besides, it is compromised by Mulan and Li Shang's potential engagement at the end of the film. In this sense, Mulan does not transcend the gender conventions and her defiance does not include a political agenda calling for women's equal rights. Boys are still the ones who lead active lives and engage in military combat and girls can only do so when they pretend to be male. Mulan's non-threatening combination of masculinity and femininity has contributed to her emergence as a role model in contemporary times.

In the film not only is Mulan a good, dutiful daughter and a wise, courageous soldier who brings honor to her family, but she is also a role model for individual accomplishment. Her mindset and action clearly convey the Western message of individual realization. Because she is "Chinese-looking yet American-acting Mulan" (Ma 142), American as well as international teenagers are able to identify with Mulan's adventurous journey away from home in the sense that it mirrors their quest for adolescent self-realization. The film's conclusion with the young protagonist successfully saving her country and family while realizing her individual identity arouses admiration among young viewers across cultures.

Disney's *Mulan* is a hybrid film in many ways: inspiration for her character and story comes from a non–Euro-American tradition and therefore ensures the heroine's exotic attributes. The film's protagonist is also a typical Disney teenager equipped with cultural hybridity and situated in a globalized world. The different elements Disney has utilized to reconfigure the heroine's tale enrich the film in important ways: adding new threads about the protagonist's personality, expanding the plot of her military adventure, and developing feminist elements in the narrative, among others.

Perhaps most importantly, Disney's film is different from all other transformations because the protagonist's gender secret is exposed earlier, and she wins the final battle as a young woman who does not need to resort to male disguise. At the victorious finale in the Imperial Palace, the Emperor as well as the Chinese people bestow recognition on a heroine, a successful *female*. Using such "cross-cultural referencing mechanisms," to borrow Chan's words, the Disney version thus has inserted a new hybrid characterization to the Mulan gallery. As a transcultural text Disneyfied, *Mulan* is neither genuinely Chinese nor entirely American (Chan 241). A representation of cultural hybridization, Disney's film transforms Mulan's tale for children as well as their families. *Mulan* indeed reflects a hybrid of cultures not only in its expression of cultural heritage as a Chinese folk story, but also in conveying the Western message of individual realization. In this sense, Disney's film presents a transnational transformation of the heroine's tale that is a result of bricolage, that is, "making something new with something old" (Genette x). Future re-inventions of Mulan will probably draw on or react to this transformed text that the Disney conglomerate has provided us.

Notes

1. *Mulan* earned over $120 million at the United States box office and more than $170 million foreign. It won or was nominated for a number of awards, including twelve nominations and ten awards at the twenty-sixth Annual Annie Awards, two Golden Globe nominations, two Grammy nominations, an Academy Award nomination, and the "Best Children's Movie" at the twenty-second Annual International Angel Award, and was well received in many countries (Kuo).

2. For an English translation of this poem, see Frankel. Frankel's translation is also available online: http://www.geocities.com/Hollywood/5082/mulanpoem.html.

3. I borrow the term "pre-feminist" from Deborah Ross, who discusses female imagination in Disney's animation world in "Escape from Wonderland."

4. For a brief introduction to Kingston, see Dong, "Woman Warrior."

5. Examples of the multidisciplinary and interdisciplinary study of Kingston's book are the articles collected in Lim and in Wong. Lim's volume includes readings of *The Woman Warrior* in such fields as history, Asian studies, gender and women's studies, writing, literature, and folklore. Wong's collection deals with genre, multiculturalism, gender, and other issues and includes debates about Kingston's work. Collectively they speak for *The Woman Warrior*'s significant influence across scholarly fields.

6. For a critical reading of Lee's book, see Dong, "Writing."

Works Cited

Ayres, Brenda. "The Poisonous Apple in *Snow White*: Disney's Kingdom of Gender." *The Emperor's Old Groove: Decolonizing Disney's Magic Kingdom*. Ed. Ayres. New York: Peter Lang, 2003. 39–50.

Brown, Corie, and Laura Shapiro. "Woman Warrior." *Newsweek* 8 June 1998: 64.

Byrne, Eleanor, and Martin McQuillan. *Deconstructing Disney*. London: Pluto, 1999.

Chan, Joseph M. "Disneyfying and Globalizing the Chinese Legend Mulan: A Study of Transculturation." *In Search of Boundaries: Communication, Nation-States and Cultural Identities*. Ed. Chan and Bryce T. McIntyre. Westport, CT: Ablex, 2002. 225–48.

Dong, Lan. "The Woman Warrior." *Encyclopedia of Multiethnic American Literature*. Ed. Emmanuel S. Nelson. Westport, CT: Greenwood, 2005. 2310–13.

_____. "Writing Chinese America into Words and Images: Storytelling and Retelling of *The Song of Mu Lan*." *The Lion and the Unicorn* 30.2 (2006): 218–33.

Flanagan, Victoria. *Into the Closet: Cross-Dressing and the Gendered Body in Children's Literature and Film*. New York: Routledge, 2008.

Frankel, Hans H., trans. "Mu-lan." *The Flowering Plum and the Palace Lady: Interpretations of Chinese Poetry*. New Haven: Yale University Press, 1976. 68–72.

Genette, Gérard. *Palimpsests: Literature in the Second Degree*. 1982. Trans. Channa Newman and Claude Doubinsky. Lincoln: University of Nebraska Press, 1997.

Halberstam, Judith. *Female Masculinity*. Durham, NC: Duke University Press, 1998.

Kingston, Maxine Hong. *The Woman Warrior: Memoirs of a Girlhood Among Ghosts.* New York: Vintage, 1989.

Kuo, Angela. "The *Mulan* FAQ." 7 Aug. 2008. <http://www.geocities.com/Hollywood/5082/mulanfaq.html>.

Labi, Nadya, Jeanne McDowell, and Alice Park. "Girl Power." *Time* 29 June 1998. 13 Mar. 2009. <http://www.time.com/time/magazine/article/0,9171,988643,00.html>.

Lee, Jeanne M. *The Song of Mu Lan.* Arden, NC: Front Street, 1995.

Lim, Shirley Geok-lin, ed. *Approaches to Teaching Kingston's* The Woman Warrior. New York: MLA, 1991.

Ma, Sheng-mei. *The Deathly Embrace: Orientalism and Asian American Identity.* Minneapolis: University of Minnesota Press, 2000.

Manuel, Dolores de, and Rocío G. Davis. "Editors' Introduction: Critical Perspectives on Asian American Children's Literature." *The Lion and the Unicorn* 30.2 (2006): v–xv.

McCallum, Robyn. "Masculinity as Social Semiotic: Identity Politics and Gender in Disney Animated Films." *Ways of Being Male: Representing Masculinities in Children's Literature and Film.* Ed. John Stephens. New York: Routledge, 2002. 116–32.

Mulan. Dir. Barry Cook and Tony Bancroft. Walt Disney, 1998.

Nguyen, Mimi "Role Models: Mulan." *San Jose Mercury News* 5 July 1998. 8 Aug. 2008. <http://www.theory.org.uk/ctr-rol2.htm>.

Ross, Deborah. "Escape from Wonderland: Disney and the Female Imagination." *Marvels & Tales* 18.1 (2004): 53–66.

San Souci, Robert D. *Fa Mulan: The Story of a Woman Warrior.* Illus. Jean and Mou-Sien Tseng. New York: Hyperion, 1998.

Wang, Georgette, and Emilie Yueh-yu Yeh. "Globalization and Hybridization in Cultural Products: The Cases of *Mulan* and *Crouching Tiger, Hidden Dragon.*" *International Journal of Cultural Studies* 8.2 (2005): 175–93.

Wong, Sau-ling Cynthia, ed. *Maxine Hong Kingston's* The Woman Warrior: *A Casebook.* New York: Oxford University Press, 1999.

Zipes, Jack David. "Once Upon a Time beyond Disney: Contemporary Fairy Tale Films for Children." *In Front of Children: Screen Entertainment and Young Audiences.* Ed. Cary Bazalgette and David Buckingham. London: BFI, 1995. 109–26.

13

Mass-Marketing "Beauty": How a Feminist Heroine Became an Insipid Disney Princess

MARC DIPAOLO

When my three goddaughters turned four in 2004, they started show-ing signs of being able to understand and appreciate movies, so I decided it was as good a time as any to introduce them to the Walt Disney films I had grown up with. Naturally, I was leery of showing them any Disney films that seemed to glorify the idea of "being a princess," or that concluded with a manly prince "rescuing" the heroine simultaneously from the forces of evil and her own independence—so I avoided showing the triplets *Sleeping Beauty* and *Cinderella*. Instead, I chose *Beauty and the Beast* (1991), a film that I remembered as being enchanting as well as boasting a strong female lead in the figure of Belle. What I did not realize at the time was that Disney's Consumer Products division had spent the last four years developing a mar-keting campaign called the Disney Princess line and had included Belle as an integral part of its merchandising initiative, doing possibly irreparable harm to the character in the process.

In the various dolls, Halloween costumes, DVDs, and video games that comprise the multibillion-dollar Disney Princess industry, Belle is featured as the brunette princess, *The Little Mermaid*'s Ariel is the redhead, Snow White is the black-haired White girl, and Sleeping Beauty (a.k.a. Princess Aurora) and Cinderella vie for position as the blonde princess. The group-ing encourages Caucasian girls of every major hair color to pick their favorite princess to identify with, thereby imagining themselves in the tiara and regal gown. For both marketing and multicultural reasons, these main five princesses are sometimes joined by the Native American Pocahontas, the Asian Mulan, and the Semitic Jasmine, but they are rarely positioned as centrally as the first five. By the time I had decided to show my goddaughters the film *Beauty and the Beast*, I discovered that they had already spent the past several months dressing as the Disney Princesses and declaring themselves royalty, often using their newfound titles as an excuse not to go to bed early or eat their greens at dinnertime.

The triplets had already known Belle from *Beauty and the Beast*, not as a fictional character, but as a sort of totem or figure of mythical, upper-class privilege and idealized femininity. But it was not the Belle I had come to know and admire—the feminist Belle of the Disney film. That Belle was an avid reader with a sly sense of humor who was capable of great warmth and noble acts of selflessness. That Belle was a liberated woman who turned down a proposal of marriage from the handsomest, most controlling and self-involved man in town, Gaston the big game hunter, to maintain control of her own destiny. That Belle confronted a pack of wolves brandishing a torch and disobeyed the Beast's command not to enter the forbidden west wing of the castle. In contrast, the Belle of the Disney Princess line is an empty-headed, dewy-eyed cipher perpetually clutching a rose to her bosom, who sings songs like "The Perfect Princess Tea" and "The Princess Dance" in spin-off videos. I was disappointed to see the feminist heroine created by screenwriter Linda Woolverton so diminished, and I second-guessed my enthusiastic desire to introduce Belle to my goddaughters.

The Disney brand name has never been synonymous with feminism, so it should have occurred to me that the moderately liberal *Beauty and the Beast* film, which provided a long-overdue feminist Disney heroine, would be an exception, not the start of a trend toward progressive depictions of women by the studio. After all, many critics accept as a given that the Disney adaptations of fairy tales are bowdlerized, antifeminist versions of older fairy tales. Child psychologist Bruno Bettelheim, in *The Uses of Enchantment*, complains that Disney's Cinderella is more passive than any other incarnation of the character, even the "sugar-sweet and insipidly good" heroine of the Perrault story that inspired it (251). And Marina Warner, in *From the Beast to the Blonde*, argues that the demonic stepmother of Cinderella has convinced legions of children that all real-life stepmothers must be equally demonic. In addition, Warner notes that the self-centered Ariel and obese Sea Witch from *The Little Mermaid* are also far from solid female role models (207, 402). However, what is frustrating here is that Disney got Belle right in its wonderful film adaptation of *Beauty and the Beast* and then proceeded to undo its own good work by marketing the Beauty character as a Disney princess, transforming her into a merchandiser's dream but a feminist's nightmare.

The Belle in the movie carries the first half of the film alone and, even when the impressive Beast shows up and threatens to overshadow Belle, she remains a central focus of audience interest and sympathy, especially in her bravery when defying Beast, who dwarfs her in size. Although the film ends with a marriage—and such romanticized endings are problematic for many feminists because of the implication that women can only be happy within the context of heterosexual marriage—the lovers develop a mutual respect by the end of the film, and they have strong enough personalities that the audience is reassured that their union will be happy and equitable.

The animated movie begins by presenting Belle as a beautiful young woman living in a provincial town in France. She is an avid reader and the daughter of a scientist; she is far more intelligent than everyone else in town and has neither close friends nor romantic prospects, least of all the egomaniacal big-game hunter, Gaston, whom she steadfastly refuses to marry. When her father disappears unexpectedly, Belle investigates and discovers that he has been captured by an enormous, bull-like figure that rules over an enchanted castle filled with subjects that have been transformed into living furniture. In an act of self-sacrifice, Belle wins her father's freedom by offering herself as a hostage instead. Once she is sure that her father is safe, however, Belle immediately begins to defy the terms of her own imprisonment, first by investigating the forbidden west wing of the castle to uncover the secret of the curse that has transformed the entire kingdom, and then by fleeing the castle. While her escape attempt fails, leading her into the clutches of a pack of wolves, it forces Beast into action, and he reveals his bravery and affection for her when he risks his life to chase the wolves away. Victorious but badly wounded, Beast collapses in the snow, near death. Here Belle gives up her chance to escape and rescues Beast in turn by dragging him back to the castle.

Following this dramatic event, both Belle and the Beast declare a truce and allow themselves to get acquainted on a deeper level. The middle of the film is replete with scenes in which the two show deference to each other, exchange gifts, and make significant sacrifices on the other's behalf. In the process, most audience members become convinced that they belong together, despite Beast's initial, unforgivable behavior, because he has become more humane while Gaston becomes more bestial. In the climactic segment, Gaston duplicates Beast's crime against Belle by placing her father in a mental institution in an effort to blackmail her into marrying him. Beast grants her leave to go free her father, even though he needs Belle's love in order to break the enchantment that cursed him. Meanwhile, Gaston leads an angry mob of torch-bearing villagers to kill Beast in his castle. After freeing her father, Belle instantly races back to the castle, just in time to see Beast fighting Gaston atop the battlements. Gaston falls to his death and Beast nearly joins him, but Belle arrives in time to save his life by grabbing onto his shirt. It is only at this moment, when Belle joins Beast willingly instead of as his prisoner, that the spell is broken and Beast and his subjects regain their lost humanity.

Because Linda Woolverton and the Disney production team worked so hard to create a Belle who is as independent as she is self-sacrificing and a Beast who is ferocious yet kindly enough to deserve salvation, the Disney cartoon shows conclusively what few other versions of the tale manage to demonstrate—that Beauty and the Beast love each other, deserve one another, and will, indeed, live happily ever after. Admittedly, the opinion of informed feminist critics is against me here. While I am impressed by Woolverton's characterization of Belle and accept both the romance and the "happy ending" on the terms that the film offers them, most feminist and deconstructionist film and literature critics would argue that I am embracing a naïve reading. They would also observe that my affection for the character suggests that I am allowing my emotions to be manipulated in a manner that is little different from the pernicious effect I myself am warning about regarding the Disney Princesses.

To put it another way, I see a large distinction between the Belle of the film and the Belle of the Disney Princesses. Most feminist critics appear to see no such distinction, and would warn that the film Belle, like the mass-marketed Disney Princess Belle, is a bad influence on impressionable young women. For example, Lara Sumera cites Belle as a potentially dangerous character because her surface feminism is essentially the bait used to trap enlightened viewers into accepting the same reactionary Disney family values dressed up in more progressive clothing. As she observes, "At first, Belle is strong, independent and intellectual. But as the film progresses, she becomes dependent and attached to the Beast, and although well read and intellectually curious, her romantic inclinations ultimately revert back to the Disney heroines of old" (46). In addition, Allison Craven argues that the film emphasizes romance over the moral development of its characters. She further points out—and I agree with her completely here—that the plot descriptions of the film on the backs of DVD and VHS copies of the film compound the problem by suggesting that Belle is the only one with anything to "learn" during the course of the film, despite the fact that Beast is the one with a tendency to take hostages.

One of the reasons it is difficult to find a literary or cultural critic who would act as an apologist for this film, as I do, is that many of them approach the subject matter with a knowledge of both art and literature that "the average American" in the mass media age does not have. I agree that, next to the books and films of Angela Carter, Margaret Atwood, Jane Smiley, and Gillian Armstrong, the Disney version of *Beauty and the Beast* does not seem even remotely feminist. However, even critics who approach the material from this vantage point have granted that Belle is an appealing character with a noticeable feminist streak at her core. And as a point of comparison, if one begins with how women are portrayed in popular culture rather than with how women are portrayed in literature or by academics, then *Beauty and the Beast* quickly emerges as a breath of fresh air. Compare the Belle of the film to the Lolitas featured in the average MTV music-video harem; the marriage-obsessed daddy's girls of reality television and films such as *27 Dresses* and *Bride Wars*; and the damsels in distress in need of rescuing by the superhero of the day. If Belle comes up short of a more ideal feminist character (such as the heroine of *My Brilliant Career*), she still stands head and shoulders above the nightmarish role models available for young women today. As rock singer Pink laments in her song "Stupid Girls," the girl who dreamed of becoming president is likely to settle for dancing in a rapper video. Ironically, even as cultural critics write that Linda Woolverton's Belle isn't feminist enough, the executives at Disney prove that their reputation as reactionaries is well-deserved as they strive, through their merchandising campaign, to strip her of the feminism that she *does* have—the feminism that I see in her and have long celebrated.

Now, one might suggest that I overreacted to my first glimpse of the commodification of my favorite Disney heroine and that my dislike of the merchandise is a bit silly. After all, the mastermind of the marketing campaign, Andy Mooney, said in an interview with Peggy Orenstein that the marketing initiative merely "gave girls what they wanted," and he cited the massive financial success of the line as proof of little girls' preexisting desire to imagine themselves as princesses. His argument nevertheless seems self-serving and too dismissive of the legitimate complaints that feminists have against his merchandise. He has also maintained that the princess fixation represents a normal phase of girlhood that is essentially harmless and soon outgrown, much like little boys' love of cowboys, cosmonauts, and gangsters. Orenstein is skeptical of Mooney's claims, and I share her skepticism. After all, it is one thing to provide products that cater to the interests of young boys and girls who love guns and gowns in the name of making a profit. It is another thing to bombard children with products that reinforce a narrowly defined definition of masculinity and femininity in our commodity culture, which sees the same mass-media marketed products for sale in the same aisles in the same chain stores all across the country.

As Orenstein writes, the pervasiveness of the Disney Princesses seems to amount to a cultural mandate for girls to dress in pink and be passive. In an article published in 2006, "What's Wrong with Cinderella?" Orenstein argues that "young women who hold the most conventionally feminine beliefs—who avoid conflict and think they should be perpetually nice and pretty—are more likely to be depressed than others and less likely to use contraception." They tend to shy away from sports because of fears that women shouldn't be athletes, and they often feel a "paralyzing pressure to be 'perfect'"—that is to get perfect grades, be thin, gorgeous, fashionable, and be liked by everyone they meet. As Orenstein concludes, "Give those girls a pumpkin and a glass slipper and they'd be in business."

Since the omnipresence of the Disney Princess advertising initiative suggests that it would be nigh impossible to avoid contact with these princess characters, or ignore them, it behooves parents to help their daughters develop a wider understanding of what they may represent, outside of being figures of glamour. Ideally, the best way for parents to undo some of the possibly pernicious influence of the Disney Princess campaign is to encourage their daughters to read and think about the older versions of the story, to consider the narratives in light of the times and cultures that produced them, and to ponder the possible relevance the tales have today.

Belle, and the *Beauty and the Beast* film she came from, is a 1990s attempt to distill and enhance the feminist elements of a story that is thousands of years old and that has appeared in a multitude of forms in a variety of cultures. The theme of the reluctant bride who gradually comes to love what is human and beautiful at the core of her hideous husband has appeared frequently enough to have been catalogued as Aarne-Thompson fairy-tale type 425.[1] These stories feature early literary examples of women in the role of adventurer, investigator, and messiah. Many of the heroines featured in these versions are praised as much for their intelligence as for their looks, and a number of them are sculptors and painters. Other versions of the heroine dare to try to escape their captors, disobey their parents, and strive to shape their own destinies. These versions of the Beauty character, and those particular plot developments, are those that most inspired Woolverton's reinvention of the tale. Other less feminist story elements, including an intrusive narrator's voice that occasionally chides Beauty for being too strong-willed, or exaggerated female villains who make the sometimes reprehensible Beast look good in comparison, are understandably absent given Woolverton's desire to update the narrative.

The multiplicity of versions of the Beauty and Beast fairy tale complicates discussion of what the character of Belle (or Beauty) means to the modern American female, not only because the Disney Princess Belle is a

revamping of Linda Woolverton's Belle, but because Woolverton's Belle is a
reaction to Beauty in her many previous incarnations.[2] On the one hand,
the Beauty and the Beast story, at its most basic and as presented in many
permutations, would seem to be an unlikely feminist parable, for it is in
many ways about the limits of a woman's power in a male-dominated world.
A complicit father surrenders his daughter to an ugly beast, often sacrificing
her to atone for a crime that *he has committed* (such as stealing a rose from a
garden), and the daughter acquiesces, either out of a misplaced sense of guilt
(because the rose was for her) or because she does not want to be disobedient to her father. The heroine is horrified by her intended husband's bestial
appearance—which varies from being bear-like to serpentine—and the Beast
often does little to earn her trust and respect. In fact, sometimes his deeds
are as monstrous as his appearance, but the heroine is still supposed to fall
for him. Over time, Beauty learns to love the Beast despite his appearance,
and her affection for him ultimately transforms him into a handsome husband she might have chosen for herself, had she been granted the power to
choose a mate.

Many of the most traditional ways of interpreting the fairy tale would
not speak to the sensibilities of the modern female reader. For example, Bettelheim argues that the Beauty and the Beast story dramatizes the moment
when a woman of marriageable age has to learn to overcome her dread of
sex in time for her wedding night. The ghastly appearance of her husband
on the honeymoon symbolically represents that fear of sex, and the climactic transformation of the beast into a handsome prince demonstrates that
sex will ultimately prove beautiful and rewarding once the woman has lost
her virginity (283). Considering that the earliest versions of the story came
to prominence in civilizations in which women's choices in marriage were
limited at best and marriages were frequently arranged by parents, the tale's
historical significance may be that female readers were encouraged to follow
Beauty's example and make the best of an arranged marriage, usually to an
older man, as Marina Warner argues (278). However, the Beauty and the
Beast tale is unusual because it grants subjectivity and centrality to a female
protagonist who thinks, feels, and is capable of growth and change. After
all, western literature is replete with "othered" female figures who are represented stereotypically as either virgins or whores and who demonstrate little tendency toward intellectual growth or complexity of personality. In this
tale-type, it is the male who is the frightening "other" figure and the woman
who is the central character.

While not the most radical version of the story, Woolverton's *Beauty
and the Beast* was part of a 1990s corrective to the reactionary 1980s, the
Reagan-Bush years during which time the women's movement lost ground

in the realm of public opinion and public policy. Beginning in the early 1990s, Hillary Clinton heralded an era of Lilith Fair musicians and films such as *Thelma & Louise*, which returned strong, intelligent women to the screen after a decade of teen-sex comedies, slasher films, and Arnold Schwarzenegger action vehicles. In this uncharacteristically progressive Disney film, Woolverton's screenplay stresses Belle's depth of character from the outset by making her physical beauty less important than her intelligence and integrity, and her two most admirable traits, her love of reading and her love for her father. The Disney *Beauty and the Beast* does what it can to grant Beauty more freedom of choice than in previous versions, by having Beauty choose to live with Beast as an act of self-sacrifice when her father would prefer she flee from Beast. In most of the older versions of the tale the father hands the daughter over as ransom and she has no choice in the matter. Beast himself treats his captive with respect, even making a gift of his enormous library when he discovers how much of a bookworm she is.[3] Thus the modern Beast treats Belle with greater respect than previous beasts, making him a more worthy object of love.

However, as kind as Beast is in his heart, especially in contrast to Gaston, he still has much to learn when he first meets Belle. Her love, and noble example, transforms him during the course of the film, awakening a goodness he never knew he had. And so Beast learns how to control his anger, shoulders his responsibility to his subjects, and learns to be less self-absorbed. Because Woolverton places the onus on Beast, not just Belle, to grow, the message of the film cannot be simplified to "women need to learn to see past ugly appearances." Instead, the film is about the dangers of self-absorption, fear, and prejudice, all of which can be defeated through a love of learning, a desire to ask difficult questions and solve mysteries, and the power of a kind heart. While Beast is asked to change more here than in previous versions, he is also a less problematic figure from the outset than previous beasts, as he is neither a rapist nor a fool, as some earlier versions of Beast are. Belle does become less self-absorbed and bitter during the course of the film, but she does not have to change as much as Beast does, nor are her faults overly critiqued. For example, no fairy shows up at the end to lecture her about the proper role of a woman, as happens in Madame Gabrielle de Villeneuve's version of the story.

In fact, as much as the two lead characters grow, the film hints that the largest problems with their lives come from external evil and not internal flaws, for the society they live in is as oppressive as it is pretty. Woolverton's story acknowledges that the tiny French town Belle grew up in is male-dominated and stifling, and Belle is angrily aware of the limits of her "provincial life." To dramatize the societal constraints placed on Belle, evil patriarchal

traits that had once been associated with both Beast and Belle's father—a
fear of women's subjectivity, a desire to dominate and own powerful women—
is displaced onto the villainous Gaston, who is ugly on the inside and handsome on the outside and is therefore Beast's opposite.[4]

Gaston represents a dangerous sexuality (he is muscular and covered
with hair), and a threat to female agency with his repeated attempts to blackmail and coerce Belle into a marriage that, in an earlier version of the tale,
might have been forced upon her by her father. In light of Jeanne-Marie Leprince de Beaumont's 1756 version of the story, which was meant to reassure
young women entering into marriage with older men, and which shows
beastly men redeemed by the love of a virtuous woman, Gaston is an unre-
deemed double of the beast both because, as Warner observes, he is genuinely evil and because Belle does not love him (316–17). However, Gaston's
presence is vitally important to the film as both a brilliant satire of patriarchal evil and as a much-needed location for all the more sinister and imperial personality traits that Woolverton shaved off the film's two other central
male figures—Beast and Beauty's father.[5] Gaston is one of the most grandly
evil males in the story's history. In previous versions, the most blatantly evil
characters are nearly all female, such as Beauty's vain sisters in Beaumont's
version and the operatically evil Venus from Apuleius's *The Golden Ass*, and
Woolverton was wise to eliminate the presence of grand female evil from
her script. A few ugly women villagers and a trio of bubble-headed blonde
Gaston groupies are the limit of feminine baseness here.

Of course, while the climactic transformation of the beast into a handsome man was traditionally a moment of comfort for women worried that
they would not love the husbands they were forced to marry, by the twentieth century the transformation took on a different, more problematic over-
tone. Many viewers who, like Belle, have grown to love the Beast as he was,
express disappointment when he returns to human form at the end of
Woolverton's film. Apparently they feel that the transformation undermines
the message that it is important to accept and love people who look different. This was also a problem for viewers of the Jean Cocteau film *La Belle
et la bête* (1946). Actress Marlene Dietrich reportedly said, "Give me back
my beast," when she saw the beast turn human at the end of that film (Kael
58). The jarring, dissatisfied feeling some viewers experience at the end of
the Disney film may have inspired DreamWorks' spoof film *Shrek*. Made ten
years after *Beauty and the Beast*, *Shrek* has in some ways eclipsed the Disney
film in popularity.

Shrek is a groundbreaking computer-animated parody of the traditional
Disney animated film that consistently mocks Disney character–types and
themes, such as romance, royalty, and the mandatory musical number.[6] Its

satire is at its most effective when it portrays the main villain, the diminutive tyrant Farquaad, as a double for Disney head Michael Eisner and when it depicts Farquaad's "magic kingdom" as a deceptively clean-cut theme park for neo–Nazis. The Fascist imagery savages Disney's financial and creative dominion over the animated film industry, children's entertainment, merchandising, and even, to a degree, childhood itself. Because Disney's far-reaching influence is stifling and limiting on so many levels, the segments set in Farquaad's domain are particularly refreshing and amusing and do not, despite the Fascist imagery, seem "out-of-line" or overstated.

Of course, when a film sets out to target Disney and its respective projects, it makes sense that such a film would take aim at one of Disney's greatest successes. The anti-heroic title character (voiced by Mike Myers), is a green ogre who falls in love with the beautiful Princess Fiona, but worries that he is too ugly to attract her. For her part, Fiona is cursed to change every night, werewolf-style, from a human into a green ogre who looks like Shrek, so the match is not as farfetched as Shrek initially thinks it is. After several scenes of misrecognition, bickering, and comedic plot twists, *Shrek* concludes by turning the audience expectation of the end of the Beauty and the Beast tale on its head: instead of both Shrek and Fiona being "cured" of Ogrehood, the two are fixed permanently in ugly/cute green bodies and live happily ever after. In the age of multiculturalism and civil rights, the traditional endings of Beauty and the Beast tale seem racist: the unique-looking beast, who is often handsomely bestial, is expected to turn into a "handsome" white man who is bland in comparison to the charismatic beast. *Shrek* challenges this reading of the fairy tale very effectively, by refusing to end in the expected way. Fortunately, the sequels do not undo this ending, and both Shrek and Fiona remain their normal green selves as they fight the Gaston-like Prince Charming and team up with the silly and annoying Disney Princesses. It is particularly refreshing, in light of the petite-blonde-Lolita standard of female beauty that Britney Spears' debut revived in the mass media, to see a plump, green heroine like Fiona on screen as the hero's main love interest and looking nothing like Cameron Diaz, the blonde bombshell who voices her.

However, as progressive as the idea of the Fiona character is, the reality is that she is not as compelling a character as Belle from the Disney version. Shrek is the viewpoint character, and Fiona is kept largely in the background. Significantly, she does not share the title of the film with her true love, as Belle does in the Disney version. Indeed the *Shrek* films seem modeled on classic male buddy films (like the *Odd Couple* or *Butch Cassidy and the Sundance Kid*) in which the female love interest is a secondary concern and primary dramatic weight is granted to the friendship the hero has with his slightly annoying friend. In the *Shrek* films there are two annoying friends, Eddie Murphy's Donkey and Antonio Banderas' Puss-in-Boots. Fiona simply cannot compete with Donkey's one-liners or Puss-in-Boots' cuteness, and she is nowhere near as strong a feminist role model as other recent Beautys, despite her occasional moment in the sun, as when she leads a Princess rebellion against the villains at the end of *Shrek the Third*. Even minor background characters, like the hilarious Gingerbread Man, manage to steal Fiona's thunder. In contrast, Belle of Disney's *Beauty and the Beast* has much more dialogue and screen time, and she is not sidelined so that the film can explore the blossoming buddy relationship between Beast and, say, Lumiere the singing candlestick. Belle's actions directly shape the plot, and her thoughts and feelings are the chief concern of her film. She has a magnetic screen presence, even when she is sharing the stage with an enormous Beast and an array of singing dinnerware. Admittedly, Belle is not given a flashy pop song when she comes on screen as Fiona often is, and Fiona seems to know more kung fu than Belle does. Still, Belle doesn't need such rock fanfare or comic-book feminist traits like kickboxing skills to outshine Fiona. For all her girl-power trappings, Fiona is nowhere near as central to the *Shrek* story as she should be and often amounts to little more than a plot device, while Belle is at least the co-star, if not the star, of her story.

My problems with the first *Shrek* film aside, its sensibilities are decidedly more feminist than those represented by the Disney Princesses, but not more so than the Disney film *Beauty and the Beast*. Just as the 1980s saw a backlash against the feminism of the 1970s, the feminism of the 1990s took a back seat to patriotism and family values in the wake of the attacks of September 11, 2001. Liberal values in general and feminist and pacifist sensibilities in particular were seen as unpatriotic in light of these attacks, and American women were asked to be thankful that they were not living in Afghanistan and thus should not complain about the inequalities that remain in American society. Suddenly, feminism was out of season. Thanks to this more conservative worldview, and the perception that those in the Millennial Generation are more Republican than the members of Generation X who preceded them, the executives at Disney seem to have felt it was better to market a more passive, domestic American Belle to the women of the twenty-first century. While Woolverton's feminist Belle was profitable for Disney in the 1990s, in the early twenty-first century she represented a financial risk akin to the uppity, anti–Bush *Dixie Chicks*, so Disney mothballed her. She was translated into a new Belle, who looked like the old one but was reduced to a two-dimensional image adorning nightgowns and handheld mirrors, or a doll to be dressed up in a variety of regal gowns. That was how, and why, Disney destroyed its own feminist hero. So, while I initially resented the first *Shrek* film for what I perceived to be a mocking of Woolverton's excellent story, in the end, I find myself inclined to agree with its central satirical thesis: the executives at Disney Studios are evil capitalists who don't care what corrupting influence they have on the youth of America in their quest to make a profit.

Despite the influence of the Disney Princesses, the original film remains available for viewing on DVD. Woolverton's screenplay remains unique in the canon of Beauty and the Beast stories and Disney films in its efforts to be simultaneously a traditional heterosexual romance film while positing the feminist notion that the relationship between Beauty and the Beast is a partnership of equals. While different readers will, understandably, prefer different versions of the classic fairy tale (and most modern students are likely to prefer *Shrek* because its overtures to feminism are more obvious), any of these is more interesting and more rewarding to consider than the self-absorbed, gaping face of Belle that is emblazoned on Disney Princess merchandise in stores across the country. Any Beauty is preferable to her, and anything that parents, educators, or young women themselves can do to become familiar with the more substantial Beauty of books and films will be doing themselves a service.

Notes

1. Examples of this type include the earliest known version, the Cupid and Psyche myth from Apuleius's book *The Golden Ass* (c. 160), as well as "The Bear Prince" (1873), "East of the Sun, West of the Moon" (1888), "The Singing, Springing Lark" (1857), and "Zelinda and the Monster" (1885). These tales and a description of this tale-type can be found at the "Beauty and the Beast" page of the *SurLaLune Fairy Tales* website, surlalunefairytales.com.

2. Plot and character elements that appear unique to Disney's rendition of *Beauty and the Beast*—most notably the handsome beast Gaston, the singing candlestick Lumiere, the beautiful enchantress, and the bookworm Beauty—can be found in earlier versions by writers such as Apuleius, Madame Gabrielle de Villeneuve, Jeanne-Marie Leprince de Beaumont, Jean-Paul Bignon, Jacob and Willhelm Grimm, Jean Cocteau, and Angela Carter.

3. In addition, this gift of Beast's library places him in direct contrast with the handsome-but-evil Gaston. The first time we see Gaston and Belle together in the film, he pulls a fairytale book out of her hand and tosses it into the mud as he proclaims his love for her. He objects to women reading because he sees it leading to their thinking and getting ideas of their own when they should be busy cooking and bearing large, strapping male children like him.

4. Gaston has the distinction of being one of the few operatic Disney villains who does not undergo a hideous physical metamorphosis before he is killed. The witches from *Snow White*, *Sleeping Beauty*, and *The Little Mermaid* are transformed shortly before being dispatched by the knightly heroes—the first turns into a crone, the second into a dragon, and the third into a giant. Gaston's transformation is not physical and is therefore subtler, but he also becomes more demonic as the film progresses, and the loss of humanity he suffers justifies his death. As obnoxious as Gaston is from the film's outset, few viewers predict that the comic boor of the opening segment will finish the film snarling like an animal and cowardly stabbing Beast in the back with a dagger before falling to his death. Looking at Gaston's "beastliness" from a slightly different angle, he does not need to magically turn into a beast at the end because, as a male, he is already "beastly."

5. Had Gaston's character not been incorporated, the film might have been populated by far too many amiable and accessible male characters. After all, a certain degree of ominousness should surround "maleness" or masculine virility in order for any Beauty and the Beast tale to satisfy an audience dramatically.

6. Based on William Steig's children's book, *Shrek* was written by *Pirates of the Caribbean* scribes Ted Elliott and Terry Rossio (with an assist from five other screenwriters).

Works Cited

Aarne, Antti. *The Types of the Folktale: A Classification and Bibliography.* Trans. Stith Thompson. 2d rev. ed. FF Communications 184. Blomington: Indiana University Press, 1995.

Apuleius. *The Golden Ass.* Trans. P. G. Walsh. New York: Oxford University Press, 1994.

Beaumont, Jeanne-Marie Leprince de. "Beauty and the Beast." *Beauty and the Beast: And Other Classic French Fairy Tales.* Trans. Jack Zipes. New York: Signet, 1989.

Beauty and the Beast. Dir. Gary Trousdale and Kirk Wise. Walt Disney, 1991.

"Beauty and the Beast." *SurLaLune Fairy Tales.* Ed. Heidi Anne Heiner. 25 June 2007. 8 June 2009. <http://www.surlalunefairytales.com/beautybeast/index.html>.

Bettelheim, Bruno. *The Uses of Enchantment: The Meaning and Importance of Fairy Tales.* New York: Random House, 1975.

Carter, Angela. *The Bloody Chamber.* New York: Penguin, 1993.

Cocteau, Jean, dir. *La Belle et la bête.* DisCina, 1946.

Craven, Allison. "Beauty and the Belles: Discourses of Feminism and Femininity in Disneyland." *European Journal of Women's Studies* 9.2 (2002): 123–42.

Grimm, Wilhelm, and Jacob. *The Complete Fairy Tales of the Brothers Grimm.* Trans. and ed. Jack Zipes. 3rd ed. New York: Bantam, 1992.

Kael, Pauline. *5001 Nights at the Movies.* New York: Holt, 1991.

My Brilliant Career. Dir. Gillian Armstrong. Madman Entertainment, 1979.

Orenstein, Peggy. "What's Wrong with Cinderella?" *New York Times* 24 Dec. 2006. 8 June 2009. <http://www.nytimes.com/2006/12/24/magazine/24princess.t.html>

Pink. "Stupid Girls." *I'm Not Dead.* CD. La Face, 2006.

Shrek. Dir. Andrew Adamson and Vicky Jenson. Dreamworks Animation, 2001.

Shrek 2. Dir. Andrew Adamson, Kelly Asbury, and Conrad Vernon. Dreamworks Animation, 2004.

Shrek the Third. Dir. Chris Miller and Raman Hui. Dreamworks Animation, 2007.

Steig, William. *Shrek!* New York: Farrar, Straus, 1990.

Sumera, Lara. "The Mask of Beauty: Masquerade Theory and Disney's *Beauty and the Beast.*" *Quarterly Review of Film and Video* 26:1 (2009): 40–46.

Tatar, Maria. *Off with Their Heads! Fairy Tales and the Culture of Childhood.* Princeton: Princeton University Press, 1992.

Villaneuve, Madame Gabrielle de. "Beauty and the Beast." *Beauties, Beasts and Enchantments: Classic French Fairy Tales.* Trans. Jack Zipes. New York: New American Library, 1989.

Warner, Marina. *From the Beast to the Blonde: On Fairy Tales and Their Tellers.* New York: Noonday, 1994.

Woolverton, Linda, adapt. *Beauty and the Beast.* Dir. Gary Trousdale and Kirk Wise. Walt Disney, 1991.

14

Four Times Upon a Time: "Snow White" Retold

STELLA BOLAKI

"Snow White" is a story of an innocent girl "with skin as white as snow," "blood-red lips," and "hair as black as ebony," who is persecuted by her evil and jealous stepmother, finds refuge in the forest living with seven dwarfs, and is ultimately saved by a prince whom she marries in the end. The best-known version of this classic fairy tale was collected by two German professors in the nineteenth-century, the Grimm Brothers, and adapted by Walt Disney in a popular animated film in 1937. This brief plot has been embellished in many ways as is evident by the numerous oral and written versions of the story that have been collected in many countries. Because fairy tales do not belong to anyone, the genre is promiscuous and infinitely flexible; tales travel from place to place and are constantly revised by successive generations. In the case of "Snow White," while most versions recycle tropes like the evil stepmother's mirror and her poisonous apple, some versions do not distinguish between Snow White's real mother, who briefly appears at the beginning of the tale, and her stepmother. Others replace the dwarfs with robbers or woodsmen or vary the methods and number of times the stepmother tries to get rid of Snow White, as well as the ways in which the heroine comes back to life after she has eaten the poisoned apple. In Disney's version, for example, Snow White awakens with the prince's kiss, while in the Grimms' version she wakes when the apple is dislodged from her throat as the coffin in which she is being carried is accidentally jolted.

While change is already part of the fluid nature of fairy tales, I see the act of transformation as a more conscious and active choice. In the essays "The Laugh of the Medusa" and "Sorties," Hélène Cixous, a French feminist critic, examines the ways in which myths and fairy tales have been used to represent women. In "Sorties," written with Catherine Clément, Cixous uses the story of "Sleeping Beauty," which is similar to "Snow White," to call on women to wake up from the sleep to which they have been sent by men. She writes that in tales like these, "Beauties slept in the woods, waiting for princes to come and wake them up. In their beds, in their glass coffins, in their childhood forests like dead women. Beautiful but passive" (Cixous and Clément 66). One way to resist the limiting depictions of women in fairy tales is through the process of writing as revision. Adrienne Rich, an American feminist critic and writer, defines revision as "the act of looking back, of seeing with fresh eyes, of entering an old text from a new critical direction" (35). Starting from this definition, we can proceed to describe feminist transformation as an act of revision that aims to expose the dubious models for female socialization that have shaped women's expectations and to put forward new ones.

While adaptation usually entails a simpler attempt to make texts relevant or easily comprehensible to new audiences and readerships, in most cases by using different media such as the cinema (Disney's *Snow White and the Seven Dwarfs* works along these lines), feminist transformations reveal the cracks and fissures "in the old bottles" of fairy tales like "Snow White" by "putting new wine" into them, to use Angela Carter's phrase ("Notes" 69). The four transformations I discuss are Anne Sexton's narrative poem "Snow White" in *Transformations* (1971), Olga Broumas's "Snow White" in her collection of poems *Beginning with O* (1977), Angela Carter's story "The Snow Child" in *The Bloody Chamber and Other Stories* (1979), and Emma Donoghue's "The Tale of the Apple" in *Kissing the Witch: Old Tales in New Skins* (1997). These four transformations of "Snow White" expose and challenge artificial gender paradigms that serve to separate women and make them enemies of themselves and each other. They do this by "exploding" traditional "bottles" of the tale.

Views differ about whether traditional fairy tales, as part of children's literature, can and should be modified to remove violence to protect children. According to the psychoanalyst Bruno Bettelheim it is dangerous to tamper with the genre's emphasis on natural consequences for behavior because these simplifications may have negative repercussions on the normal maturation process of children, on whom fairy tales are influential. Two critics who have written extensively on fairy tales and who are strongly opposed to efforts to reduce tales to static formulas and universal archetypes are Jack Zipes and Marina Warner. They are both committed to understanding fairy tales within their historical context, since they believe that stories are the products of specific material conditions. Therefore, they expect fairy tales to be continually retold to reflect new social, cultural, and political contexts and values.

Because the feminist versions that I examine address adults rather than children, the question of their transformation may seem to be less problematic. Still, feminist transformation raises another issue, namely how politics can enter a genre like the fairy tale, which is "dedicated to the pleasure principle," in Angela Carter's words, without destroying its magic (*Virago* xii). After all, magic is necessary not only for children but for adults. Transformation, to recall Rich's idea of looking *back* to see *with fresh eyes*, entails a process of rearranging the known and the new. In Susan Sellers' view, the familiar ingredients of fairy tales operate as "compass points around which we can weave new and different stories" (30). This means that transformations of fairy tales do not lose their power to guide us in our choices, alleviate fears, or help us deal with psychological crises, as Bettelheim argues, but they suggest new directions and routes. The process of transformation defined in this way is not devoid of creativity or magic, and it can breathe new life into the genre. It can be compared to the activity of *voler* (with its double meaning of stealing and flying), which Cixous defines in "The Laugh of the Medusa" in the following way: "Women take after birds and robbers. They enter a room and take pleasure in jumbling the order of space, in disorienting it, in changing around the furniture, dislocating things and values" (Cixous 356–57). Warner and Carter mirror Cixous's metaphor in their references to "the blue chamber where stories lie waiting" (Warner 418) and the more gothic "Bloody Chamber" of Carter's short story title. These adjustments, however, are capable of leaving traces so that the landscape is permanently changed. Let us examine how these four writers transform the landscape of "Snow White" with their revisions.

***

> Suddenly one day the mirror replied,
> Queen, you are full fair, 'tis true,
> But Snow White is fairer than you.
> Until that moment Snow White
> had been no more important
> than a dust mouse under the bed.
> But now the queen saw brown spots on her hand
> and four whiskers over her lip
> so she condemned Snow White to be hacked to death.
> Bring me her heart, she said to the hunter,
> and I will salt it and eat it.
>
> —Anne Sexton, "Snow White" (4)

Anne Sexton's *Transformations* includes sixteen revisions of fairy tales by the Grimms and, being among the first modern attempts to rework classic tales, has set an example for revisions to come. As a whole, the collection retains the most familiar ingredients of the Grimm tales—in the case of "Snow White" the three attempts by the stepmother to kill Snow White, the presence of the dwarfs, and the dislodging of the apple—but Sexton updates them by rooting them in twentieth-century America, as becomes evident by her allusions to consumer culture and her peculiarly American language.

"Snow White," like all the tales in *Transformations*, begins with a prologue that seems to replace the conventional moral associated with fairy tales. In this case, the opening lines set the tone of the entire poem: "No matter what life you lead / the virgin is a lovely number" (3). The narrator, identified in the first story of the collection as "a middle-aged witch," whose project is to "transform the Brothers Grimm" (2), ironically comments upon virginity and the ways it determines the market value of women. Sexton describes Snow White as a "doll" "rolling her china-blue ... eyes open and shut" according to a preset script (3) and as a "dumb bunny" (7) who consistently falls into her stepmother's traps and depends on others for salvation. The poet's irony is pervasive. After her stepmother's second attempt to kill her, Snow White revives miraculously thanks to the timely arrival of the dwarfs. Sexton captures this moment of resuscitation with the following words: "[Snow White] was as full of life as soda pop" (6). Given the way Snow White is portrayed, the reader's empathetic identification with the heroine, which fairy tales usually elicit, is constantly being undermined. Snow White's maturation—contrary to Bettelheim, who interprets each of the heroine's rebirths in the classic tale as an attainment of "a higher stage of ... understanding" (214)—is rather an education in submissive femininity.

Under a patriarchal system, according to Sexton, every woman's fate is predetermined: "But, oh my friends, in the end / you will dance the fire dance in iron shoes" (4). Snow White is finally metamorphosed into the wicked queen (her stepmother), as the ending of the poem makes clear through the similarities it has with the opening: "Meanwhile Snow White held court, / rolling her china-blue doll eyes open and shut / and sometimes referring to her mirror / as women do" (8). This outcome seems to be consistent with feminist critics Sandra Gilbert and Susan Gubar's classic interpretation of "Snow White" in "The Queen's Looking Glass," according to which "the angel and the monster are twin images" of a single woman. In their view, the wicked stepmother represents a later stage of development, an inescapable fate for her innocent daughter (44).

Although Sexton cautions against the effects of passive femininity, her heroines do not gain any real insight into their plight. To borrow the title of the study by feminist critic Rachel DuPlessis, Sexton does not "write beyond the ending" of the traditional fairy tales. In accordance with her own description of her versions as "enlarged paper clips" (Sexton 2), she blows the tales up to "push [their] implications further and further" (Harries 127).

***

> Don't curse me, Mother, I couldn't bear
> The bath
> Of your bitter spittle.
> No salve
> no ointment in a doctor's tube, no brew
> in a witch's kettle, no lover's mouth, no friend
> or god could heal me
> if your heart
> turned in anathema, grew stone
> against me.
> —Olga Broumas, "Snow White" (71)

The collection of poems entitled *Beginning with O* by Olga Broumas, a Greek-American poet and a lesbian feminist, includes, among other poems, seven revisions of fairy tales in poetic form.[1] The poems as a whole are the product of what Broumas describes as a commitment to "a politics of transliteration" in her poem "Artemis" (24). Elizabeth Wanning Harries, who discusses *transliteration* and *reframing* as two important narrative strategies employed in old tales and recent fairy-tale revisions alike, argues that Broumas's poetic revisions are best categorized as transliterated, which she defines as the activity of zooming in on "apparently peripheral details, transforming them into new centers of meaning" (136). To Harries, Sexton's versions of fairy tales are examples of the second strategy, reframing, for she uses "an exterior frame" that allows her to narrate her stories from the satirical perspective of a middle-aged witch. Unlike Sexton's sardonic poetry, which draws on American consumer culture, Broumas's poetry is steeped in Greek myth and is characterized by lyrical qualities, such as musicality.

Other than the references to the apple and the mirror and of course its title, Broumas's "Snow White" bears little resemblance to the popular Grimms' tale or Disney film. The poem opens with three generations of women—Snow White's grandmother, Snow White's mother, and Snow White—sleeping peacefully while the father is off fighting a war:

> Three women
> on a marriage bed, two
> mothers and two daughters.
> All through the war we slept
> like this, grand-mother, mother, daughter [69].

This maternal lineage is shattered when the father returns home; his presence breaks the circle of "women loving women" as the following lines suggest: "A woman / who loves a woman / who loves a woman / who loves a man" (69). Nancy Walker is right to note that in Broumas's transformed fairy tales "men are not rescuers, but rather intruders" (60).

In the next stanza of the poem, Snow White, who has meanwhile married, following the "normal" socialization pattern for women in patriarchy, emerges from her trance only to discover that her husband is an "alien instrument ... for a music I couldn't dance" (70). She also learns that her mother's fatal apple is in fact a "gift." This gift brings a new knowledge to the heroine, one that allows Broumas to interrogate the inevitable heterosexual ending of the tale. This alteration in turn forces the reader, in Ellen Rose's words, to "consider the possibility that lesbianism is not deviant but a natural consequence of the undeniable fact that a woman's first love object, like a man's, is her mother" (221). In the end, mother and daughter become the "two halves" of a single apple (Broumas 70). There is no rivalry in this version, and the mirror, which has traditionally stood for female jealousy, becomes something else, as Snow White asks her mother to "receive" her with the following words: "I'm coming back / back to you / woman, flesh / of your woman's flesh, your fairest, most / faithful mirror (71). Unlike the ending of Sexton's version, in which Snow White perpetuates her mother's destructive fate by submitting to the patriarchal voice of the magic mirror, Broumas's heroine contemplates a mirror that reflects the mutual love between mother and daughter.

***

So the girl picks a rose; pricks her finger on the thorn; bleeds; screams; falls.

Weeping, the Count got off his horse, unfastened his breeches and thrust his virile member into the dead girl. The Countess reined in her stamping mare and watched him narrowly; he was soon finished.

Then the girl began to melt. Soon there was nothing left of her but a feather a bird might have dropped; a bloodstain, like the trace of a fox's kill on the snow; and the rose she had pulled off the bush. Now the Countess had all her clothes on again....

—Angela Carter, "The Snow Child" (92)

Angela Carter, an English novelist and journalist, includes a radical revision of the Snow White tale in *The Bloody Chamber,* a brief but unsettling version entitled "The Snow Child." The tale opens with a Count (the father in the traditional tale) going riding with his wife in a snowy landscape. Carter dispenses with common motifs such as the mirror, the apple, the dwarfs, and the prince, to focus on what is more important, namely the dependence of both the Countess and her stepdaughter on the Count. She draws on a German folk version of "Snow White" in which Snow White's birth is the direct outcome of the father's rather than the mother's desire, which is what most revisions choose to foreground. This desire is, however, articulated in more or less similar terms: just like the Queen in Grimms' version, the father asks for a girl "as white as snow, ... as red as blood" and as "black as that bird's feather" (91), and as soon as this is uttered, Snow White is miraculously created. The rest of the tale complicates this innocent wish for a daughter, however, with its explicit sexual violence and dark humor.

The Countess, who instantly hates Snow White, is portrayed in black furs and shining boots with scarlet heels, a description which immediately places her as Snow White's opposite (92). In reality, however, the two women are not as different as they may seem. Carter exposes the objectification of women under patriarchy in the figures of both the Snow Child and the Countess, both of whom are dependent on the Count. Snow White is created out of the Count's wish; a product of a male fantasy, she is cast as "the perfect woman," both pure and passionate, as the white and red colors suggest. This woman, however, cannot exist in reality, which is why she is portrayed melting back into her primary ingredients at the end of the tale. The Countess is also the product of the Count's desire, but she is aware that she can be replaced by a younger woman any time she stops being her husband's object of desire. This is why she immediately perceives the child as a threat. Carter makes this obvious when she shows the Count pitting "his women" against one another in the tale.

In what is consistent with the plot of the Grimm tale, but not with Disney's version, the Countess tries to get rid of the Snow Child three times. Her method, however, is very different: each time she drops one item from her outfit and asks the girl to bring it back to her, the Count intervenes, protecting the girl while promising his wife new clothes. Each time, the possessions of the Countess are magically transferred to the naked girl until roles are completely reversed and the naked girl stands fully dressed. It is clear, then, that the two women are interchangeable and that the Count has the final word over these transactions. The Count also has the final word over Snow White's destiny. At the end of Carter's version, Snow White dies after she pricks her finger on the thorn of a rose, and melts as soon as the Count rapes her in front of his wife.

The most important revision in Carter's version, which makes the tale explicitly sexual, is that the Count has sex with the dead child. In an interview Carter notes, "The tales in my volume *The Bloody Chamber* are part of the oral history of Europe, but what has happened is that these stories have gone into the bourgeois nursery and therefore lost their origins" (qtd. in Gamble 138). It was the Grimm Brothers who camouflaged explicit references to sex and violence and polished the crude language of some of the tales they collected because they found them inappropriate for children. They justified their editing work on the premise that they wanted their collection to serve as "a manual of manners" (Tatar 373).

For Carter, however, "the toning down of sexual situations and the reluctance to include 'indelicate' material ... helped to denaturize the fairy tale" (*Virago* xvii).

The practice of editing or removing such material goes against the main characteristics of the fairy-tale genre, namely its orality and fluidity; the project of "improving" the tales through standardization so that they can be acceptable to children or to a middle-class audience means that the many different voices and perspectives they represent become muted. This is not to suggest that in the original version of "Snow White" the Count had sex with the child, but it could explain why Carter chooses to make the sexual elements latent in fairy tales explicit in her own version.

However, as critics have suggested, using pornographic material has its own risks. What if the illicit material functions merely as an enticing device that prevents a critical response to the tale in that, not unlike magic in fairy tales, it does not seek to engage the reader on an intellectual level? Soman Chainani has read "The Snow Child" alongside *The Sadeian Woman*, Carter's bold response to the work of Marquis de Sade, which was published in the same year as *The Bloody Chamber*. Viewing it as an "erotic fable" (221), she argues that the pornographic material is just the surface of the story. Carter, like Sexton, provides points of reflection that allow the reader to see what is being concealed under fairy-tale and pornographic models alike, namely female complicity to patriarchy and passivity. Chainani's discussion of "The Snow Child" in terms of a surface plot and a subtext seems consistent with Carter's famous description of her revisionist project: "I am all for putting new wine in old bottles, especially if the pressure of the new wine makes the bottles explode" ("Notes" 69). Whether Carter manages to rewrite the tale so that it escapes the binary division of the innocent daughter and the jealous stepmother, which is the structure or the "bottle" within which "Snow White" traditionally operates, is open to debate. The use of pornographic elements sustains the predator-prey dichotomy, which Carter also examines in *The Sadeian Woman*. However, the fact that the Count has sex with the dead child in Carter's version is proof that both Countess and child are products of male desire; clearly the Count has not wished for a child but for a sexualized object to replace his older, and for that reason easily dispensable, wife.

***

As the story went, my mother sat one day beside an open window looking out over the snow, embroidering coronets on a dress for the christening of the child she carried.... Just then the needle drove itself into her finger, and three drops of blood stained the snow on the ebony window frame. My mother said to her maid, The daughter I carry will have hair as black as ebony, lips as red as blood, skin as white as snow. What will she have that will save her from my fate?
                    —Emma Donoghue, "The Tale of the Apple" (43)

Emma Donoghue's "The Tale of the Apple," a transformation of "Snow White" told through first person like Broumas's poem, allows the reader to penetrate the heroine's private world. Donoghue, an Irish-born writer who lives in Canada, does not make an effort to place the tales she rewrites in a new context by making them more contemporary, which is what both Sexton and Disney do, though in different ways. She retains both the simple language in which fairy tales are usually rendered and their unspecified settings, but the inner confessional narrative challenges the flat and distanced perspective of the Grimms' tale. The most striking innovation in Donoghue's collection is the use of a "receding series of frames" (Harries 130). Every tale in her book is connected to the next one as a character in one tale becomes the narrator of the following one, until we reach the final tale ("The Tale of the Kiss"), which is left to "the reader's mouth" as an invitation to develop it further (Donoghue 228).[2]

"The Tale of the Apple" opens with Snow White's real mother wishing for a daughter and with her subsequent death in childbirth, but it focuses on the relationship between Snow White and her stepmother. The daughter, unlike the versions by Sexton and Carter, is aware of the ways in which patriarchy conditions her life and articulates this realization with an unparalleled self-awareness: "I know now that I would have liked [my stepmother] if we could have met as girls ankle deep in a river. I could have loved her if, if, if" (45). As Cixous writes in "The Laugh of the Medusa," "Men have committed the greatest crime against women. Insidiously, violently, they have led them to hate women, to be their own enemies" (349). In Donoghue's tale, the king, like the Count in Carter's version, functions as an arbitrator; he plays the two women off against each other and plants the seeds of jealousy and competition: "Two such fair ladies, he remarked, have never been seen on one bed. But which of you is the fairest of them all?... Tell me, he asked, how am I to judge between two such beauties?" (46). As in Broumas's version, the King breaks the developing bond between the two women. He keeps his wife locked in her room and forbids her to go walking with his daughter. His wife is instructed not to "do anything except lie on her back and wait to find herself with child, the child who would be his longed-for son" (47).

Like Broumas, Donoghue subverts the ideology implicit in traditional versions of "Snow White" according to which mother and daughter will necessarily become rivals for the father's love, but unlike the former she does not resort to myth or draw explicitly on a lesbian mythology. What seems to fuel the two women's antagonism in her version, in particular after the King dies, is not the stepmother's anxiety that she is not as pretty as Snow White but her insecurity that she will lose the throne. In her chapters on stepmothers in *From the Beast to the Blonde*, Marina Warner demystifies the image of the "wicked stepmother" by restoring it to its historical and social context, in other words the patrilineal system of the nineteenth century (218–40). Throughout her study, Warner brings to the surface the ways in which some of the fundamental stereotypes of fairy tales, in particular the pathological hatred between stepmother and daughter, can be illuminated by examining the material circumstances of the time such as the laws of dowry, land tenure, feudal obedience, domestic hierarchies, and marital dispositions (xix). In "The Tale of the Apple," the Queen's insecurity is explained in the tale that follows, "The Tale of the Handkerchief," in which the stepmother reveals that she had been born to the maid of the queen and had herself been maid to the queen's daughter.

After Snow White leaves the castle and finds refuge with a gang of woodsmen, the stepmother tries to locate her, not in order to kill her, as in traditional versions, but because she has missed the things they used to do together. She is portrayed in a realistic way as a real woman with feelings rather than as an envious witch, which is how she is constructed in the Disney film. Lace, comb, and apple make their appearance, as in the Grimm version, but not as lethal weapons. What they evoke is radically different. When the stepmother tracks Snow White down for the first time and laces her corset, Snow White confesses, "I shut my eyes and it felt like old times" (52). The second time they meet, she lets her stepmother comb her hair while she pleads with Snow White: "I haven't had a night's sleep since you left; ... it feels like dancing in shoes of red-hot iron. Will you come home now?" (52–53). It is not only the Queen who feels this attachment. Her stepdaughter, too, admits that the image of her stepmother haunts her and that when she pictures the Queen's life, it seems "strangely familiar.... We were living the same kind of life" (51). On tasting the one side of the apple on the stepmother's third visit, she experiences mixed feelings: "fear and excitement locked in struggle in my throat ... I fell to the ground" (54). When she brings herself back to life, she discovers that the apple is not poisonous: "It was the first apple of the year from my father's orchard" (55).

Armed with this knowledge, Snow White decides at the end of the tale to return to her mother despite the woodsmen's strong objections.

> There was a good Queen who pricked her finger with a needle, watched blood fall on snow, gave birth to a girl-child named Snow White, and lived to raise her. And sometimes when this Queen looked into the mirror of her mind, she passed in her thoughts through the looking glass into a forest of stories so new that only she and her daughter could tell them.
> —Gilbert and Gubar, "The Further Adventures of Snow White" (403)

Feminist transformations of fairy tales, as the analysis of the four revisions of "Snow White" has shown, range from simple and extensive plot interventions, which reconfigure power relations and imagine alternative endings, to highly sophisticated versions, which employ complex narrative techniques that foreground the tales' own artificiality and fictionality. In *Postmodern Fairy Tales,* Cristina Bacchilega sees the latter as specifically "postmodern" tales. Postmodern literature often deconstructs master texts using techniques such as intertextuality and parody. Whether we call them "postmodern" or not, feminist revisions of fairy tales by contemporary writers succeed in cracking the "flat" mirror of patriarchy, which, in the words of Bacchilega, "conflates the natural with the ideological" (33). However different the four transformations examined here are in the plot elements they choose to foreground and the formal techniques they use, such as innovative framing and varied point of view, they all stress the need to explode the so-called natural assumptions of the traditional tale. In this way, they question "the immutability and invincibility" of any kind of "mirror" that perpetuates female rivalry and passivity (Bacchilega 38). Among the alternatives they put forward are the bond between mother and daughter, the need to question heterosexuality as the normal socialization pattern for women, and, ultimately, love as a generous gift.

Feminist revisionist projects affirm that there will always be another story to put up against the worn tales of the fathers of folklore, like the Grimms, and to challenge patriarchal values, but they should not be seen as denying the pleasure, wonders, and optimism of the fairy tale as a genre. Transformations of fairy tales, as I hope this analysis has demonstrated, "offer a way of putting questions, of testing the structure as well as guaranteeing [the genre's] safety" (Warner 411). They do that by investing common motifs with fresh meanings and by generating new stories on the basis of older ones.

If there are weaknesses in these four revisions of "Snow White" it is that they are not obviously concerned with envisaging alternatives that might satisfy the needs of different groups of women. In "The Further Adventures of Snow White," Gilbert and Gubar wander into a new "forest of stories" in order to address this issue. Their funny and ironic variations of "Snow White" are intended to capture the continuously shifting historical landscape around gender issues and the diversity of literary responses that such changes elicit. One of their versions, for instance, interrogates whiteness by having Snow White discover that she is Black (367). However, even transformations of fairy tales that change the race of a character or characters would disguise differences within Black communities and across varieties of geographical locations. This is why I find Bacchilega's call to rethink the intersection of gender issues with "local" ones a very useful tool for future rewriting of fairy tales, especially when taking into consideration "Disney's naturalized colonialism" (145–46).

Bacchilega refers to a musical, "Once Upon One Time," written by Lisa Matsumoto and directed by Tamara Hunt, which was produced at Kennedy Theatre in Honolulu in 1991. Giving her readers a chance to savor its language through a short extract, Bacchilega shows how the musical reflects "'local' experience" in both its language (Hawaiian Pidgin) and its themes, which relate to a specific community of young people growing up in Hawai'i (145–46). This is an example of exploiting the potency of fairy-tale discourse, in particular its fluidity and capacity for transformation, to make the genre more dynamic and more inclusive. There is room to plant more trees in the forest of stories. What are the further adventures of Snow White and of other fairy-tale protagonists going to be like? This is left to future generations of feminist readers and writers to imagine and shape.

Notes

1. In the epigraphs to her revisions of "Cinderella" and "Rapunzel," Broumas acknowledges her debt to Sexton.
2. The tales are linked by a question and answer, in italics, which is placed on a page of its own at the beginning of each story. "The Tale of the Apple" follows "The Tale of the Rose," which is the story of Beauty and the Beast. In this story, Beauty addresses the Beast (who is revealed to be a woman in disguise) with the following words:

> Another summer in the rose garden I asked,
> Who were you
> Before you chose a mask over a crown?
> And she said, Will I tell you my own story?
> It is a tale of an apple [39].

Works Cited

Bacchilega, Cristina. *Postmodern Fairy Tales: Gender and Narrative Strategies*. Philadelphia: University of Pennsylvania Press, 1997.

Bettelheim, Bruno. *The Uses of Enchantment: The Meaning and Importance of Fairy Tales*. Harmondsworth: Penguin, 1976.

Broumas, Olga. "Snow White." *Beginning with O*. New Haven and London: Yale University Press, 1977. 69–71.

Carter, Angela. "Notes from the Front Line." *On Gender and Writing*. Ed. Michelene Wandor. London: Pandora, 1983. 69–77.

_____. *The Sadeian Woman: And the Ideology of Pornography.* London: Virago, 1979.

_____. "The Snow Child." *The Bloody Chamber and Other Stories.* London: Vintage, 1979. 91–92.

_____, ed. *The Virago Book of Fairy Tales.* London: Virago, 1990.

Chainani, Soman. "Sadeian Tragedy: The Politics of Content Revision in Angela Carter's 'Snow Child.'" *Marvels & Tales* 17.2 (2003): 212–235.

Cixous, Hélène. "The Laugh of the Medusa." *Feminisms: An Anthology of Literary Theory and Criticism.* Ed. Robyn R. Warhol and Diane Price Herndl. Houndmills: Macmillan, 1997. 347–362.

_____, and Catherine Clément. "Sorties." *The Newly Born Woman.* Trans. Betsy Wing. Manchester: Manchester University Press, 1986. 63–132.

Donoghue, Emma. "The Tale of the Apple." *Kissing the Witch: Old Tales in New Skins.* London: Hamish Hamilton, 1997. 43–55.

DuPlessis, Rachel Blau. *Writing Beyond the Ending: Narrative Strategies of Twentieth-Century Women Writers.* Bloomington: Indiana University Press, 1985.

Gamble, Sarah. *Angela Carter: Writing from the Front Line.* Edinburgh: Edinburgh University Press, 1997.

Gilbert, Sandra M., and Susan Gubar. "The Queen's Looking Glass: Female Creativity, Male Images and the Metaphor of Literary Paternity." *The Madwoman in the Attic: The Woman Writer and the Nineteenth-Century Literary Imagination.* New Haven: Yale University Press, 1979. 3–44.

_____ and _____. "The Further Adventures of Snow White: Feminism, Modernism, and the Family Plot." *No Man's Land: The Place of the Woman Writer in the Twentieth Century, Volume 3, Letters from the Front.* New Haven: Yale University Press, 1994. 359–403.

Grimm, Wilhelm, and Jacob. "Snow White." *The Complete Fairy Tales of the Brothers Grimm.* Trans. and ed. Jack Zipes. Expanded ed. New York: Bantam, 1992. 196–204.

Harries, Elizabeth Wanning. *Twice Upon a Time: Women Writers and the History of the Fairy Tale.* Princeton: Princeton University Press, 2001.

Rich, Adrienne. *On Lies, Secrets, and Silence: Selected Prose 1966–1978.* New York: Norton, 1979.

Rose, Ellen Cronan. "Through the Looking Glass: When Women Tell Fairy Tales." *The Voyage In: Fictions of Female Development.* Ed. Elizabeth Abel, Marianne Hirsch, and Elizabeth Langland. Hanover: University Press of New England, 1983. 209–227.

Sellers, Susan. *Myth and Fairy Tale in Contemporary Women's Fiction.* Houndmills: Palgrave, 2001.

Sexton, Anne. "Snow White." *Transformations.* London: Palgrave, 2001. 3–8.

Snow White and the Seven Dwarfs. Dir. David Hand. Walt Disney Productions, 1937.

Tatar, Maria. "Sex and Violence: The Hard Core of Fairy Tales." *The Classic Fairy Tales: Texts, Criticism.* Ed. Tatar. New York: Norton, 1998. 364–373.

Walker, Nancy A. "Twice Upon One Time." *The Disobedient Writer: Women and Narrative Tradition.* Austin: University of Texas Press, 1995. 45–83.

Warner, Marina. *From the Beast to the Blonde: On Fairy Tales and Their Tellers.* London: Vintage, 1994.

Zipes, Jack. *Don't Bet on the Prince: Contemporary Feminist Fairy Tales in North America and England.* Aldrershot: Gower, 1986.

15

Mermaid Tales on Screen:
Splash, The Little Mermaid, and Aquamarine

CHRISTY WILLIAMS

Mermaids are powerful symbols of transformation. Part woman, part fish, they embody hybridity. But the mermaid also stands, as it were, as a symbol of female sexuality and desire—both as object of desire and as desire personified. In popular American culture, the mermaid has taken on the additional symbol of female rites of passage and pubescent change from girl to woman. As noted by Susan White, mermaid films in the late twentieth century revolve around "painful 'growth' experiences" that address the fears and experiences of growing up female (186). Tied to that are issues of sexuality and finding one's voice in a patriarchal society where daughters' voices are too easily dismissed. As scholars have noted, the best-known and most influential retelling of the mermaid tale, Disney's *The Little Mermaid* (1989), does not offer a solution to the difficulty of coming of age as a woman, for Disney's singing, wanting mermaid must first give up her voice to find her place.[1]

Disney's mermaid, Ariel, at first seems very much to want her father to listen to her—to hear her voice—but he can only seem to do so when what he hears does not threaten patriarchal order. When Ariel wants independence, he destroys her collection of human artifacts. When Ariel wants to marry a prince, he gives her legs, a sparkling blue dress, and a rainbow. He finally hears her voice once she has risked her life (not to mention her friends' and family's lives) for the love of a man. The film is problematic for a variety of reasons, as most essays on it demonstrate. The usual concern expressed, and one that I share, is the extent of the sacrifice Ariel must make to get her man.[2] Also worrying is the iconic power the film has as a part of the Disney marketing machine, for Ariel is very clearly sold as a role model to young girls (she is rebellious, after all, and doesn't wait around to be rescued by the prince—she rescues him from death at least twice). Despite her strength as a heroine compared to other Disney female leads, she embodies self-sacrifice as a necessary component of acceptable femininity. But what is also troubling for me is the extent to which Disney's film has eclipsed other mermaid stories. There is very little room for other mermaids when Ariel takes center stage, and she outshines the other mermaids who stand in her shadow. As such, alternatives to Disney's pseudofeminist mermaid are found wanting.

An obvious comparison is to the story that inspired Disney's film, Hans Christian Andersen's fairy tale "The Little Mermaid." Andersen's mermaid shares a desire similar to Ariel's, but her sacrifice is greater—she suffers painful and permanent bodily mutilation, and she dies for her desire. Other films have taken Andersen's story and updated it for contemporary audiences, also shifting the nature of the mermaid's desire and sacrifice. The films *Splash* (1984) and *Aquamarine* (2006) follow similar stories of a mermaid who comes to land looking for love and in doing so learns something about what it is to be a human woman. Andersen's story is the only one with an unhappy ending—all of the other mermaids find love—and he demands more of his mermaid than the films do. But in contrast to Andersen's and Disney's tellings, the mermaids of *Splash* and *Aquamarine* retain their voices on land; they express their desires, symbolically preserving the autonomy lost to the silent mermaids. All four texts center around transformation—physical, emotional, psychological, spiritual, and cultural—but do so to different ends. In transforming Andersen's story for late twentieth- and early twenty-first-century audiences, the three films address pertinent issues about how love and sacrifice are represented when tied to female bodies and how female gender is acquired and performed.

Andersen's fairy tale "The Little Mermaid," though not the first mermaid tale, is arguably the most well-known.[3] Andersen's mermaid leaves her ocean home for the human world in search of an immortal soul, which can be gained through the love of a human. She sacrifices her voice to do so, but fails to win the love of her prince and commits suicide. However, the mermaid's suffering, sacrifice, and good deeds grant her the chance of obtaining a soul. Andersen's story of sacrifice has been transformed by many writers and filmmakers into a story of true love. The spiritual aspects of the tale are usually replaced by romantic love and the goal is to find a soul mate, not a soul. Andersen's tale is steeped in self-sacrifice, and the underlying theme is that through suffering, one can achieve one's dream. Love is the nameless mermaid's means to an end: through the joining-by-marriage with a human the mermaid will be able to share her husband's immortal soul. Although hope is held out, as the mermaid has the possibility for a soul as a Daughter of the Air, it will take her approximately 300 years to obtain one, and she is likely to continue to suffer because her penance is extended by the naughtiness of children she tries to help. Andersen's story was published in 1837, so it will be 2137 before the mermaid can hope to have a soul. There is no mention of a soul in any of the transformations discussed here, and each movie abandons the religious overtones in favor of the desire for love. Both *Splash* and Disney's *The Little Mermaid* focus on the marriage plot found in Andersen's story. *Aquamarine*, however, focuses on the love between friends, despite the mermaid's preoccupation with "true love's first kiss."[4] Yet all keep Andersen's emphasis on self-sacrifice as the ultimate evidence of one's love for another, thus alluding to the Christian ideal of selflessness important to Andersen's story.

Splash, the earliest of the three films, presents an independent mermaid who seeks out her own prince rather than waiting for him to rescue her. Madison, the heroine of the film, is the initial rescuer. She is a child when she meets Allen, who has jumped overboard at Cape Cod, and apparently she falls in love at first sight. As an adult, she rescues him from drowning at Cape Cod and comes to land to be with him after finding his wallet. If she does not return at the next full moon, in six days, she will remain human.[5] Except for the identity of the mermaid, the action of the story is reversed from Andersen's, with the mermaid's quest transferred to the prince. The gender reversal is a common way of retelling classic fairy tales. In this reversal, however, the genders of the main characters remain intact, while the plot movements associated with the characters are switched. This variation removes the emphasis on self-sacrifice as a model for women, though Madison is relegated to the role of victim by the end of the film so that Allen can become her rescuer. However, as with the other two films, the severity and significance of the protagonist's sacrifice is drastically different from Andersen's.

Allen, not Madison, is the protagonist of this mermaid tale, as it is the story of his development. Allen is having personal problems—he is the responsible brother and lacks the fun his older brother Freddie finds in life. Allen does not take risks, and much of the film depicts him learning to let go of his fears and becoming who he wants to be. Allen, despite being shown as the responsible one, must grow up and learn to make a commitment. His commitment is dramatic, for in the end he joins Madison, sacrificing his normal, respectable life on land for love under the sea. Madison, however, risks all for love in coming to land to be with Allen, for she is captured and becomes the test subject of scientists who see her as a fish, not a woman with rights and feelings. After Madison is captured, Allen rejects her as a "fish," but soon comes to his senses and realizes that he loves her, instigating his acts of risk-taking and commitment.[6] Both characters choose to give up their families and the way of life they have always known. Madison, however, is threatened with violence and humiliated, but she does not choose this as Andersen's mermaid does, and so it is not a "sacrifice." As in the Disney film, sacrifice does not equal physical pain or suffering for the protagonist of *Splash*. Instead, Allen sacrifices comfort and stability. Allen loses his brother when he joins Madison in the sea, but he also loses the responsibility of running the company, friends he has no connection with, and his fear of drowning and risk-taking. Freddie helps to engineer Allen's leap into the sea and supports the familial separation. With Freddie's encouragement, Allen's choice does not amount to much of a sacrifice.

Released five years after *Splash*, *The Little Mermaid* is seemingly the most straightforward of the three films. Ariel, Disney's mermaid, wants to leave her father's underwater kingdom to make a name for herself in the human world, about which she shows a clear obsession and very little accurate knowledge. But she abandons that desire upon falling in love with a handsome human man, Prince Eric, whom she saves from drowning. Once she falls in love with Eric, she seeks out the sea witch, Ursula, and makes a bargain—her voice for legs. She has three days to make the prince fall in love and kiss her or she loses everything. After a crash course in dating from Ursula and Sebastian, a crab who is her appointed protector, Ariel seems to be successful. At this point, Ursula intervenes and steals Eric for herself. In the subplot of the film, Ursula uses Ariel's desire to usurp King Triton as ruler of the sea. Ursula of course fails and is killed, and Ariel regains her voice and marries her prince. The sacrifice of Andersen's mermaid is replaced by risk-taking that has no dire consequences. Ariel regains her voice, marries her prince, and reunites with her family.

Ariel has been both praised for her feisty defiance of her father and lamented for her obsession with a cute boy and unwavering ability to acquiesce to his desires. Unlike previous Disney princesses such as Snow White who waits for her prince to come, Ariel goes out and gets her prince. Laura Sells, arguing for feminist glimmers in the film, points to Ariel's success as contrasted to Andersen's mermaid. Ariel has both her man *and* her voice by the end of the film, suggesting that she has moved beyond the attractive object she is throughout most of the film (185). In contrast, Deborah Ross argues that "[w]hatever Ariel might *say*, or sing, what we see her *do* is flee a world of infinite possibility to settle in the land of the banal. Her fantasy is a sort of anti-fantasy. Yes, she gets her legs, she makes her stand, she marches—but only down the aisle, to marry some guy named Eric" (60). Though more active than the earlier Disney fairy-tale heroines, Ariel is still defined by her relationship to men. She leaves her father's home for her husband's, and she abandons her own quest for self-discovery when an attractive man enters the picture. The film presents a model where physical beauty is more important than self-expression; a woman's value is based on how she is perceived by men, with beauty as the maker of great value; and the appropriate role for women is being submissive to a man, first one's father, then one's husband. The marriage plot, in addition to Ariel's virgin/whore contrast to Ursula, the only other significant female in the movie, is the strongest means of crushing Ariel's early show of independence and self-concern.

Aquamarine, based on an Alice Hoffman novel of the same name, appears to diverge the furthest from Andersen's plot, but its critique of popular conceptions of romantic love parallels Andersen's story in ways that the earlier mermaid films do not. The film focuses on the two girls who befriend the mermaid, Aquamarine. In this version, the mermaid comes to land to prove to her father that love exists as part of a pact made to enable her to escape an arranged marriage. Unlike her predecessors who seek marriage, Aquamarine is trying to escape it, which sends a very different message to its young female audience than does Disney's film. This mermaid does not sacrifice anything, but must make the "hot" lifeguard Raymond fall in love with her in three days to prove that love exists, the same time frame Disney's mermaid has to complete the same task. The sacrifice is made by the two girls, Hailey and Claire, who befriend her. Claire, like Allen, must overcome her fear of the water specifically and life more generally to help her friend. More importantly, the girls must decide to forgo making a wish (granted by Aquamarine as a reward for helping her) to prevent Hailey and her mother from moving to Australia. Both girls learn to put aside their selfish desires and their fears—of the water and risk for Claire and of the move for Hailey—in order to help someone they love, Aquamarine and Hailey's mom. The love that Aquamarine seeks resides not in the romantic relationship she develops with Raymond, but the friendship she finds with the girls. While Claire, Hailey, and Allen must learn to put their own desires aside to help someone they love, Ariel learns no such lesson, as her desire is the very hallmark of the film.

This latest transformation of "The Little Mermaid" shows a shift in how love and sacrifice are perceived. When Aquamarine first meets Raymond, she asks him if he loves her, and he replies, "No, but I think you're hot," which contradicts the earlier "true love" model presented by *Splash* and *The Little Mermaid*. At the end of the film, Aquamarine repeats her question and Raymond stutters: "Well, I mean, we've had one date. Don't get me wrong. I like you." He is not able to fall in love with Aquamarine after knowing her for only three days. This version harkens back to Andersen's tale, in which love is not achieved in an instant, and the repetition of the kiss-in-three-days task offers a direct comment on the Disney formulation of love. As Roberta Trites points out, turning "the process of human love into a rushed affair" has the effect of equating love with "physical sexuality." Whereas Ursula tells "Ariel the prince must 'fall in love with you—that is—kiss you'" (Trites), *Aquamarine* challenges that assertion by demonstrating that sexual attraction is not love. If all it took was sexual attraction, then Aquamarine would have no problem, but this film suggests that true love is far more complex. Unlike Andersen's story, in which divine intervention is necessary to keep the absence of romantic love from being fatal, in *Aquamarine* the idea of love is expanded to include nonromantic relationships between friends and among family. Sacrifice is still a part of this love, but it's a matter of sacrificing selfish desires, not one's self. Whether this suggests a change in American audiences' ideals of love or a change in how audiences *should* see love, this is a noteworthy divergence from previous mermaid transformations.[7] It broadens the story and opens readings of Andersen's story from romantic love to platonic love.

There is no evidence in Andersen's story that the prince feels sexual or romantic attraction for the mermaid. She is depicted as his pet, sleeping on a cushion outside his door; as his companion, dressed in boy's clothing so she can follow him wherever he goes; and as his child, someone he must care for (Andersen 228). Sheldon Cashdan explains that "[t]he prince's emotional response to the Little Mermaid is more like that of a brother for a sister than that of a lover.... His love is more platonic than sexual" (168). She is the one who has romantic feelings, but even then, they are not sexualized or very adult, despite the obvious sexual interpretation of the mermaid needing her fins parted to make a man love her. She is in love with the prospect of gaining a soul, not the prince (Andersen 224). Part of the "sad" ending of Andersen's version, that there is no such thing as love at first sight, is contradicted by the ending of *Aquamarine*. The result is the same—the prince does not love the mermaid because he has not had the opportunity to fall in love with her—but it is not sad for Aquamarine and certainly not fatal. The girls who befriend Aquamarine know her much better than Raymond does and do love her, as evidenced by the lengths they go to help her. It is not the kiss but the female bonding and friendship that save Aquamarine. Much like the sisters in Andersen's story, who demonstrate sisterly love by trading their hair for a way to save the little mermaid, sacrifices and risks are taken by family and same-gender friends, not romantic conquests. As Trites has pointed out, the Disney film "destroys" the strong female characters and female-female relationships in its emphasis on the marriage plot.

Gender alliance is strong in all of the versions except Disney's. Even in *Splash*, male-male relationships form the support system for the protagonist: Freddie takes risks for his brother, as does Walter Kornbluth once he sees the result of his previous selfish actions (he is the scientist who reveals Madison's identity as a mermaid to the world). But Ariel is without a female connection in her world. Her sisters barely factor in the tale, and her friends, Flounder the fish, Sebastian the crab, and Scuttle the seagull, are all male. She has no mother or grandmother to turn to. Her only female companion is Ursula the sea witch, who is deliciously evil. Ursula exudes sexuality, as pointed out by both Cashdan and Marina Warner. Warner notably describes Ursula as "what the English poet Ted Hughes might call 'a uterus on the loose'" (403). She is sex personified and represents a very powerful woman who will do anything to get what she wants. This, in all honesty, makes her very much like Ariel. The difference between the two women is that Ariel's desire for marriage is validated by her society and Ursula's desire for power is not. Both go to extreme lengths to get what they want, but only Ariel's actions, which do not threaten the patriarchal order of either her father's or Eric's kingdom— or that of Disney and the United States—is allowed to succeed.

Laura Sells argues that Ursula's danger comes from her gender performance (182). Gender performance is a theory made popular by Judith Butler in *Gender Trouble*, who argues that gender norms are constructed by society. Ursula, who was based on the famous drag queen Divine, teaches Ariel to perform woman (Sells 182). The performance does not require language, so Ariel will not need her voice, and Ursula robustly sings about the use of body language. While this scene demonstrates that femininity is about appearance, its campy drag nature highlights the reality that femininity is an act, not an innate trait that comes with having female genitalia. Kerry Mallan and Roderick McGillis explain that "while she demonstrates for Ariel the ways to use her feminine charms to lure men, [Ursula's] camp drag performance highlights the fraudulence of her purportedly natural feminine talents" (14–15). Performativity is the repetition of "words, acts, gestures, and desire" deemed feminine or masculine and recognized as feminine or masculine, and the means by which gender is constructed (Butler, *Gender Trouble* 173). It is not, however, a "single or deliberate 'act'"—a performance like that of an actor assuming a role, which describes what is happening in the scene where Ursula teaches Ariel to perform woman (Butler, *Bodies* 2). But drag performance, which this scene parodies, is particularly useful in demonstrating that gender is constructed because "[*i*]*n imitating gender, drag implicitly reveals the imitative structure of gender itself*" (Butler, *Gender Trouble* 175). In a drag performance, the disconnection between the male body of the performer and the feminine persona shows that femininity can be put on, and therefore taken off.

For Sells, this gender performance is where Disney's film makes a feminist claim: Ursula "destabilizes gender," thus revealing it to be a construct (181). This is certainly a subversive position for a Disney film to take, and it draws on the transformative appeal of the fairy tale. For Ariel, a successful performance means marriage and the ability to move up in the world (though a princess under the sea, she sees the human world as better). But unlike Sells, I see this gender performance safely contained by the marriage plot. Ursula, after all, pays dearly for her challenge to patriarchal authority in the form of King Triton. She does teach Ariel to perform woman, but Ariel does not do anything with that knowledge other than get married. She does not even get to be the one who kills Ursula; that privilege belongs to Eric. Gender acquisition is a key part of the mermaid's transitions to land in *Splash* and *Aquamarine* as well. After all, to win a human mate, they too must learn to be human women. But without the drag element, the equivalent scenes are rendered as less dangerous and therefore do not require the spectacular squashing that Ursula does. Like Ariel's performance, Madison's and Aquamarine's is safely contained by heterosexual romance. But unlike Ariel's lessons, Madison's and Aquamarine's are less-conscious performances of femininity, making them much closer to what Butler describes. The gender performance in Disney is certainly direct, but that makes it more easily contained. Because gender acquisition, and the implication that gender is constructed, is more normalized in both *Splash* and *Aquamarine*, the performativity carries a more subversive edge.

Madison, in *Splash*, similarly learns to perform her gender through the acquisition of popular culture via Bloomingdale's and television—the mermaid is created by the world she wishes to inhabit. She is made to fit in not by her sacrifices of fins and voice, but by her ability to adapt and assimilate the culture presented to her. When leaving Allen's apartment, dressed in his suit and speaking only one word—Bloomingdale's—Madison, while a sexual being, is not yet a "woman"; she is without gender. Much like Andersen's mermaid, she dons the trappings of the most convenient gender. Andersen's mermaid is dressed in girls' clothes when the prince wants a dancing partner and boys' clothes when the prince wants a companion for horseback riding (Andersen 227–28). Madison learns to perform her gender at Bloomingdale's with the aid of a saleswoman, a credit card, and television.

Consumerism teaches Madison what it is to be a woman, and this demonstrates a fear that many critics, whether feminist or not, have of Disney movies and fairy tales specifically, and popular culture more generally. Gender is taught in *Aquamarine* through teen magazines, *Cosmogirl* and *Seventeen*, and trips to the mall. Hailey and Claire are still girls, not yet women, as is evident from their clothing. They do not dress like sexualized women, but wear one-piece bathing suits and cover-ups. They do not wear makeup or carry purses or any of the other adornments of women adopted by the villains of *Aquamarine*, the popular girls who are ultimately jealous of Aquamarine's seemingly natural and breezy beauty and confidence. Aquamarine gives the girls the confidence that they cannot find in the fashion magazines and competitive woman-against-woman culture the magazines and their schoolmates endorse. The gendered bonding, not the competition taught by Ursula, Bloomingdale's, and *Cosmogirl*, supports the characters' transformations. But the competitive and beauty-centered lessons are not unique to contemporary film. In Andersen's tale, the grandmother, the Dowager Queen of the merpeople, tells the mermaid that "one can't have beauty for nothing" and dresses the mermaid like her sisters and the adult mermaids—with lilies in her hair and oyster shells painfully attached to her tail (220). The grandmother is also teaching the mermaid what it means to be a woman— her beauty is gained through pain.

In Disney's *The Little Mermaid* the subversive gender performance suggested by Ursula is undercut by the film's adherence to traditional values that beauty and femininity are of utmost importance and that a girl's only desire should be to get married. But in *Aquamarine* these same values are questioned. The lessons learned about femininity are rendered ridiculous on screen as they are shown to be ineffective and part of a phase. Claire and Hailey are playing at being women, as evidenced by their frequent giggling. The villains are the girls who are successful in donning traditional femininity. This rejection of femininity based on conventional beauty for the sake of obtaining a man suggests an alternative to Ariel, and even Madison. Madison has won her prince before learning to become a woman, but she still becomes a conventional beauty for the sake of fitting in. Aquamarine does the same, but Claire and Hailey do not.

Disney's *The Little Mermaid* is the most popular of the three films discussed here and, as stated earlier, has supplanted Andersen's tale in popular culture as *the* mermaid story. Indeed, the Disney Corporation's aggressive marketing of its animated film through product tie-ins ensures market saturation of Disney's vision of "The Little Mermaid." From dolls and remote control cars to dishes and linens, Disney provides constant reminders that Ariel, not Andersen's nameless heroine, is *the* little mermaid. Twenty years after Ariel first sang of her desires to become part of the human world of "stuff" and to be "the girl who has ev'rything," she has clearly become part of our world of commercialism and has her own line in Disney's popular Princess collection.[8]

When I have read Andersen's tale with my students, most expect Ariel to marry Prince Eric and are shocked when the mermaid dies in the end. They also tend to prefer Disney's film, as they find Andersen's "sad." Andersen's mermaid, when faced with a prince who is about to marry someone else, is given the chance to regain her fins by plunging a dagger into the prince's heart. She falters and throws herself overboard, apparently committing suicide rather than hurting the one she loves. The wedding of Ariel to Prince Eric presented in Disney's film, complete with beautiful rainbow, is clearly the cheerier event. Even Andersen's insistence on divine intervention in the form of the mermaid becoming one of the Daughters of the Air as a reward for her sacrifice does not triumph over the unsatisfactory situation of a girl who gives up her home, family, friends, autonomy, voice, tongue, fins, pain-free existence, and ultimately her life, only to fail.

But what is the use in deeming Andersen's tale superior to Disney's, as is the common conclusion among critics? That judgment does not help us to understand any of the versions better or explain why these particular motifs are popular. These three films are not just versions of "The Little Mermaid" updated for new audiences; they are transformations that use "The Little Mermaid" story to engage popular culture. Each film, particularly *Splash* and *Aquamarine*, clearly recognizes the importance of popular culture in forming female identities and governing how we view love. The sage flirting advice given by the teen magazines in *Aquamarine*, such as the "fluff and retreat" strategy (fluff his ego then retreat), mimics the advice given by Ursula in *The Little Mermaid*: "It's she who holds her tongue who gets her man." Each tale offers ideals of what true love is, whether it is love at first sight or friendship, and demonstrates that sacrifice is intertwined with love. For Andersen, sacrifice of one's total self—identity, body, and life—is the ultimate act of love, both for the prince and the God alluded to by the promise of an immortal soul. Sacrifice is not nearly as drastic in any of the films—no one dies for the one they love; however, putting the needs of another before one's own selfish desires is a theme of each film.

Ultimately, these films are transformations of multiple texts, not just Andersen's. The later films refer to the earlier ones and Hollywood conventions, and they engage a variety of cultural conversations about gender. They go back to Andersen for various plot points, themes, and motifs, but they are stand-alone texts first. *Splash*, Disney's *The Little Mermaid*, and *Aquamarine* create new stories that promote happy endings, the value of strength and confidence, the need to think of others, and the importance of friendship.

They also critique the popular culture of which they are a part and engage feminist discussions of gender acquisition and performance, taking a stand on what it means to be an American woman. Comparing the stories and noting how they differ offers a rich view of how the crucial elements of love and sacrifice are represented. The comparison also demonstrates a cultural shift in how these concepts are tied to gender. Together these four texts open each other up to a more complex reading than does comparing any one of the three films to Andersen's alone.

Notes

1. Susan White, Laura Sells, Deborah Ross, and Marina Warner, among others, have addressed the issue of voice and sacrifice in mermaid retellings.
2. White in particular addresses post-colonial as well as feminist concerns in her essay "Split Skins: Female Agency and Bodily Mutilation in *The Little Mermaid*."
3. Andersen's tale is not based on a specific folktale. Unlike "Cinderella," "Snow White," and other fairy tales well-known to contemporary American audiences, there is no specific folkloric predecessor, but Andersen's fairy tale draws on mermaid lore. Marina Warner identifies "varied strands of oral and written tales in Eastern as well as Western tradition, about undines and selkies, nixies, Loreleis and Mélusines" as sources from which Andersen could have drawn (396). Plot elements of "The Little Mermaid" can also be found in previous mermaid tales, like *Undine*, a novella published in 1811 and based in German folklore (Zipes 107). In this tale, a water sprite falls in love with a human knight, but can only marry him if she has a soul. After her sacrifice to gain a soul, she marries the knight but is betrayed by him. The basic plot elements of a water creature wanting to have a soul and to marry a human are not original to Andersen, but as Zipes has explained, "Andersen transformed the tale into a Christian miracle narrative that was intended to celebrate the power of Christian salvation" (107).
4. The quotation here is from Disney's *Sleeping Beauty*, not *Aquamarine*, but it is an apt description of what Aquamarine is searching for. She needs to prove that love exists and expects to find that proof in a kiss.
5. In "Making a *Splash*," a documentary on the DVD, Ron Howard describes a deleted scene that shows Madison making a deal with a sea witch to transform herself, which is a direct reference to Andersen's plot, even if Howard and producer Brain Grazer do not say so.
6. White provides a Freudian reading that equates Allen's revulsion at the mermaid body to his rejection of "aggressive" female sexuality (186).
7. The two-decade span between the 1980s films (*Splash* and *The Little Mermaid*) and *Aquamarine* saw a number of feminist interventions in popular American culture. Not the least of these is that the model 1980s heroine—powerful, sexy, and a slave to consumerism, typified by Madison and Ariel—has been replaced by a variety of strong female types, thanks in part to the 1990s popularization of "girl power" and third-wave feminism. The number of feminist issues addressed in the popular media exploded in the late eighties and nineties (for example, in television shows like *Designing Women* and *Murphy Brown* and in the music of artists like Cyndi Lauper and Queen Latifah) and complicated the career woman-or-housewife, sexpot-or-saint dichotomies that informed 1980s films like *Splash* and *The Little Mermaid*.
8. A. Waller Hastings attributes the success of Disney's *The Little Mermaid* to the aggressive marketing of the film's product tie-ins and the "more conventional happy ending than Andersen's original" (89).

Works Cited

Andersen, Hans Christian. "The Little Mermaid." 1837. Trans. R. P. Keigwin. *The Classic Fairy Tales*. Ed. Maria Tatar. Norton Critical Edition. New York: Norton, 1999. 216–32.
Aquamarine. Dir. Elizabeth Allen. Perf. Emma Roberts, Joanna "JoJo" Levesque, Sara Paxton, and Jake McDorman. Twentieth Century–Fox, 2006.
Butler, Judith. *Bodies That Matter: On the Discursive Limits of "Sex."* New York: Routledge, 1993.
_____. *Gender Trouble: Feminism and the Subversion of Identity*. New York: Routledge, 1999.
Cashdan, Sheldon. *The Witch Must Die: The Hidden Meaning of Fairy Tales*. New York: Basic, 1999.
Hasting, A. Waller. "Moral Simplification in Disney's *The Little Mermaid*." *The Lion and The Unicorn* 12.1 (1993): 83–92.
The Little Mermaid. Dir. Ron Clements and John Musker. Perf. Jodi Benson, Samuel E. Wright, Pat Carroll, and Christopher Daniel Barnes. Walt Disney, 1989.
"Making a Splash." *Splash: 20th Anniversary Edition*. DVD. Touchstone, 1984.
Mallan, Kerry, and Roderick McGillis. "Between a Frock and a Hard Place: Camp Aesthetics and Children's Culture." *Canadian Review of American Studies* 35.1 (2005): 1–19.
Ross, Deborah. "Escape from Wonderland: Disney and the Female Imagination." *Marvels & Tales* 18.1 (2004): 53–66.
Sells, Laura. "'Where Do the Mermaids Stand?': Voice and Body in *The Little Mermaid*." *From Mouse to Mermaid: The Politics of Film, Gender, and Culture*. Ed. Elizabeth Bell, Lynda Haas, and Laura Sells. Bloomington: Indiana University Press, 1995. 175–192.
Sleeping Beauty. Dir. Clyde Geronimi. Perf. Mary Costa, Bill Shirley, and Eleanor Audley. Walt Disney, 1959.
Splash. Dir. Ron Howard. Perf. Tom Hanks, Daryl Hannah, Eugene Levy, and John Candy. Touchstone, 1984.
Trites, Roberta. "Disney's Sub/Version of Andersen's *The Little Mermaid*." *Journal of Popular Film & Television* 18.4 (1991): 145+. *Communication & Mass Media Complete*. EBSCO. 4 June 2009.
Warner, Marina. *From the Beast to the Blonde: On Fairy Tales and Their Tellers*. New York: Farrar, Straus and Giroux, 1994.
White, Susan. "Split Skins: Female Agency and Bodily Mutilation in *The Little Mermaid*." *Film Theory Goes to the Movies*. Ed. Jim Collins, Hilary Radner, and Ava Preacher Collins. New York: Routledge, 1993. 182–95.
Zipes, Jack. *Hans Christian Andersen: The Misunderstood Storyteller*. New York: Routledge, 2005.

About the Contributors

Antje S. Anderson is chair of the English Department at Hastings College in Nebraska. Her research interests include the British novel, particularly the Victorian novel, and she is working on the cross-currents between nineteenth-century British and German novels, including the reception of Dickens in Germany and the influence of German fiction on George Eliot. Her interest in film adaptations (and transformations) began when she discovered them as a superb teaching tool.

Stella Bolaki holds a Ph.D. from the University of Edinburgh, where she teaches courses in English and American literature. Her research interests lie mainly in the field of contemporary American literature, with a focus on multiethnic fiction and feminist theory. Essays have appeared or are forthcoming on topics as diverse as cultural translation, queer diasporas, and narratives of community, trauma, and disability in the work of Jamaica Kincaid, Sandra Cisneros, Maxine Hong Kingston, and Audre Lorde.

Alissa Burger is a recent graduate of the American Culture Studies program at Bowling Green State University. Her scholarship focuses on film, literature, gender studies, and innovative transformations, such as those achieved by the multiple versions of the Wizard of Oz narrative. Alissa's research interests also include critical film theory; representations of gender, power, and magic; and the role of music in popular culture.

Marc DiPaolo, a lecturer in English and film at Oklahoma City University, is a specialist in British literature and film. He is the author of *Emma Adapted: Jane Austen's Heroine from Book to Film* and co-editor of the literature anthology *The Conscious Reader*. DiPaolo has contributed chapters to the books *A Century of the Marx Brothers* and *The Amazing Transforming Superhero!*, and he writes the autobiographical blog "The Adventures of Italian-American Man" for I-Italy.

Lan Dong is an assistant professor of English at the University of Illinois at Springfield. She holds a Ph.D. in comparative literature and is the author of *Reading Amy Tan* (Greenwood) and several journal articles and book chapters on Asian American literature and film, children's literature, and popular culture. She is completing a book manuscript on Mulan.

207

Phyllis Frus is chair of the Department of English at Hawai'i Pacific University. She is the author of *The Politics and Poetics of Journalistic Narrative* (Cambridge University Press). Her most recent article, in the *Journal of Popular Film and Television*, uses intertextuality to read two biopics of Truman Capote. She is working on a guide to the many genres of "reality" film, tentatively titled "True Stories on Screen: A Viewer's Guide to Fact-Based Film."

Marni Gauthier, an associate professor of English at SUNY Cortland, specializes in contemporary American literature and film. Her work has been published in *African American Review, Modern Fiction Studies,* and *English Language Notes,* and in the Nevada Humanities Committee Halcyon Series. She is completing a book on contemporary historical fiction and global truth-telling that treats novels by Don DeLillo, Toni Morrison, Michelle Cliff, Bharati Mukherjee, and Michelle Cliff.

Devin Harner is an assistant professor of English at John Jay College of Criminal Justice/City University of New York where he teaches journalism, film, and contemporary literature. His article on musicality, memory, and allusiveness in the Northern Irish poet Cieran Carson's memoir, *Last Night's Fun,* was published in *An Sionnach.* His essay "YouTube's Budget Travel Through Time and Space—Yours and Mine," appeared in popmatters.com's special "Pixelated Brain."

Laurie F. Leach, professor of English at Hawai'i Pacific University, is the author of *Langston Hughes: A Biography* (Greenwood), and essays in such journals as *Studies in the Literary Imagination; LIT: Literature, Interpretation, Theory: South Central Review; Biography;* and *Romance Notes.* Her current project is an analysis of intertextual connections between "Meditations on History" and *Dessa Rose* by Sherley Anne Williams and *The Confessions of Nat Turner* by William Styron.

Cathlena Martin, a Ph.D. candidate at the University of Florida, researches children's culture through literature, comics, film, and new media. She teaches communication arts at Samford University and professional communication and business writing at the University of Florida online. Her publications include chapters in collections on *Peter Pan* and video games, play in *Ender's Game,* using wikis in the college classroom, and adaptation in children's texts. Further details at www.cathlena.org.

Jennifer Orme is completing her doctoral studies at the University of Hawai'i. Her dissertation project, "'Trust Me, I'm Telling You Stories': Storytellers and Desire in Contemporary Fairy-Tale Fiction and Film" examines narrative desire and the representation of storytelling in fairy-tale fiction and film produced in the last thirty years. She has presented at conferences in the U.S. and the U.K. and is the assistant review editor for *Marvels & Tales.*

Anne M. Reef is a Ph.D. candidate in textual studies at the University of Memphis. She holds a B.A. in English from the University of the Witwatersrand in Johannesburg, South Africa, and an M.A. in English from the University of Memphis. Her research, conference papers, and publications focus on contemporary South African texts. She is the winner of the 2007 Children's Literature Association Best Graduate Student Essay Award.

Deborah L. Ross is a professor of English at Hawai'i Pacific University, specializing in British literature and issues of gender and power in narrative. She is the author of a book on early women writers and the history of the novel, *The Excellence of False-*

hood; several critical articles on subjects ranging from Shakespeare to Disney; and more recently, cultural commentaries and creative essays about her family.

Julia Round lectures in media and communication at Bournemouth University, U.K., and edits the academic journal *Studies in Comics*. She has published and presented work internationally on cross-media adaptation, the graphic novel, the application of literary criticism and terminology to comics, and the presence of gothic and fantastic motifs and themes in this medium. Further details at www.juliaround.com.

Christy Williams is an instructor of English at Hawai'i Pacific University and a doctoral candidate at the University of Hawai'i. She specializes in fairy-tale studies, focusing on the gender and narrative interventions made by contemporary and postmodern fairy tales. Her work on fairy-tale retellings can be found in the journals *The Comparatist* and *Marvels & Tales* and the collection *Fairy Tale Film and Cinematic Folklore*. She is the 2009 winner of the Elli Köngäs–Maranda Student Prize from the women's section of the American Folklore Society.

Index